INDIA
A BIRD'S-EYE VIEW

INDIA
A BIRD'S-EYE VIEW

EARL OF RONALDSHAY

GYAN

Published by

GYAN

Gyan Publishing House
5, Ansari Road
Daryaganj, New Delhi-110002
Phone: 011-47034999, 9811692060
E-mail: books@gyanbooks.com

Distribution Network
gyanbooks.com
India, USA, Canada, UK, Australia

ISBN: 978-93-7447-485-3 (PB)

First Published, 1906

2nd Impression 2026

Printed at: Gyan Press, Delhi.

INDIA: A BIRD'S-EYE VIEW

Author: EARL OF RONALDSHAY

INDIA

A BIRD'S-EYE VIEW

Plate I.

THE IMAGE OF THE SUN GOD AT KONĀRAK.

(See page 257.)

INDIA
A BIRD'S-EYE VIEW

BY THE

EARL OF RONALDSHAY

P.C., G.C.S.I., G.C.I.E.

HON. D.LITT. CALCUTTA ; HON. D.L. DACCA ; HON. D.LITT. LEEDS
PRESIDENT OF THE ROYAL GEOGRAPHICAL SOCIETY

AUTHOR OF
'SPORT AND POLITICS UNDER AN EASTERN SKY' ; 'ON THE OUTSKIRTS OF EMPIRE IN ASIA' ; 'A WANDERING STUDENT IN THE FAR EAST' ; 'AN EASTERN MISCELLANY,' AND 'LANDS OF THE THUNDERBOLT'

CONSTABLE AND COMPANY LIMITED

LONDON · BOMBAY · SYDNEY

1924

PREFACE

I AM often asked by persons wishing to know something of India what they should read. The answer is not so simple as might be supposed, for India can be viewed from so many different angles. Experience suggests, however, that what the majority require, particularly those contemplating a visit to India whether for business or for pleasure, is something in the nature of a bird's-eye view. They want more than a mere narrative of travel, however vivid the pen pictures which it contains and however graphic the description of the experiences of which it tells, and something less than the studies of specialists which treat with a weight of technical knowledge which alarms if it does not repel, of particular aspects of the case. And it is a bird's-eye view, therefore, that I have set myself to present.

This phrase is not, of course, to be interpreted too literally, since descriptions of the actual scenery and outward appearance of peoples and buildings occupy but a small part of the whole. Such a picture would fall short of what is demanded. Man with his capacity for accumulating records of events, from which has developed his historical sense ; with his gift of imagination, whence he derives his enjoyment of aesthetic values; with his adaptation of himself to his environment as displayed generally by the control which he exercises over nature and in particular by his industries and commerce; with his speculative faculty which has given birth to his philosophies; man, in short, with his varied outlook upon the universe demands a picture of more than the mere outward appearance of things. The bird's-eye view which he requires is a mosaic of diverse pieces—a composition of historical, pictorial, statistical, and ethnographical vignettes.

This then is what I have tried to do—to bring together vignettes of Indian history; glimpses of Indian architecture and archaeology; sketches of the social and industrial economy of her peoples; indications of the modes in which their religious thought has found expression; illustrations of their unceasing war with their environment, particularly in the matter of climate and disease—to construct a mosaic which will present to the man who wishes to know something of this huge and varied land, whose recent history has been bound up so intimately with his own, an intelligible conspectus.

The pages which follow are concerned for the most part with external things, for one must acquire familiarity with that which lies open to one's gaze before one can hope—or, indeed, before one is likely even to desire—to probe beneath the surface. The final chapters are an exception to this general statement, for in them I have touched upon one aspect of the inner life of India. I have done so because the particular belief to which I have therein alluded—that in reincarnation and its cause—is universal among the Hindus and colours their whole outlook upon life. No volume, therefore, which aims at giving a faithful picture of India would be complete without some reference to it. Elsewhere I have written of one of the most powerful influences which have gone to fashion the Indian outlook upon life—the teaching of Sidartha Gautama, the Lord Buddha.[1] The subject-matter of the final chapters of the present volume is complementary to much that is contained in the latter, for they set forth the Indian theory concerning the past and the future of man—the theory of a pitiless and inexorable repetition of existence, an ever-recurring cycle of birth, old age, death, and re-birth, from which it was Buddha's mission upon earth to seek and to find an avenue of escape. Of both volumes it may be said, therefore, that they conduct the reader to the threshold of another world—the world of thought as distinct from the objective world of experience. There for the time being I leave him. If he is tempted to push his exploration across the threshold into this unfamiliar but fascinating world, these two volumes may be of assistance in equipping him for his journey. If, on the other hand, he is content to confine his journeyings to the broader highways of more familiar country, the pages which follow will, I hope, prove adequate to his purpose. To assist him in picturing the scenes of which they tell, I have made a selection from a number of photographs which I have taken at various times in different parts of India.

In one or two places I have availed myself of the permission granted me by the editors of the

[1] In "Lands of the Thunderbolt," Messrs. Constable & Co., 1923.

"Nineteenth Century and After" and of the "Empire Review," to reproduce matter which has already appeared in those publications. The greater part of Chapter XIV. was originally written as a contribution to the January number of the former in 1923, while certain passages touching upon the life and teaching of Buddha were included in an article in the September issue of the latter during the same year. And I gladly take this opportunity of acknowledging my indebtedness to their respective editors for the courtesy which they have thus shown me.

RONALDSHAY.

January 1924

CONTENTS

CHAPTER IX

CHAPTER X

CHAPTER XI

CHAPTER XII

CHAPTER XIII

CHAPTER XIV

CHAPTER XV

CHAPTER XVI

CHAPTER XVII

CHAPTER XVIII

ILLUSTRATIONS

CHAPTER I

WHAT IS INDIA ?

In attempting to give a description of India which will possess a reasonable degree of interest for the general reader, it is a little difficult to know how much to take for granted. What sort of picture does the average man conjure up when he thinks of India ? When he does so is it with a conscious knowledge, for example, that of the 440,000,000 of British citizens who constitute the British Empire 320,000,000 are Indians ? Or that in spite of Great Britain's far-flung dominions in five continents, the loss of India would mean a shrinkage in the Empire from 13,250,000 to less than 11,500,000 square miles ? Is his picture anything more than a smudge of red upon the map of Asia ?

By a curious chance the first debate which I ever attended as a member of the House of Commons was the annual debate on the Indian budget, when a desultory discussion took place upon what struck me as the rather bewildering motion, that Mr. Speaker should leave the chair. The principal participant was the Secretary of State, Mr. (afterwards Lord) Morley. And to any one impressed with the magnitude of the task which Parliament had undertaken towards 320,000,000 British subjects of India when it had assumed responsibility for their good government, his opening words were as startling as they were picturesque. "The Indian Secretary," he remarked, "is like the aloe which blooms once in a hundred years, for he only troubles the House with speeches of his own once in twelve months."

It is not so very long ago that Sir John Strachey wrote that the first and most essential fact that could be learned about India was that there was no such country. It is unlikely that he propounded so profound a paradox merely for the sake of being paradoxical. He was anxious to dispel a popular and perfectly intelligible error, namely, that of the man who, when he thought on India, visualised it as a country like Great Britain instead of as a continent like Europe. The analogy presented by Europe is not an exact one, but it is sufficiently near the mark to serve the purpose of one. The author of the report on the Indian census of 1911, while insisting on the necessity of regarding India as a continent, or collection of different countries, did so half apologetically on the ground that the remark was "trite." It may be so to those who habitually study Indian official publications. The average man does not; and nine people out of ten still talk of the People of India when they mean the peoples of that continent. One may quote statistics, then, without being charged with pedantry.

For a start, imagine a region the size of all Europe exclusive only of Russia, stretching over twenty-eight degrees of latitude and forty degrees of longitude, with a population of 320,000,000 practising nine great religions and speaking 130 different dialects belonging to six distinct families of speech. That is India looked at from the point of view of the statistician. But statistics are dry bones. If they are startling, as Indian statistics are, they merely bewilder; if they are commonplace they leave one cold. If their meaning is to bc grasped they must be seen clothed with flesh and blood. And that means hard and extensive travelling. When within the space of a few months, for instance, one has been brought into contact with the business-like Parsi of Bombay, the indolent and easy-going Burman, the courtly and cultured Brahman of Southern India, the primitive Kohl or Bhil of the jungles of Central India, the emotional and subtle-minded inhabitant of the towns of Bengal, the cheery hill-man of the Eastern Himālayas, the great landholders of the United Provinces and the Punjab, the proud aristocracy of Rajputana, the wild Afridi of the North-West Frontier and the picturesque chieftain of Baluchistan, then it is that statistics as to race and language begin to assume definite meaning and reality.

Wise men tell one that it is impossible to generalise about India ; and in the main the wise men are doubtless right. One does not generalise about Europe, and in some respects Europe is more homogeneous than India. And, indeed, it does not require a man of outstanding wisdom to tell one that in the case of a region stretching over forty degrees of longitude and twenty-eight degrees of latitude, generalisations are only likely to hold good, subject to large qualifications. Nevertheless there are certain rough generalisations which may be made. Thus it may be said that India is essentially an agricultural country, and the correctness of such an assertion cannot be disputed. Seventy-two per cent of the population, or approximately 219,000,000, are dependent upon agriculture in one form or another for their livelihood. The population as a whole lives in small country towns and villages. There are in the whole of the huge continent less than 750 towns with a population of 10,000, and only thirty towns with a population of 100,000 and upwards. And the general accuracy of the statement is not invalidated by the fact that in Calcutta and Bombay India possesses the second and third cities of the British Empire.

Again, take the case of climate. It may be said in a general way that India is a hot country; and the fact that there are parts of India where cold weather is experienced during certain seasons, and other parts where a winter of almost arctic severity prevails, does not disprove the general contention. If India were not a hot country, it is unlikely that her people would consume round about 2,000,000 miles of cotton cloth every year, as in point of fact they do. In the year 1913–14 they took from the looms of Great Britain alone over 1,750,000 miles of grey, white, and coloured cloth.

The assertion may also be ventured that as a general rule the outstanding characteristic of Muhammadan architecture is its simple grandeur of outline, its purity, and its stateliness, while Hindu architecture is characterised by an amazing exuberance of ornamentation and an elaborate intricacy of design. While there is a suggestion of austerity about the one, there is often a hint almost of meretriciousness about the other.

Lastly, in the domain of philosophic thought it is undoubtedly the case that, excepting in those regions which are dominated by the creed of Islam, the doctrine of *Karma* and Transmigration—of which more later—exercises an almost universal sway.

These are generalisations, and they are unquestionably true. But having made them by way of protest against a too rigid interpretation of the statement that one cannot generalise about India, let me hasten to add that I subscribe to it on the whole. I recognise fully the amazing diversity of the continent; and, indeed, it is

Plate 2.

THE PEARL MOSQUE AT DELHI.

"... the outstanding characteristic of Muhammadan architecture is its simple grandeur of outline, its purity and its stateliness ..."

to this very diversity, presenting as it does such rich studies in contrast, that is attributable no small part of its singular charm.

Take an example. There are in North-West India, both east and west of the Indus as it makes its way across the plains towards the sea, great tracts of desolation. In particular there is the Daman—a dusty stretch of sun-scorched wilderness running from the Indus banks to the mountains which rise tier upon tier from the edge of the trans-Indus plains to the highlands of Afghanistan. There are probably many similar tracts in the North-West Frontier Province and in the Punjab, and I merely take the Daman as an example, because I happen to have travelled across it myself. In the middle of it stands Dera Ismael Khan, and away to the west, at the foot of the first mountain range, a small frontier post near the mouth of the Gomal Pass, called Tank. The light railway which now connects these two places had not then been built, and apart from these two symptoms of human existence I can recall little but an impression of desolation triumphant. It is an unlovely patch of Nature at her crudest—hard, staring, and blistered by the sun. The most poignant sensation which a contemplation of it excites in the mind is that of unquenchable thirst. In the Daman "men drink once a day, and the cattle every second day. Washing is an impossible luxury."[1] It might easily be imagined that such a land would excite nothing but feelings of repulsion. Yet, curiously enough, this is not so. With all their disabilities these waste places possess an attraction which the traveller who is familiar with the desert unexpectedly finds inherent in it. Perhaps it is due to an exhilarating sense of freedom which is produced by an ever receding and apparently

[1] Captain Crostwaite.

limitless horizon. Perhaps, too, the untainted atmosphere reacts favourably upon one's physical organism, whilst the great cool silence of night descending like balm upon a weary and jaded spirit is responsible for a feeling of strange content. Certainly the gold and crimson glory of the sunset or the graceful symmetry of the palm tree of an occasional oasis, silhouetted darkly against the westerning sky, afford generous response to one's aesthetic cravings. Probably it is a combination of all these things that redeems the character conventionally given to the desert.

This, however, is somewhat beside the point. My object for the moment is to present a picture of Indian scenery typical of large areas of the continent where the annual rainfall does not exceed three or four inches, and then to remind the reader that it is in this same India that he must seek for the wettest climate on earth. At Cherapungi in the Khasia hills in Assam the normal annual rainfall is little short of 450 inches. In the year 1899 the rain gauge there recorded 641 inches, including a fall of over 150 inches in the month of June alone. On the 14th of June 1876 over 40 inches of rain fell at the same place in the course of twenty-four hours. In Assam and Bengal generally there are over ninety recording stations with an annual fall of more than 100 inches. In Baluchistan, on the other hand, out of a total of sixty-one recording stations nine only show an annual average of 10 inches and upwards, the highest figure reached being at Shahrig in Thal Choliali, where a fall of 12½ inches may be expected in the course of a twelvemonth, and the lowest at Jhatput, where 3 inches is as much as can be counted on in any one year. At Cherapungi rain falls in a normal year on one hundred and sixty-one days; at Jhatput on six days only.

A further aid towards realising the magnitude of the contrast afforded by different parts of the Indian continent is provided by the forestry statistics. In the North-West Frontier Province and in Baluchistan the areas under forest amount to 1·8 per cent and to 1·4 per cent of the respective provinces; in Assam to 44·5 per cent, and in Burma to 64·4 per cent. To which may be added the figures of the annual output of timber and fuel, amounting for Baluchistan to 254,000 cubic feet, for Assam to 13,445,000 cubic feet, and for Burma to 100,775,000 cubic feet.[1] One would have to travel far before finding elsewhere a parallel to such contrasts in the physical conditions even of a continent.

Nor is the contrast between the peoples at each end of the civilised scale less striking than that between the tropic luxuriance of one part of India and the sterile aridity of another. In the peoples of India is to be found an ethnologic pageant epitomising the gradual growth of civilisation through centuries of time. At one end of the scale are men of the finest culture who have reached dizzy heights in the realms of speculative thought; at the other, men whose religion has not yet outgrown the stage of the crudest superstition. At this end the bow and arrow represents the highest achievement in the domain of mechanical invention; at the other we are presented with the spectacle of an Indian scientist contriving and constructing apparatus of such "exquisite refinement"[2] as to excite the astonished admiration of the scientists of the West. It is, indeed, a long way from the bow and arrow of the aboriginal Kohl or the primitive plough of the Indian peasant to the "Resonant Recorder" of Sir Jagadis Bose, recording automatically

[1] Figures for the year 1918–19.

[2] The words are those of Professor Patrick Geddes.

measurements of time as short as a thousandth part of a second.

What has been said hitherto is sufficient to show the falsity of any attempted analogy between India and any one of the countries of Europe, and has indicated tentatively that a nearer analogy would be that between India and Europe as a whole. It remains to point out the limitations to which even this latter attempt at comparison is necessarily subject. The most pronounced characteristic which distinguishes one European country from another is undoubtedly language. That is to say, the boundaries of the different States of Europe coincide generally with a line where the language spoken by the people of one of the coterminous states ceases and the tongue common to the subjects of the other begins. In India the boundaries of the different countries, or provinces, are purely arbitrary. They are based neither on linguistic nor on ethnological considerations. They are either purely accidental or are based, broadly speaking, on grounds of administrative convenience. This has been strikingly illustrated in recent years by the way in which the boundaries of huge provinces have been swept away and set up elsewhere by the mere stroke of an official pen. In 1905 the Government of India took a large slice out of the huge territory known as the Presidency of Bengal, welded the severed portion with the adjacent territory of Assam, built it a capital and endowed it with a Government, and the new province of Eastern Bengal and Assam came into being. In 1912 the greater part of the new province, which had made great progress during the short term of its independent existence, became once more the victim of an official *ipse dixit*, and was reincorporated in the presidency, while, as a result of the facile removal of other landmarks on the west, the new province of Bihar and Orissa was created. On the other side of India another example is provided by the North-West Frontier Province, which was carved out of the Punjab by Lord Curzon's Government in 1901.

I am not here concerned with the fierce controversies which raged round these reorderings of the map. I merely mention them as illustrations of the artificial nature of the constitution of the different provinces of India. It may, indeed, be urged with some force that the arbitrary character of the divisions is inevitable, for it would be practically impossible to devise a scheme under which the peninsula could be divided up on an ethnological or linguistic basis. This becomes clear when it is remembered that the successive waves of immigrant stock with which the continent is largely peopled have been controlled by peculiar geographical conditions. The vast mountain system of the Himālayas has formed a formidable barrier between India and the rest of Asia. Invasion, when it has taken place, has followed the path of least resistance, and has poured through narrow passages in the mountain barrier. These occur mainly in the north-west, and each successive stream of invasion, after pouring through the defiles in the mountains, has spread fan-like over the plains which stretch away far and wide from their foot. For the same reason each successive tide of invasion has flown over the same ground, leaving its impress upon the whole sphere of its influence without obliterating the racial deposits of earlier inundations. A confused medley has been the result, which is strikingly illustrated by the present distribution of language. Hindi, for instance, is widely spoken in five different provinces in British India, as well as in two large groups of native states; but though widely spoken, it is only *one* of the languages spoken in each. The Central Provinces and Berar is one of the five provinces in question, and eight other languages are spoken by appreciable portions of its inhabitants. Assam furnishes a remarkable example of linguistic heterogeneity. Here nearly half the people speak Bengali and one-fifth Assamese, while the remaining two-fifths speak ninety-eight different tongues, each of the following being spoken by a fraction not less than one per cent of the population: Hindi, Manipuri, Bodo, Naga, Khasi, Garo, Mihir, Mundari, and Lushei. One may venture to doubt whether such confusion of tongues can be paralleled even by the classic example of linguistic promiscuity.

But it is when we come to the political position that the analogy with Europe fails altogether. When the British came to India they found a land torn with internal strife. Inter-state war with its inevitable tendency towards disintegration was the normal condition of the peninsula; peace with her sister progress was abnormal. So it had been for generations. If we try to form a mental picture of Indian history we see a confused procession of kingdoms taking shape and dissolving again after the manner of the changing mosaics of a kaleidoscope. Here and there great figures stand out—the founders of dynasties or the architects of kingdoms—marking the flight of monarchies fugitive across the centuries. At one moment we pause breathless in our review, dazzled by the magnificence of some unusually brilliant reign; at the next we find ourselves contemplating the ruins of all this greatness subsiding amid a welter of anarchy and confusion. In the fourth century B.C. Chandragupta and in the third century Asoka arrest our gaze—the former famous for his achievement in wresting an empire from the generals of Alexander, the latter for his patronage of Buddhism, which gave it the impetus resulting in its becoming one of the greatest religions of the world. In the second, fourth, and seventh centuries A.D. we catch passing glimpses of great sovereigns in Kanishka, Samudragupta, and Harsha; and in the eighth century we witness the rise of the celebrated warrior clans of the Rajputs, destined to leave so deep an impress upon the fortunes of Hindustan. During the centuries of their dominion Buddhism was attacked and vanquished by Hinduism, which now attained its golden age and reached the acme of its speculative greatness in the persons of Sankara and Ramanuja, the famous commentators on the Vedanta system of philosophy. Yet scarcely have we grasped something of the meaning and the greatness of the Rajput sway than we become aware of new forces pouring through the narrow portals of the North-West Frontier, conquering, slaying, and proselytising, assailing Hinduism with the fierce fanaticism inspired by a new monotheistic and vigorously militant creed. With the Muhammadan conquests in India we inevitably associate the fierce figure of Mahmūd of Gazni in the eleventh century and the gorgeous epoch of the Moghul dynasty, whose stately palaces and tombs remain to this day, bearing silent witness to the glories of their reign. Towards the close of the Moghul period we see the rise of the Marathas of the Deccan, and once more we witness the spectacle, so familiar in the long history of India, of a great empire sinking to impotence and finally disappearing from the annals of the land.

Romance there is in plenty to colour these fleeting pictures of the mind; but if we base our impressions on hard fact it is War, the fruit of fierce and striving ambition and of the clash of rival creeds, that casts its shadow over the whole, and like some spectral showman ushers across the stage, kingdom after kingdom in an ever-recurring cycle of birth and death, greatness and impotence, growth and decay.

Nor does the early period of European ascendancy in the East differ in this respect from the eras which preceded it. Spain and Portugal, France, Holland, and Great Britain fought fiercely for dominion, and it was not until a single Power emerged triumphant from the contending nations that a decisive hour in the history of India struck. Great Britain achieved what numberless competitors through past ages had striven for in vain—the hegemony of the continent.

To this position we can find no analogy. We must be content to regard it as unique, and to examine it as we find it—a vast experiment in the science of government being carried on before our eyes in the strangely equipped laboratory of the East, in a manner and on a scale never before contemplated and for which no precedents can be invoked. This is India from the most interesting and at the same time the most fateful point of view.

CHAPTER II

FIRST IMPRESSIONS

One's first impressions of India are usually formed at Bombay; and no more lovely gate-house to the wonderful land to which it gives entrance could be wished for than the verdant city, encircling the blue waters of its splendid harbour. In the streets of the city itself one scarcely notices the trees; but look down upon it as it lies spread out like a map beneath you from some point of vantage upon Malabar Hill, and it is the buildings that shrink into the back-ground, lost in a green bower of trees.

It was in the winter of 1898–99 that I first set foot in Bombay, two years after plague had made its sinister appearance in the land and before the Improvement Trust had got to work upon its beneficent task of cleansing and reconstructing the city. What the advent of this scourge meant to India may be dimly imagined from a bald statement of the number of deaths caused by it, amounting to 10,500,000 in something less than a quarter of a century.

My impressions formed then were those of the average cold-weather visitor, and it was not until some years later that I discovered a side of Bombay which does not usually impress itself upon the casual visitor, a side of the city which provides a picture harder in outline and darker in hue than that aspect of it which, with its rich colouring and attractive novelty, catches the eye of the traveller, grim but substantial and full of a solid material reality, the characteristics of modern industrial progress. Of this picture I then saw only the shadow in a heavy pall of smoke-haze that hung like a curtain over the land across the bay. And I was but dimly conscious of the fact that behind that murky curtain there lived and laboured a vast industrial community whose pulses throbbed to the ceaseless whirr of the spindle and the palpitating crash of the loom. I had occasion later to visit some of the great cotton mills which have brought wealth and squalor hand in hand to the city, and a mere stroll through the damp and enervating atmosphere which pervades them was enough to explain and justify the agitation which arose early in the present century for factory legislation.

On the occasion of my first visit I went in company with other visitors to see the sights: the markets and the polyglot crowd that frequented them, the Arab stables, the Towers of Silence, and the Caves of Elephanta. Before the Great War cut off the supply from the Persian Gulf, the Arab stables were certainly a feature of the city, for neither in Asia nor in Europe could one have found their counterpart. This was, in fact, the one and only market in existence for the sale and purchase of this famous breed. There were 3000 ponies in the stables when I visited them, one dealer alone possessing a fine racing string of seventy-five animals. According to the dealers—fine, upstanding men of Arabia, of proud and dignified bearing—a flea-bitten grey was the most highly prized of all, such ponies having the reputation of being the quietest and best of the breed.

The Towers of Silence necessarily attract the attention of the newcomer on account of the novelty of the idea of giving over the dead to the fowls of the air rather than to the slow disintegration of the tomb. Moreover, the Parsi community, to which this method of the disposal of the dead is peculiar, is small in number and is mainly concentrated in Bombay, so that one is not likely to come across elsewhere the curious, low, circular towers surrounded by trees on whose branches groups of vultures brood expectantly. If the fluttering of these sombre scavengers as they alight on the grating on which the corpse is laid causes an involuntary shudder, the peace of this strange garden amid the golden light of the sunshine, as it brings its great powers of purification to bear on all around, quickly restores one's equanimity.

A stroll towards sunset on the beach which sweeps in a wide semicircle from Colāba to Malabar, reminds the stranger further that he has entered a land where the religious uniformity of Europe no longer prevails. In the rows of attentive figures standing with book in hand, gazing earnestly across the waters to the sinking sun, he will recognise the devout descendants of the faithful followers of Zoroaster, who, throughout the weary days of their exodus from the land of their birth, kept the sacred fire burning till at the end of their wanderings they could establish and feed it in the new home of their choice.

A trip across the waters of the bay to the island on which are situated the famous rock-cut temples of Elephanta is likewise instructive. In the course of it one may see the palatial residences of great industrial magnates, reminders of the success with which, in Bombay at any rate, Indians have imbibed the commercial spirit of the West. For unlike Calcutta, where, as one discovers later, the immense mills of the jute industry are almost exclusively in the hands of

Europeans, the cotton mills of Bombay are the property of Indians. It was a Parsi who built the first Indian cotton mill in Bombay in 1854, and despite the excise duty upon Indian cotton products, round which has raged from time to time so fierce a controversy, Bombay to-day can boast its merchant millionaires. And then one comes to Elephanta and its great cave temples—a splendid husk of that grain which is of the real fibre and substance of India—a thing not of the earth earthy, but of the spirit. These cave temples, with their splendid columns and their titanic sculpture dating back a dozen centuries and more, cannot fail to impress even the least instructed visitor. But some acquaintance with Indian symbolism discloses something of their meaning and significance, and enables one to take a glimpse into that world which he who seeks to understand India must strive to enter—the intangible world of the spirit, built up through the centuries by the powerful religious impulses of her peoples. A massive shrine foursquare to the cardinal points of the compass, with eight guardian figures 15 feet in height, one on either side of its four entrances, encloses a symbol which later on becomes familiar in connection with temples dedicated to Shiva throughout the land, the *lingam*, emblematic of the mysterious reproductive power of Nature. The shrine itself containing this emblem stands for the earth and all that therein is. Another great panel of stone represents Shiva as the Lord of Creation, engaged in a mystical dance, whereby he sets the universe in motion. Later, in Southern India, one will come across this same conception wonderfully wrought by the temple image-makers in bronze, and learn something of its deep philosophical significance. For the time being one has seen enough to set one thinking, even if one is not yet in a position

Plate 3.

A CAVE TEMPLE AT ELLORA.

". . . encloses a symbol which later on becomes familiar in connection with temples dedicated to Shiva throughout the land.

to appreciate the dictum of Mr. E. B. Havell, that the sculpture of Elephanta reflects the lofty idealism and intellectuality of the Upanishads.[1]

* * * * *

It is convenient to leave Bombay by night, and on stepping into one's railway carriage one realises that one has cause for gratitude to the early railway builders in India, who, out of consideration or caprice, laid their track on broad and generous lines. The $5\frac{1}{2}$-foot gauge of the greater number of the Indian railways allows of a roomy compartment on whose broad seats, running lengthwise on either side of the carriage, one can spread one's bedding and lie at ease. If the journey is made during the winter months, the first night, during which one scales the sides of the Ghāts Mountains by steep gradients, is likely to prove unexpectedly cold after the damp heat of Bombay, and a warning to have a thick blanket or quilt at hand is one which is well worth heeding.

The disadvantage of leaving Bombay by night is that one thereby misses by far the most picturesque portion of the journey, for after scaling the Ghāts and emerging on to the plateaux of the Indian hinterland one will find little of note in the scenery. Hour after hour one travels monotonously across a dusty landscape. It leaves upon one's mind the impression of a land of vast spaces, and, to the rather fastidious taste in rural scenery bred by the trim hedges and neatly enclosed fields of Great Britain, it appears preposterously untidy. The villages seem to consist of fortuitous collections of houses of sun-dried bricks, thrown together with no regard to the modern science of town-planning. They are usually half-buried in trees, which, whether deciduous by nature or not, always seem to be in

[1] "The Ideals of Indian Art."

leaf. This provides us with one of the minor contrasts of India, for, except for this unexpected behaviour on the part of the trees, greenness in any form is the last thing suggested by a winter landscape in Central or North-West India. Later on, a more leisurely tour through an Indian district will enable one to observe large differences in the character and construction of these small centres of agricultural activity, in precisely the same way as a lengthened stay in China proves to one the unreliability of one's first impression that all Chinese are exactly alike in physiognomy. There are, for example, villages which aspire to the dignity conferred by the title "municipality," whose corporate life is ordered by a board composed of the chief residents, with power to impose rates and to take action in a variety of directions conducive to the general well-being. I recall an attractive example of this type of village-municipality in the United Provinces, styled an "Act XX. town" I think, a hamlet with a minimum population of fifteen hundred, possessing all the picturesqueness of a typical Indian village, but in addition well-planned streets, surprising tidiness, and a population the comfortable circumstances of whose lot were plainly apparent. But these are features of rural life which cannot, of course, be detected from the window of a railway carriage.

The probability is that one's first impressions, induced by what one sees as one travels from Bombay to Delhi, let us say, will be vague. The glare of the sun outside produces weariness of the eye, and the dust with which everything inside becomes smothered causes the kind of discomfort and annoyance which distracts one's attention. One's faculty of observation becomes blunted by the monotony of the landscape and with ennui produced by the petty physical discomfort of which one is never altogether unconscious. And it is only by degrees, after a succession of journeys broken by welcome halts at places of special interest, that one finds that one has arrived at certain rough conclusions which seem to be capable of more or less general application. The train of thought already set in motion at Bombay by the spectacle of the religious practices of the Parsis is early reinforced by a conspicuous notice at the railway stations, which apprises one of the fact that drinking-water for Muhammadans and Hindus is kept separate. This seems to indicate something more than a mere absence of religious uniformity; it suggests a wide gulf between the adherents of two great schools of religious thought.

Another conclusion on a matter which at first sight may appear to be somewhat trivial, but which later is seen to be of no small importance, is that the cow is pressed into the general service of Indian humanity, to perform all those tasks which are undertaken by the farm-horse in England. Yet another conclusion is forced upon one during one's early days in the land, namely, that laughter is singularly rare in the people as a whole, that their bearing is characterised rather by a submissive sadness, which may easily be mistaken for a disagreeable taciturnity. At first sight one finds an adequate explanation of this latter characteristic in environment. A blistering sun, the ever-present spectre of drought leading in turn to famine and pestilence, the monotonous life of the multitude with its narrow outlook—a hard, hand-to-mouth existence, in which the morrow holds out no prospect of any mitigation of the toil of to-day; all these things, which go to make up the sum-total of the average peasant's joys and woes, seem sufficiently well calculated to banish inordinate merriment and to give to existence the sombre tint of a half-tone engraving.

But later on, when one begins to understand the mental attitude of the people towards the problems of life and death, one realises that one is witnessing here one aspect of a peculiar psychology which is by no means wholly due to physical causes. One discovers here the first signpost which directs one to the Indian side of the gulf which separates the deeper thought of the East from that of the West. To the Indian, life is a very minute episode in an eternity of existence. Behind the present, unnumbered lives stretch back into the dim and receding past; ahead lies an ever-expanding vista of lives still to come. The idea prevalent among Western peoples that life is the great present reality to be made the most of, and that the future that lies beyond it is dim, shadowy, and unrealisable—an abstraction, consequently, of little immediate interest or concern—is altogether alien to the Indian mind. To the Hindu peasant all existence in this world is suffering and sorrow. His ambition is not to prolong it, but to escape from it. Why then, it may be asked, does such an outlook upon life not lead to suicide on a large scale? The answer is simple. Suicide does not put an end to life; it merely leads to rebirth, and so prolongs it. And the nightmare which assails the Hindu is not death, but the inexorable recurrence of life. It is the perpetual cycle of birth, life, death, and rebirth that preys upon his mind, and paints existence for him in colours of infinite gloom. It is to this problem that the great thinkers of India have directed their minds; and the "way of emancipation" is the promise of the gospels which they have preached to suffering mankind. Existence, then, gives little enough cause for rejoicing; but more than this, to find enjoyment in life is, in the view of the more extreme schools of thought, to draw tighter the cords that bind a man to it. So certain is this that for the Jain ascetic who has renounced the world, laughter is a positive sin. "If he laughs even once, some punishment will follow, and if he persists in the indulgence, it will lead to his rebirth."[1]

But if much time and more thought are required before one can begin to form conclusions about India, its amazing diversity at least will be brought home to one at the very outset of one's investigations if one is prepared to embark upon an extensive programme of travel. It is, indeed, difficult to give any adequate idea of the wonderful medley of sensations which crowd themselves upon one in the course, for example, of a triangular journey from Bombay to the heart of the Punjab, thence east across the United Provinces and Bihar to Calcutta; from Calcutta to Madras and on to the southern apex of the peninsula at Tuticorin, and from the Southern Presidency back to Bombay across the stony highlands of the Deccan. It must be experienced to be understood, and no description can serve the purpose of anything more than a rough introduction. Before reaching Delhi or Lahore, one may call a halt in order to visit one or more of the historic feudatory states of Rajputana, over which still hangs the picturesque atmosphere of an era of autocracy, fast dissolving on all sides of them, under pressure of the democratic tendencies of present-day movements in British India. No traveller who has once seen them can forget the pink-and-white buildings of Jeypore, or the cut-glass work and the suggestion of romance conjured up by what still survives of the ancient city of Amber hard-by; or the shimmering white splendour of the palace at Kotah or the charm of its ruler; or again the mediaeval picturesqueness of the little city of Bundi, built steeply and

[1] "The Heart of Jainism," by Mrs. Sinclair Stevenson.

cunningly in a cleft in a mountain range. Here undoubtedly is a link with bygone days; and it was altogether in accordance with the fitness of things that it should have been the Raja of Bundi who, so recently as 1897, appeared at the Great Durbar held at Delhi in that year in the court-dress of the Moghuls, "to the amazement of a generation that had almost entirely forgotten the Moghul court and its fashions."[1] The traveller is not likely to have the time or the opportunity of visiting more than a few of the Native States, but such glimpses as he obtains will reveal the existence of an India differing very materially from British India and covering as much as a third of the Indian continent.

In the course of such a journey as I have suggested, the traveller will discover for himself something of the wide range of the climate to which reference has been made in the previous chapter, for he will pass from the dry and dusty plains of the north-west through the intermediate zone—half green, half drab—of the United Provinces, into the steamy atmosphere and semi-tropical vegetation of Bengal. Farther south in Madras, he will find the India of his preconceived ideas—the land of palm trees, emerald-tinted rice fields, and mosquitoes; of brown-skinned, scantily-clad humanity, of rich colouring and of a climate enervating and sensuous, inducing a languorous repose. And the contrast as he passes from such surroundings to the torrid and desiccated uplands of the Deccan will not easily be forgotten. If he wishes to see those marvellous transformations wrought annually by the advent of the monsoon, when that which before appeared to be desert is converted, almost in a night, into a vast rolling sea of green, he must be ready to

[1] Sir T. W. Arnold in his Birdwood Memorial Lecture, delivered at the Royal Society of Arts on May 26, 1922.

travel in the months of July and August, and he must be prepared to put up with the teasing discomfort produced by an exasperating alliance between heat and moisture.

But it is the buildings of the land that bulk most largely among one's first impressions. Hindu and Muhammadan, Buddhist and Jain have all given concrete expression in rock, in marble, in brick, in wood, and in stone, to the wonderful variety of conception which they have formed of that which lies, or is thought to lie, beyond the world of everyday experience. Temples, mosques, and viharas are the finger-posts directing one along a fascinating road in quest of the conclusions which the most religious-minded peoples on earth have arrived at concerning the WHY of the universe and the destiny of man. In the first instance it is, no doubt, the outward form of the buildings and the symbols and images which they contain—the architectural appeal which they make—that claims attention, rather than any philosophical significance which they may possess. Nevertheless, with a little trouble one may learn much from these mute chroniclers of Indian thought and Indian history; and no observant traveller will be content to pass them by, even at first sight, as mere examples of architectural design. Let us visit some of them and pick up something of the story which they have to tell.

CHAPTER III

WHAT THE BUILDINGS HAVE TO TELL

THE diversity which is so striking a characteristic of the climate and geography of India is equally apparent in her architecture. One marvels at the delicacy of detail and design which the old Jain sculptors hammered out of their blocks of white marble, seen at their best, perhaps, in the Dilwara temples at the summit of Mount Abu in Rajputana. And then one strikes the splendid structures of red sandstone and white marble which Delhi, Agra, and Lahore have inherited from two centuries of Moghul domination. And one sees in them the embodiment of great and lofty ideas. There is nothing petty in the architecture of the Moghuls. Spaciousness and purity of line seem to be their outstanding characteristics. The ideas for which they stand seem to have been born of the freedom of vast spaces acting upon broad and vigorous minds.

Away, many days' journey even by express train, in the hot vapour-laden atmosphere of the south-east of the peninsula, one finds oneself in a completely different architectural world. The buildings here are large like the mosques and the tombs and the pillared halls-of-audience of the Moghuls. But with their size, their similarity ceases.[1]

[1] I am aware that the expert will find in the buildings of the Moghuls features which were evolved from earlier Hindu designs; but I am now

Nothing, indeed, could be farther apart in style than the Dravidian temples at Madura, Conjeeveram, Srinangam, Tanjore, or Trichinopoly, and the mosques and palaces of Delhi and Agra. The space within the four walls of the Sri Meenakshi Sundareswaral temple at Madura is approximately 830 feet by 730 feet. The walls are high, but the feature of all these temples which immediately arrests the attention is the huge pyramidal tower, rising story above story over the elaborate gateways into the enclosure, commonly called *gopuram*. The south gopuram of the temple at Madura rises 150 feet above the street below, a mad medley of imagery in stone, brickwork, and brightly coloured plaster. One is told that this bewildering profusion of figures represents the more popular of the deities, personages, and events met with in the Hindu sacred books; but it is difficult to believe that any can have been left out from so crowded a series of galleries. Within the enclosures are a sacred tank, rows of cloisters, *mandapams* or halls of assembly for the delivering of discourses, the holding of philosophical or religious discussions, the recitation of the great epics, the singing of sacred songs or the holding of the temple dance, and numbers of shrines. In an inner enclosure in the centre stand the shrines of Shiva Sundara or Shiva the beautiful and his spouse Meenakshi, the fish-eyed, the daughter of a Pandya king, born with three breasts, one of which fortunately disappeared when she met Shiva, by whom she was destined to be wed.

Such buildings as these catch the eye from afar. They tower above the earth, immense structures outlined sharply against the turquoise

---

writing from the point of view of the layman who compares the impression created on his mind by the one with that created by the other.

background of the Indian sky. There is, however, another type of temple less noticeable from afar, but well calculated to arrest the attention when once discovered. This is the cave temple, a specimen of which—that of Elephanta—greeted us at the very gateway of the continent. The first people to hew their sacred places out of the rock cliffs upon the hillsides were the Buddhist monks, thanks to the religious fervour of the Emperor Asoka, who planned and executed some at least of these, destined to become enduring monuments to his missionary zeal, more than two centuries before the Christian era. At Ajanta there exists an amazing series of such excavations, wholly Buddhist. But the example of the Buddhists was copied later both by Hindus and Jains; and at Ellora in the State of Hyderabad, may be seen, side by side, hewn out of the face of a vast and lofty scarp of rock, "curved like Shiva's moon-crest" and facing the setting sun, a most remarkable series of Buddhist retreats and Hindu and Jain temples, stretching for more than a mile in length. Near the centre of this great scarp stands a temple which immediately arrests the eye; "for instead of making a horizontal excavation into the hillside, the master masons here cut down into the sloping hillside from above, quarrying a pit varying in depth from 160 feet to about 50 feet, and leaving in the middle of it a detached mass of rock from which they sculptured a full-sized double-storied temple—solid at the base, but with the first floor completed internally and externally."[1] It is known as the Kailasa temple, for it is a representation in stone of a wonderful vision conjured up in the minds of the master builders who conceived it, of the Himālayan abode on Mount Kailasa of the great god Shiva. And

[1] "A Handbook of Indian Art," E. B. Havell.

Plate 4.

A DRAVIDIAN TEMPLE.

"The feature which immediately arrests attention is the huge pyramidal tower, commonly called *gopuram*."

one cannot but marvel as one gazes at it, at the soaring imagination and the technical skill which combined to create so splendid and unique an edifice. But having satisfied one's astonishment and admiration one may turn with profit to the earlier works of the Buddhist monks, less striking in dramatic effect, but containing a key, nevertheless, to much that is of paramount importance to any one who seeks to understand something of the heart of India. These Buddhist caves are of two distinct types; in one of them one sees a place of residence—the *vihara* or monastery of the order; in the other a hall of assembly—the *chaitya* or chapter-hall of the brethren. The finest example of this latter type at Ellora is known as the Visvakarma Cave. It is of a comparatively late date, probably of the seventh century A.D., and has lost something of the simplicity of earlier examples. The main plan of construction is, however, constant in all the chaityas of the Buddhists and gives the key to their origin and purpose. In design they resemble a Christian church, for they consist of a nave with aisles on either side formed by two rows of pillars. The nave terminates in an apse, and the aisles are carried round the back of the apse so as to form a passage-way round the whole of the central part of the building. Its object was, in fact, to permit of the circumambulation of the main building by bands of pilgrims. In place of the altar of the Christian church, the Buddhist chapter-hall contains a monument roughly hemispherical in shape, known as a stupa, the cenotaph of Buddha. Here, then, we have a hall of assembly of simple design with nothing in the way of furniture beyond a cenotaph, the whole surrounded by a corridor. What is the story which these things have to tell? If we begin our inquiry by tracing the stupa in its form of a Buddhist cenotaph to its source, we find ourselves carried at one stride back across the yawning gulf of time to a day nearly 500 years B.C. The ancient records which have now been rescued from the dusty limbo of past and forgotten things provide us with the material which enables us to paint a picture of the events of those early days. Let us try to do so.

In the shade of a plantation of sāl trees we see a man lying at the point of death—a venerable figure of eighty years, the leader evidently of some cause or mission, for he is surrounded by a group of his immediate followers, grief-stricken and clearly apprehensive for the future of their cause, now that they are faced with the prospect of the loss of their revered Master. Not far from the grove is situated a small town—little more, in fact, than a large village, such as one may see in many a rural tract of the India of to-day, for the spokesman of the disciples grumbles at this selection of "a little wattle-and-daub town, a town in the midst of the jungle,"[1] as the death-place of his beloved Master. It is nevertheless the capital of an Aryan tribe of aristocratic lineage—a tribe of the great Khatriya or warrior caste, the Mallas of Kusinara; a tribe, moreover, ruled on a democratic basis by an assembly of the representatives of its own people. And while the disciples are gathered round their dying Master, drinking in his last words spoken to them in the sāl plantation on the outskirts of Kusinara, it happens that the Mallas are assembled in their mote-hall for the transaction of public business. The scene as one pictures it is a dramatic one. The discussion is suddenly interrupted, and a hush falls upon the assembly as a man in the garb of a

[1] Quoted by Mr. B. C. Law in his "Ksatriya Clans in Buddhist India."

wandering friar is seen approaching. He is easily recognised by the assembled Mallas, for it is Ananda, the spokesman of the disciples of the sage Gautama, who, during a long lifetime spent in preaching and in good works, has acquired a widespread reputation for wisdom and piety throughout the land occupied by the kingdoms of Kosala, Magadah, Kosambi, and Avanti, and the neighbouring republics—those of the Mallas, the Kalamas, the Sakhyas, and the Moriyas, and the powerful Vajjian confederacy of the Licchavis and the Videhas. On learning from Ananda the news of the approaching death of his Master, the assembly breaks up and the Mallas flock to the plantation outside their town to pay homage to the renowned teacher ere he breathes his last. It is one of the great moments of the world's history, for it marks the close of a career which has since left its imprint upon millions of the human race. The dying man, as he gazes back over the years that are gone, sees in the far-off days of childhood a boy brought up with loving care in the well-to-do household of an aristocrat of the Sakhya tribe. Next deeply imprinted upon his memory he sees the sensitive feelings of the same young man subjected to a rude shock by a dawning realisation of the hardness of life for those beyond the shelter of the loving home in which he has himself been nurtured. Of the years that followed this discovery, which drove him forth from home and family in search of a solution of the problem of the sorrow and suffering of all existence, he next sees a picture, years of struggle and sustained endeavour, of the trial and ultimate rejection of the austerities and penances of extreme asceticism, of long periods of introspection, and, finally, of the great moment of revelation when the cause of sorrow and suffering was flashed upon his mind, and the way of escape therefrom became clear. His mind lingers, perhaps, upon the first great sermon in which these illuminating flashes of insight were formulated for the salvation of mankind, and then travels on over the succeeding years of a ministry which has brought into existence a band of followers, the founders, as we now see, of the greatest monastic order in the world. And so he comes back to the present, the years of intense and fruitful struggle behind him—years which had seen the young man of a small Aryan tribe dwelling amidst the forests of the Himālayan foothills become a world-wide teacher of men, the Enlightened One, the Buddha. And knowing that the hour of his death is at hand, he gives orders as to his funeral: "As men treat the body of a King of Kings, Ananda, so should they treat the remains of a Tathāgatha."

It fell to the Mallas of Kusinara to accord him the funeral customary amongst these Aryan tribes in the case of persons of distinction. And having in due course carried through the ceremony of cremation, they damped down the funeral pyre with water scented with all sorts of perfumes, and collected the bones and placed them in their mote-hall, surrounding them with "a lattice work of spears and with a rampart of bows." And news of the death of the Exalted One was noised abroad, so that requests were made by the rulers of the neighbouring kingdoms and the assemblies of the republics for portions of the relics. "The Exalted One was a Khatriya and so are we," ran the claim. "We are worthy to receive a portion of the relics of the Exalted One. Over the remains of the Exalted One will we put up a sacred cairn." So the remains of Buddha were divided into eight portions and distributed amongst the applicants, and cairns were raised over each portion and over the vessel in which the relics had been collected, and over the embers of the funeral pyre. Thus there were ten cairns in all.

The stupas which we see alike in the Buddhist chapter-halls of to-day—such an one has been built in Calcutta within the last few years for the reception of a relic found in Southern India, and presented by the Government of India to the Mahabodhi Society—and in those ancient halls hewn out of the living rock at such places as Ajanta, Karle, and Ellora, represent the sacred cairns raised up over the funeral ashes of Buddha. Yet the stupa was not a creation of Buddhism, and we may, if our curiosity incites us to further investigation, trace back its history to a still earlier day. When Ajattasatru, King of Magadah, and the spokesmen of the republican tribes declared that they would raise up cairns over the ashes of the departed sage, they were not the authors of some novel plan for honouring the dead; they were but carrying out Buddha's own instruction to Ananda, that his remains should be treated as men treated those of a King of Kings, or person of distinction. Research has shown that amongst these Aryan settlers it was customary to expose the bodies of ordinary men in a public place reserved for the purpose, that they might there be destroyed by animals or disintegrate in the course of time, much as the bodies of the Parsis are disposed of at the present day. But the bodies of more distinguished persons were cremated and cairns raised over the ashes, as was done in Buddha's case. The practice has been traced far back into early Vedic times, and in the dome-shaped structure of the Buddhist stupa Mr. Havell sees a copy of the domical hut built of bamboo or wooden ribs of the chieftain of the clan or tribe. It is a reasonable assumption, he thinks, that at the funeral of distinguished men in early Vedic times, models of their abodes were made as temporary homes for the departed spirits during that period when, in accordance with Vedic ritual, the sacrificial worship of their relatives and descendants for three generations was required to help them on their way from the earthly to the extra - terrestrial spheres.

And just as the Buddhist stupa provides a key to early Aryan custom in the treatment of the dead, so does the Buddhist chapter-hall, in which the stupa is enshrined, afford an indication of the nature of the early Aryan polity, of which tribes like the Mallas and the Licchavis, provide examples. For the chapter-halls of the Buddhist monks were clearly copied from the mote-halls of the Aryan tribes. Buddha himself was a great admirer of the republican system of government amongst the Licchavis. "Have you heard," he asks Ananda, "that the Vajjians hold full and frequent public assemblies?" And upon Ananda saying that this was so, he added, "So long, Ananda, as the Vajjians hold these full and frequent public assemblies, so long may they be expected not to decline but to prosper." And the word *sangha* used of the Order of Buddhist monks, is the word used also to denote the corporations of such tribes as the Mallas and the Licchavis. It serves, in fact, as a key to much that is of extraordinary interest in the ancient polity of Vedic India. Panini, the great grammarian of the seventh century B.C., was at special pains to explain its meaning, namely, a collection of individuals combining for a particular purpose, or, as we should say, a corporation. And it was freely used to denote a great variety of corporations such as trade and craft guilds, religious orders, municipal and village assemblies, and larger political organisations—forms of government, that is to say, other than monarchical.

The Sangha of the Licchavis is a case in point. It was oligarchic rather than democratic, for it seems to have been a parliament of the heads of a number of clans, or groups of families, of which the tribe was composed. Each such chieftain was the ruler of a principality which was in many respects autonomous, but which was subject to the Sangha in the more important matters. The Sangha of the Licchavis, therefore, was a federation of the chieftains of the clans, exercising sovereign power over the state as a whole. There were, however, other political Sanghas of a more democratic type, and while the religious order of the Jains, known as the Jain Sangha, was modelled by its founder Mahavira, who was himself a Kshatriya of Vesali, the capital of the Licchavis, upon the political Sangha of that tribe, the Buddhist Sangha was modelled on the more democratic organisations. The point of chief interest, however, to which our inquiry as to the origin of the Buddhist chapter-hall has led us, is the existence in these early days of a large number and variety of institutions of a representative type, not merely in the administrative but in many other spheres, showing that the principle of collective control and responsibility was a strongly-marked characteristic of the Aryan people. One is curious, naturally, as to the kind of procedure governing the conduct of affairs by such bodies; and it is somewhat strange that while there are many references in the ancient literature to different types of corporation, it is only in the Buddhist books that we find any account of the procedure adopted for the transaction of business. There are good grounds, however, for assuming that the rules of procedure in force in the Buddhist Sangha were framed in accordance with those ordinarily in use in the case of Sanghas generally, for Buddha makes use of a number of technical terms without considering it necessary to explain them. Had he himself been the author of them, it would obviously have been necessary for him, as Professor D. R. Bhandarkar has pointed out,[1] to give some explanation of their meaning.

The description of the procedure given in the Buddhist books shows how remarkable is the resemblance between that of the assemblies of two thousand five hundred years ago and of those of the present day. The dignity of the assembly was arranged for by the appointment of a special officer, whose duty it was to see that members were accorded seats in accordance with their status and seniority. There was also a special officer, corresponding to the parliamentary "Whip" of the present day, who was charged with the responsibility, when necessity arose, of seeing that a quorum was secured. When the meeting had assembled, the member initiating business announced the motion which he desired to submit. The motion was then placed formally before the assembly for discussion. In some cases this was done three times, in others only once. If the members observed silence, the motion became the resolution of the Sangha. If there was discussion and difference of opinion was found to exist, the matter was decided by the vote of the majority, the voting being by ballot. In the case of members prevented by illness or other disability from attending in person, provision was made for the recording of absentee votes.

It will be seen from what has been written above, that the chapter-hall of the Buddhists is the product of a people with whom the principle

[1] In his Carmichael Lectures in 1918, in which he deals in an interesting and scholarly manner with the various systems of administration in force amongst the Aryans in India in these early days.

of the collective direction and control of affairs was a tradition. But besides conveying down the centuries news of the polity of ancient India, it, like the stupa, carries us back also to the ritual of the sacrifice, the earliest known form of the religion of the Indo-Aryan people. If the chapter-hall of the Buddhists had been nothing but a hall of assembly, there had been no need for the surrounding corridor. What was the purpose and origin of this feature of the building? Its purpose, as has been indicated, was to enable pilgrims to walk round the stupa, keeping it always on their right, without interfering with those assembled in the hall. But why this circumambulation of the stupa? The answer given by Mr. Havell is that in this Buddhist custom is to be found the adaptation of a practice derived from Vedic sun worship. The early Aryans when they processed round their altars from left to right were treading the path of the supreme law—that which governed the rising up and the going down of the sun. Gautama, while changing its precise significance, retained the symbolism of the wheel of the law, and with the symbolism there remained the ritual.[1] Hence also, as I have shown elsewhere, the strangely literal manner in which in those Indian border-lands where the curious form of Buddhism known as lamaism is found, the people interpret the phrase "turning the wheel of the law," and the meticulous care with which they circumambulate their stupas (chortens) and other kindred monuments.[2]

We have travelled far from Ellora in our dive into the past. Let us return for a moment to the Visvakarma Cave, that we may take note for future reference before leaving it, of an inscription in the characters of the eighth or ninth century

[1] See Mr. E. B. Havell's "Handbook of Indian Art."
[2] See my "Lands of the Thunderbolt."

A.D., the translation of which runs as follows: "All things proceed from cause; this cause has been declared by the Tathāgatha; all things will cease to exist; this is that which is declared by the great Sramana." Its meaning will become apparent later when we consider the Buddhist doctrine. For the moment we may occupy ourselves with a continuation of our inspection of types of Indian architecture.

These are not exhausted by caves and buildings. There is yet another type, which may be described as a compromise between an excavation and an edifice. Striking examples are to be seen at Māmallapuram, better known, perhaps, as the Seven Pagodas, on the seashore sixty miles south of the city of Madras. Unquestionably the pleasantest way of visiting Māmallapuram is, as I did, to drift with the breeze, aided, when necessary, by a gang of coolies with a tow-rope, down the canal which runs south from Madras. With the descent of the sun a great peace came upon the land, stretching away on all sides to the horizon, uninterrupted save by fields of softly waving paddy and sombre clumps of palm trees. I fell asleep in a vague and shadowy world lit only by the winking night-lights strewn across the velvet curtain of the sky; I was awakened in a world of vivid colour, a strip of golden sand dividing a land of emerald from an azure sea. Between my house-boat on the canal and the ocean there stretched a strip of level ground, from which rose a curious outcrop of boulders and ridges of felspathic gneiss—the raw material of the strange series of temples upon which I now gazed. The most interesting were the monolithic temples, fashioned—for they were not built—somewhere about the fifth or sixth century, out of the huge boulders which the workmen found ready to their hand. These shrines, known as *raths*, are, as Mr. C. S. Crole observes in his "Manual of the Chingleput District," very like Buddhist buildings, and his conclusion is that in them are to be seen "petrifactions of the last forms of Buddhist architecture and the first forms of that of the Dravidian."

Not far from these stands another silent record of the product of India's brooding thought. On the perpendicular face of a cliff of rock, 96 feet in length and 43 feet in height, is sculptured in deep relief a remarkable picture—the most remarkable of its class, according to Ferguson, to be found in India. It is usually known as the "Penance of Arjuna," and depicts an episode in the great Hindu work, the "Mahabharata," a stupendous epic eight times as long as the "Iliad" and the "Odyssey" combined, describing the war between the Pandavas and their cousins the Kauravas for the over-lordship of the land of Bharatvarsha. The particular episode supposed to form the subject-matter of this remarkable panel is one based upon an ancient and deep-seated belief of the Hindus in the efficacy of asceticism in obtaining for man control of supernatural powers. While in exile in the forest before the great battle of Kurukshetra, which was to restore to the Pandavas their lost kingdom, Arjuna, one of the five Pandava brothers, practised austerities in order to win from the gods celestial weapons, and obtained from Shiva, amongst other boons, the matchless bow named Gandiva. The figure, thought to be that of Arjuna, is seen in the posture of an ascetic on the left of a cleft in the rock, which has skilfully been made use of to introduce the snake deity Vasuki, the Naga Raja and his daughter Ulupi rising from their kingdom in the depths to do homage to Arjuna. Shiva with a mace stands to the left of Arjuna, and the remaining spaces of the rock surface are filled with animals, ascetics, and celestial beings, all attracted by the fame of the austerities practised by Arjuna. The elephants of the great god Indra—and it is worth remarking that the capital of Bharatvarsha was called Hastinapura, after Hastin the elephant and mount of Indra—bulk largely in the lower right-hand portion of the bas-relief, and come like all the rest to gaze upon Arjuna.

This great record of a famous episode hewn in the rock at Māmallapuram makes a noble introduction to one of the great literary treasures of India. When one has had time to dive into it, one discovers sandwiched into an enthralling epic story a profound philosophical treatise, known as the Baghavād Gita, the most universally treasured of all the sacred volumes of the Hindus even at the present day. But a consideration of this remarkable volume must be postponed to a later stage.

It is perhaps unnecessary to explain that the brief references to some of the buildings which press themselves upon the notice of the traveller wherever he goes in India are not in any way intended to constitute studies in architecture or archaeology. The buildings mentioned have been selected at random amongst those which I have seen myself for one purpose, and one purpose only, that of introducing the visitor to the wonderful diversity of style of the edifices raised over a vast span of time to the known and unknown gods of Indian belief, which in its turn testifies to the prolixity of conception of the unseen world which has flourished upon Indian soil. Whence came these successive waves of immigrant stock which have given to India so rich a store? That question has been briefly answered already in the opening chapter of this volume, wherein it has been shown that the great gateway into India has

Plate 5

ROCK SCULPTURE AT MĀMALLAPURAM.

". . . a cleft in the rock which has skilfully been made use of to introduce the snake deity and his daughter rising from their kingdom in the depths."

always stood, until the conquest of the sea opened up a new and far wider doorway, in the tangled labyrinth of the mountains on the north-west. It is well, then, at this early stage to bring this ancient highway under examination.

CHAPTER IV

THE NORTH-WEST FRONTIER

BROADLY speaking, the North-West Frontier may be said to run from the heat-laden plains of Makran, whose southern shores are washed by the Arabian sea, in a direction slightly east of north up to the pine-clad highlands of Kashmir. Politically, and to a large extent also ethnographically, this huge tract of desert and mountain falls into two distinct parts, marked off by the Gomal river. The southern portion comprises the great block of territory known as Baluchistan, which forms a rough square bounded by Sind on the east, Afghanistan on the north, and Persia and the Arabian sea on the west and south respectively, with a wedge-shaped excrescence projecting from its north-east corner. North of the Gomal the frontier region consists of a long strip of uninterrupted mountain of varying width, inhabited by Pathan or Pashtu-speaking tribes.

A very fair idea of the physical characteristics of Baluchistan may be gained by climbing any of the hills which rise abruptly from the plateau round Quetta. My own bird's-eye view of the country was obtained from the precipitous sides of a peak called Takatoo, whence I gazed down upon a scene happily described by Mr. D. de S. Bray as "a chaotic jumble of mud-coloured mountains, for all the world like a bewildered herd of Titanic camels." The whole country is outside the monsoon area and has an annual rainfall of about 9 inches, with the result that the rivers which loom so large in the map exist for a brief period in the year only. Nor is it only in the matter of rivers that the map shows symptoms of indulging in unconscious irony. The lakes painted in limpid blue create expectations of something very different from the "gloomy swamps of reality," and a laborious journey of 500 miles across the crude expanse of desiccated hill and scorched plain which lies between Quetta and the Persian frontier taught me to regard with grave suspicion the "refreshing oases of green and the named localities innumerable" which appear in the map and which seem to have been inserted chiefly with the object of bearing witness to the meticulous industry of the draughtsman.

The whole country revels in contrasts. "The winter cold of the uplands baffles description," while to give some idea of the midsummer heat of the Kachhi plain even so graphic a writer as Mr. Bray finds himself compelled to fall back upon the hackneyed local proverb which hints at the superfluity of Hell "to depict that burning, fiery furnace." The land likewise possesses an altogether extraordinary potential fertility; but by an unfortunate dispensation of Providence the one agent necessary to convert the potential into actual—namely, water—is for the most part lacking. Where it can be applied you can grow what you please; but often enough "Nature is so perverse that where there is land there is no water, and where there is water there is no land." [1]

Its people fit appropriately enough into the somewhat rough and unfinished setting with which Nature has provided them. Their occupa-

[1] The quotations are from Mr. Denys Bray's census report on Baluchistan for 1911.

tions are simple—chiefly agriculture, camel-driving, and flock-owning—and the standard of their civilisation is primitive. Made up in the main of Baluchis, Brahuis, and Afghans, they are picturesque in appearance and manly in their bearing. To men of the type of Sir Robert Sandeman, who may be said to have been the founder of Baluchistan as it exists to-day, they made a powerful appeal, and the influence which he exercised over them was undoubtedly based largely upon the homage which they themselves instinctively paid to a virile and sympathetic personality. That some decades of contact with the system of administration introduced by Sir Robert Sandeman and carried on by his successors has done something to soften and improve the primitive ethics of the tribes is shown by a report issued by the agent to the Governor-General early in the present century, wherein it is stated that "in the Magasi country a decision of the Shahi jirga disallowing the custom under which the revenge due on a guilty man can be taken on his relations if the offender has absconded, has been recorded and will be treated as a leading case."

Those whose lot it has been to live and work in Baluchistan find more of interest and attraction in its wild spaciousness than would appear probable from a mere bowing acquaintance with the country and its inhabitants; but it is no longer in Baluchistan that frontier problems present themselves in their most poignant form. It is in the long, sinuous stretch of rugged mountain land that runs from the Gomal valley to the Swat river that is to be found what one of India's viceroys has described as "the most critical, most anxious, and most explosive section" of the entire land frontier of the continent. It is here that the real interest of the frontier centres, for it is in this stretch of intractable country with its difficult and wayward peoples that are to be found the conditions governing the broad principles of frontier policy and creating the host of subsidiary local problems which add immeasurably to the complexity of the whole question.

In Baluchistan British administration runs up to the Afghan boundary; north of the Gomal, except at one or two points, it stops considerably short of it. The frontier here consists, therefore, of a belt of territory enclosed between two boundary lines, known as the administrative frontier and the political frontier. British administration ceases at one; Afghan administration begins at the other. Between the two the tribes enjoy political and municipal independence. The political frontier was arrived at by agreement with the Amir of Afghanistan in 1893, and is sometimes known as the Durand line. It has never been demarcated in its entirety. The administrative frontier coincides roughly with the boundary which we took over from the Sikhs, but has undergone small alterations from time to time as local circumstances have demanded. The distinctive characteristics of the tribes inhabiting this wild borderland are selfishness, vanity, treachery, vindictiveness, and general lawlessness. Their attitude towards one another is one of thinly-veiled antagonism which may at any moment break out into open hostility. This inter-tribal aggressiveness is only overruled by religious fanaticism and the fear and hatred excited by the smallest suspicion of foreign interference, so that it is said of the Afghans of the frontier that they are never at peace except when they are at war. Asked by a British officer what would be their attitude in the event of war between Great Britain and Russia, a party of tribesmen answered: "We would just sit up here on our mountain tops watching you both fight, until we saw one or other of you utterly defeated; then we would come down and loot the vanquished till the last mule! God is great! What a time that would be for us!"[1] It would indeed, for their favourite pastime is raiding and thieving.

One would hardly expect that the duty of keeping watch and ward over these troublous marches would be a popular one. The life of a frontier officer is hard, and he treads daily on the brink of eternity. Yet despite its obvious drawbacks the fact remains that these endless ranges of rugged, granitic, mesozoic, and tertiary rocks rising from lower levels covered with wind-blown deposits, do possess the power of inspiring in those whose lot is cast among them an extraordinary enthusiasm. At first one is rather puzzled to find the explanation. The unending tangle of cliffs and peaks limned in hard outline against the sky are not always beautiful, though they are generally impressive. Closer acquaintance proves that they do contain spots of marvellous beauty, where the views to be obtained under different effects of light and shade are such as to stir the deepest chords of one's aesthetic sensibility. Who is there, indeed, among those who have experienced it, who will not testify to the indescribable delight of long days of glorious toil among the mountains, followed by night beneath the stars crowned with the golden glory of the dawn? The world slumbers, all Nature is at rest, and then there comes the first faint stirring of the breeze among the trees: the soft, cool caress upon one's cheek as it passes by, a perfumed herald of approaching day. Slowly the black draperies of night fall away. There is no colour yet; all is black and white with innumerable

[1] T. L. Pennell, M.D., "Among the Wild Tribes of the Afghan Frontier."

intermediate shades of grey—a giant etching on the canvas of the sky—a marvellous monochrome. The silence of the night is broken; something scurries among the pines; the note of a bird trembles on the air. While one gazes spellbound the monochrome becomes irradiated under the influence of a magic brush. The chilly whiteness of the distant snows softens and glows pink and gold. The dark shadows which veiled the mountains to the west creep slowly down to the valley bottom. The trees become green, the mountain torrents limpid, the smell of incense rises from olive-coloured tufts of wormwood, and from far below spirals of blue-grey smoke rise lazily from the abodes of men. Day has come.

Such is the wonder of the dawn. An artist may paint it; a master of words may describe it; but who can explain it? The material of the picture is simple enough, crude elemental substances for the most part—rock and stone, earth and conglomerate, humidity congealed by low temperature, wood and fibre coloured by chlorophyll, all tinted, perhaps, as a result of the effect of varying quantities of vibrations known as light waves; but the whole, when analysed by the chemist and the physicist, a mere collection of energy and matter in different forms. To the beasts of the field and the fowls of the air it is this; to primitive man it is probably little more; but to the man who has eyes to see and ears to hear and a soul to feel it is something infinitely more—it is the far-off reflection of a splendour which is not of earth; a token of the divine in man.

It is experiences of this kind which confound the man who holds that the alpha and omega of the universe are explicable upon a naturalistic basis, and a naturalistic basis alone. He may argue that the instruments by which the beauty of the dawn is conveyed to the perceiving mind—the eye and the ear—are the products of natural selection; and there is no need to waste time in disputing the cogency of his reasoning, for the eye and the ear possess an indubitable survival value. But no one, surely, will claim a survival value for his aesthetic emotions, for a mere capacity for appreciating natural beauty can have no influence one way or the other upon the shaping and the preservation of the individual or the species. Are we, then, to designate the whole gamut of our aesthetic experiences an accidental by-product of the play and interplay of natural forces which shape the evolution of the human race? So improbable an assumption will scarcely carry conviction to an impartial inquirer. Such a person will surely find that his aesthetic experiences fit far more readily into a theistic frame, whether his conception of the divine approximates to the monotheism of the Christian or the mystic pantheism of the intellectual Hindu. And he will care little that his theories or beliefs are not susceptible of the empirical proof without which, on a naturalistic view, knowledge cannot exist. His experience is his, and no amount of learned disputation can rob him of it or of that which he derives from it.

I do not suggest that the average warden of the marches habitually subjects his feelings to this kind of analysis, but I do suggest that the circumstances of his life are such that he frequently experiences the species of spiritual exaltation induced by solitude amid the grandeur of Nature, and that such experience is one of the factors that go to make the magic of the frontier. No doubt there are many others which are less subtle, and therefore more easily analysed. Life on the frontier, for example, unmistakably drags a man out of the rut of conventional existence. Its mountains and valleys share with the desert an atmosphere of large-hearted freedom. One lives here close to Nature and far removed from artificiality. Life is full of the breadth of vast spaces and the vigour of the strong, clean breath of the hills. The absence alike of the amenities and the restraints of civilisation breed a buoyant self-reliance. Its rock-crowned keeps pulse with passion—but passion that is virile and keen, and that is redeemed by its surroundings from the cramped pettiness that haunts the emotional passages in the drama of human existence in cities. The Afridi slays and is slain with wild enjoyment, and this attitude towards fundamentals is contagious. His ethics are based upon a literal belief in the righteousness of taking an eye for an eye and a tooth for a tooth; and this simple view of the right method of ensuring the perpetuation of justice upon earth gives his personality an acute interest. It is recorded in a casual entry in the pages of the Khyber political diary for the month of June 1907, how an old feud between the Zarif Khel and Hakim Khel sections of the Khusrogi Zakka Khel was finally disposed of by the former killing three of their own men in order to square their account with the latter. So signal an example of the meticulous care with which the requirements of an unwritten code are observed cannot fail to exact a measure of admiration which need not be more than tempered, surely, by a perusal of a subsequent observation appearing somewhat in the nature of a postscript in the same record, from which we learn that the Zarif Khel "had also the inheritance of the large estates of the deceased for their second object in view."

It may sound improbable, in view of what has been said as to the characteristics of the tribesmen, that they should add their quota to the attraction of the frontier. Nevertheless I have little hesitation in saying that this is the case. The Pashtu-speaking man of the hills is selfish, vain, treacherous, vindictive and cruel, and outward and visible signs of these characteristics are sufficiently abundant. Women without noses are comparatively common in tribal territory—victims of marital jealousy and vindictiveness; the roll of Englishmen who have lost their lives through Pathan treachery is a long one. A typical instance came under my notice when I was camped on the borders of the Mahsud country in 1900. A young English officer with a party of native troops was in pursuit of a band of Mahsud marauders. One of the robbers fell wounded among the rocks, and the remainder made off. The Englishman went forward to take and succour the wounded man. He lay hidden among the rocks, and the Englishman passed by without seeing him. Whereupon the wounded man, stealthily raising his rifle, shot him dead through the back.

This act of treachery might perhaps be attributed to racial fanaticism. Not so the fell blow by which Mohammed Ashgar died. This man, we are told, had amassed much property by raiding, and throughout Tirah generally was much respected and liked. Like most men of the border, he carried on an hereditary feud, and for the most part he walked abroad with caution. Relying, however, upon the fact that his three enemies had given security that they would suspend the feud for a time, he proceeded to a tribal assembly without followers. It was soon seen that he had taken too much for granted. His enemies had hired a fourth man, who deliberately shot him in open durbar. It is recorded that as the people did not know how many of those present were interested in the murder, "no one moved or protested until the meeting broke up in the usual way." It is, perhaps, only fair to add that this peculiarly cold-blooded piece of treachery "caused a great stir in Tirah."

In the ordinary way the blood feud, of course, calls for no comment. It is a necessary product of the "eye for an eye and a tooth for a tooth" conception of justice. And little difficulty is usually experienced in temporarily suspending a feud when more important matters are toward. The following entry in the Khyber political diary, dated May 18, 1907, provides a sufficient indication of the usual state of affairs regarding the institution: "Now that the Afridis have returned to their homes in Tirah they have reopened their private feuds, and are prosecuting them vigorously. No less than five men were killed during the week." Episodes such as this are merely examples of the working of the rule that a life must be given for a life. And if, as we are so fond of saying, the exception proves the rule, the Mahsuds obligingly provide it. The chalweshtis, or tribal police appointed by the jirga to carry out its orders, are inviolable while engaged upon their duties, and in the event of their causing death while in the execution of them, the blood feud does not lie.

As for selfishness, it is so deep-rooted and so widespread that it may confidently be taken into consideration when a forecast of the behaviour of any particular tribe or clan has to be made. Thus when punitive measures against the Zakka Khel were in contemplation in 1906, the Political Agent wrote: "There is, of course, the possibility of an outburst of what we call fanaticism, but what the tribesmen call patriotism, and this might unite all sections in a last struggle against us; but the dominating characteristic of the Afridi, his overpowering selfishness, gives reason to believe that he would sacrifice his neighbour to save himself."

Specific instances of this unpleasing trait may be observed any day. One Usman, a Zakka Khel bad character, fearing punishment at the hands of the tribe, crossed the border into Afghanistan until such time as the storm blew over. The behaviour of his friends provided matter for a brief but instructive passage in an official report. "His neighbours," wrote the Political Officer, "are grazing their cattle in his crops." Yet with all his many unpleasant traits, he is a strange bundle of contradictions. In many respects he resembles a wayward child. With all his treachery he pays inviolable respect to the laws of hospitality. Should circumstances so turn out that a man found his most deadly enemy his guest, his life would be sacred. It is probably due to the sanctity of the laws of hospitality that one finds, side by side with natural treachery, an astonishing capacity for loyalty. The most remarkable example of loyalty on a large scale is contained in the story of the Khyber Rifles. It was obvious that the trials to which the men composing the corps might be subjected would be great, and it has been officially admitted that the experiment was viewed "with mistrust by many and with misgiving by all." Yet through all the trials with which they were beset, save only in one, they stood the test. That one supreme trial in which they were found wanting was an issue of the world war—a thing incalculable in its ramifications and one which wrecked the calculations of many besides those who built upon the capacity for loyalty of the wild tribes of the Indian borderland. Until this grim and incalculable terror came upon mankind, the honour of the Khyber Rifles remained untarnished. During the operations against the Zakka Khel in 1908, not a man deserted and not a rifle was lost. They had eaten the salt of the sirkar, and to their hosts they remained faithful—

even unto death. The nature of the test is sufficiently indicated by the official appreciation: "This corps, which is mainly composed of Afridis, including some 350 Zakka Khel, had to take part in an expedition against a people to whom the men were bound not only by race and religion, but by the closest ties of blood. Indeed in many cases in the expedition, brother was fighting against brother and son against father."

Doubtless the personal influence of the British officers of the corps was to a great extent responsible for the splendid record of the men. The personal element counts for much with the frontier tribes. Like the children they are, they are peculiarly susceptible to such influence. And herein lies the source of the attraction which they possess for men of strong and sympathetic natures. Force of character counts everywhere; but the influence which a man's character exerts upon those around him is seldom so palpable as it is upon the frontier. Here a man becomes conscious of his power. He sees the effects of his influence in the devotion which he not infrequently inspires in those who serve him. He feels it in the presence of the tribal jirgars which he may be called upon to meet. In his official dealings with the tribes he is conscious that there lies behind him a great tradition. He is treading in the footsteps of men who have left great names behind them—great because of their reputation for justice, uprightness, sympathy, and understanding. It is by these men and by him that Great Britain and all that Great Britain stands for is judged. He is the guardian of the honour not only of the Government which he directly represents, but of his race.

CHAPTER V

AN HISTORIC HIGHWAY

THE formidable nature of the great natural rampart which encircles India on the north-west should now be apparent. What of the gateway giving entrance through its guardian walls?

A little north of latitude 34, a natural cut in the mountains runs for a distance of twenty miles from Jamrud on the edge of the trans-Indus plain, through the outer range at right angles to its axis, to an open spot at Landi Khana on the frontier of Afghanistan. It is known as the Khyber Pass, and its peculiar importance is derived from the fact that it forms a connecting link in the chain of communication between the Kabul river valley and the plains of India. The value of this historic highway possesses all the elements of permanence, since it rests on a stable geographical basis rather than upon changing political circumstances. The Kabul river valley provides us, in fact, with a remarkable example of the decisive influence which geographical conditions are capable of exerting upon the making of history. Until the coming of sea power in comparatively recent times, it constituted practically the only channel through which could enter the many influences which have played so large a part in shaping the destinies of India. It provided the main inlet through which flowed the tide of migratory Aryan stock which eventually took root in the fertile soil of the Ganges Valley and gave to the world the rich gift of Indian thought and civilisation.

Many centuries later, though still three hundred years before the Christian era, the spirit of a great Western civilisation was borne along its stony bottom in company with the armed legions of Alexander of Macedon. Any one who takes the trouble to stroll through the museum at Peshawar may see at a glance the mark thus left by Greek culture upon the art of India. The Gandhara collection of sculptures and relievoes here on view bears the unmistakable impress of Hellenistic genius. The theme of the artists is purely Indian, namely, the life of Buddha, but many of the decorative features which figure in the bas-reliefs depicting the legends associated with the Teacher's life, are purely Greek. Here one will notice Corinthian capitals and pilasters, there a scroll of vine leaves and bunches of grapes. In another place one meets with an essentially Greek idea represented by kneeling tritons, or again by a winged marine monster. But perhaps the most striking offspring of Greek art and Indian piety is to be found in the images of Buddha himself. It would seem, indeed, that their very existence is due solely to Greek influence, for the absence of any actual representation of the great Teacher in the older monuments, in which his presence is conventionally indicated by some sacred symbol, makes it clear that it was contrary to Indian practice to depict his person. " It is," as Dr. Spooner suggests, " as though the figure of Buddha himself had been deemed too holy for representation until the Hellenistic artists of Gandhara, familiar with the comprehensive pantheon of Greek art, came to the assistance of the Indian Buddhist and tutored his first attempts at portraying the divine."[1]

[1] " Handbook to the Sculptures in the Peshawar Museum," by Dr. D. B. Spooner, Ph.D.

A thousand years after Christ, we see another conqueror—Mahmūd of Gazni—treading in the footsteps of Alexander, and opening another momentous chapter in the life story of the continent. Mahmūd was out for plunder. His attitude towards India was the instinctive attitude of all hillmen towards men of the plains. He swooped down with his fierce and fanatical legions upon the Rajputs, whom he met and defeated at Peshawar. And for a little space, as the life of nations goes, he fought and plundered right royally.

Many incalculable things sprang from this first tumultuous incursion of the fighting legions of Islam. With successive waves of Muhammadan invaders there swept through the mountain passes fresh thoughts and new ideals. The shock of impact was not physical merely, but mental also. The polytheism and pantheism in which the whole land was steeped was challenged by a pure and aggressive monotheism. The tired pessimism of Hinduism found a formidable rival in a new religion of hope. The quickening force thus introduced into the thought of India was not without effect. The ferment of mind resulting from it found expression in the teaching of two great Indian figures of the fifteenth century, Kabir and Nānak. And out of it arose in due course the powerful community of the Sikhs.

Nor was the invasion of Mahmūd less fruitful regarded from a more material point of view. He was the forerunner of the Moghul dynasty, the splendour of whose sway is, perhaps, unsurpassed in the annals of the world, as witness the wonderful legacy of architectural beauty bequeathed by them to a fortunate posterity. If, as must surely be the case, a lovely building is but the embodiment in wood or stone of a beautiful idea—itself the fleeting reflection of the divine flashed in moments of inspiration upon the mind of man, from some far-off and dimly apprehended realm of spiritual splendour—then must we conclude that the cultured classes of Moghul times were not only endowed in high degree with the vision that transcends the bounds of earth, but were fortunate also in being able to command the technical skill, without which their artistic genius could never have been given concrete expression for the delight and benefit of mankind.

It may also be thought not unworthy of remark that among other results accruing from this first incursion of Islam through the narrow passage way of the Khyber Pass, is the addition of something like 70,000,000 Muhammadans to the vast tally of those owning allegiance to the British crown.

To-day the Pass plays a less historic part. A state of equilibrium has been reached between the vast reservoirs of Central Asia and the great basin of the Indian plains. Like water, the human flood in obedience to natural law has found its own level. The basin has long since filled up, and such movement as there is through the channel provided by the Pass represents little more than surface ripples blown now this way, now that, by the passing breeze.

Yet the Pass, though no longer the scene of great migratory movements, responding for the most part to impulses which were instinctive rather than consciously purposive, is still, as it was before, the main land thoroughfare between India and Central and Western Asia. To say that it is not to-day the highway of nations or of armies, is not to say that it is not capable at any moment of becoming so. The British statesman who, towards the close of the nineteenth century, penned the despatch defining the policy of Great Britain towards the frontier, was haunted by a knowledge of its possibilities. From first to last, he was at pains to lay stress upon the determination of the Government to abstain from interference in the lands beyond its administrative border. Nevertheless he felt himself compelled to order that in any readjustment of the relations between the Government of India and the Afridi tribes, the safety of the Pass was to be "a paramount consideration." Whether viewed from the standpoint of existing obligations towards the Amir of Afghanistan or from that of the protection of British subjects, the maintenance of the Khyber Pass as a safe artery of communication and of trade must be "an essential measure." [1]

Military opinion, naturally enough, leaned towards the view that the object aimed at could best be attained by placing the Pass under effective military control. Of the two great highways between India and Afghanistan—the Khyber and the Bolan—the latter was already in military occupation. If we were to be in a position to advance, in case of necessity, to a strategical line running from Kabul to Kandahar and to fulfil the guarantee which we had given for the integrity of Afghanistan, the obvious policy, it was argued, was to assume similar control over the former. Various proposals were made—the construction of important works at Landi Kotal, their occupation by regular troops, and the laying of a railway through the Pass.

The scheme finally adopted fell short of these suggestions. By an agreement made with the Afridis in 1881, the safety of the Pass had been entrusted to the Afridi tribe, whose headmen provided a body of men for patrol and escort duties. In theory, this corps was under the control of, and responsible to, the tribal council; in practice control over it came to be exercised

[1] Despatch from Lord George Hamilton, Secretary of State for India, to the Government of India, dated January 28, 1898.

more and more by the political officer in charge of the Khyber Pass. By putting this corps on a more regular basis, by paying it, arming it, and officering it with British officers, the Government of India assumed authority over the Pass with a minimum amount of disturbance of existing arrangements. The force which was thus raised for duty in the Pass became a regiment known as the Khyber Rifles, consisting of two battalions each six hundred strong, with headquarters at Landi Kotal. It was placed definitely under the control of the Political Officer in the Khyber and was supported in case of necessity by a flying column of regular troops based on Peshawar. Nor, until a new situation was created by the short-lived third Afghan War, which broke out quite unexpectedly early in the summer of 1919, was the proposal for the construction of a railway proceeded with. Up to that time you might travel as far as Jamrud, nine miles from Peshawar on the road to the Khyber, by rail; but there you discovered that you had reached railhead, and if you desired to enter the Pass itself, you had to do so by road. It was well worth doing.

The road is a British road, metalled and admirably graded, over the whole of whose twenty miles you may travel swiftly and smoothly in a motor car. Half-way between Jamrud and Landi Kotal it passes the fort of Ali Masjid, perched on an isolated hill which rises in the middle of a wild ravine, and later it debouches on to a comparatively open space on which are scattered a few small villages in the midst of patches of struggling cultivation. Here on the north side of the road stands the fort of Landi Kotal—the ultimate outpost of Great Britain in the direction of Afghanistan. A short distance beyond the fort the political frontier is reached, and British rule and metalled roads come to an abrupt end.

The ethics of the Khyber are interesting. The road passes through the country of a people with whom raiding and plundering are at once a business and a pastime, and the cultivation of blood feuds an hereditary preoccupation. Yet it is an unwritten law, which possesses all the inviolability of the laws of the Medes and Persians, that no man shall shoot another man so long as he be on the road. Whence it comes about that the observant traveller will notice long, deep trenches running from such small villages as are to be seen in the neighbourhood right up to the metalled road, so that safe access may be had to this curious *via sacra.*

Nevertheless, the hook-nosed traders with their kafilahs of shaggy camels who journey between India and Afghanistan, take nothing for granted in the Khyber Pass. On two days in the week—Tuesdays and Fridays—the strong arm of Great Britain stretches out over the Pass and lifts a warning finger against all would-be law-breakers. Patrols of military police piquet the heights above the road, the sharp-shooters of the Khyber Rifles, who man the chain of block-houses from Jamrud to Landi Kotal, maintain a sharp look-out, and escorts drawn from the same force accompany the ascending and descending caravans. On these two days, and on these two days only, do the kafilahs take the road. Here and there on the mountain sides you may notice rows of small cairns of carefully whitewashed stones, five, six, seven, or eight cairns to the row. These give the rifleman in the nearest block-house the exact range—500, 600, 700, or 800 yards. It is significant that little things of this kind cause no comment in the Khyber Pass.

At the time of which I am writing, before the

Plate 6.

THE KHYBER PASS.

". . . the hook-nosed traders who journey between India and Afghanistan."

third Afghan War, you might have noticed other scratchings on the mountain sides. These marked the *tracé* of the railway which was proposed but was not then built. It would have run up to the Afghan frontier, and in Afghanistan railways were taboo. Railways are dangerous things for buffer states; that, at least, is the view of the buffer state itself, which looks, moreover, with grave suspicion and dislike upon any railway that even approaches its frontier. Many years ago Russia pushed a line south from her trans-Caspian system. It ran up against the Afghan frontier as against a blind wall, and there it remains to this day. From the south-east Britain pushed her line of railway, driving it through the Khojak range to the desert sands on the Afghan frontier beyond, and there it too remains. A little short of Jamrud on the Peshawar—Jamrud line, a branch wandered off in a north-westerly direction. This was the beginning of a project much talked of at one time, and known as the Loi-Shilman railway.

The idea was that it should follow the Kabul river and debouch on to a small open space on the far side of the no man's land that lies between the administrative and political frontiers, thus providing an alternative route to the Khyber Pass. It was pushed by an enterprising and insistent soldier, and it was delayed by an autocratic and strong-minded Secretary of State who wanted the signature of the ruler of Afghanistan to the Anglo-Russian Convention of 1907. In the result we got neither the railway nor the signature. Construction as far as Torsappa, twenty-three miles from Peshawar and eight or nine miles beyond the administrative frontier, had been sanctioned in 1905, and rails were actually laid to within four or five miles of this spot, when it attracted the unfavourable attention of the House of Commons, with the result that orders were issued that work on it should cease. I believe that something like £500,000 was spent on the project altogether; but when I last visited the spot in 1912, the metals so laboriously laid were about to be taken up again—another sad example of the fate which overtakes all railway enterprise directed towards unwilling buffer states.

It was unfortunate for the advocates of the scheme that the surveys carried on beyond Torsappa, or "mile 300" as it came to be known, were made at a time when that part of the frontier was stirred by one of its periodic spasms of unrest. The impunity with which the Zakka Khel inhabiting the country south of the Khyber had, for some years past, flouted the authority of Great Britain, was having its effect upon neighbouring tribes, and notably upon the Mohmands to the north of the Pass. This unrest among the Mohmands was attributed by critics in the House of Commons to the surveys for the railway, which was described by Sir Charles Dilke as part of a project for constructing a cantonment at Torsappa, "in connection with which 6000 men were to be stationed 6000 feet above the level of the sea in a hopeless spot where there was not a blade of grass for miles." It was, of course, denied by the Government that there was any definite evidence to show that the surveys of the proposed railway were the cause of the Mohmand rising. It was even stated that the Mohmands nearest the country surveyed had remained entirely friendly. Yet a dispassionate study of published documents makes it difficult to believe that the prospect of the penetration of their country by a railway had not the effect of a strong irritant upon the Mohmands in their existing state of disaffection.

It is significant that the Mohmands were joined

in their rising by a considerable body of Afghan subjects who had earlier shown opposition to the examination of the railway alignment by a railway expert, Mr. Johns, at Smatzai and Shinpokh. At the end of November 1907, the Political Officer in the Khyber telegraphed that a strong force of Khuda Khel and Khwaizai Mohmands were holding the left bank of the Kabul river and were determined not to allow the railway survey to be made. And when the cause of a rising of the Mohmands and Afghans, which broke out in the following spring, was officially attributed to fear of an intention on our part to invade their territory, it became clear that the critics had reasonably good grounds for the conclusions which they drew. And so until after the third Afghan War, at any rate, the railway project remained in abeyance.

Such, then, is the great gateway through which has passed the long procession of those who, through the centuries, have made their way with such momentous results to the far-stretching plains of Hindustan. Longer than most of the historic highways of the world, it has resisted the attack of the railway engineer. And if the soldier and the man of commerce find cause for satisfaction at the prospect of its early capitulation, the man of more romantic temperament who is untroubled by utilitarian considerations will, perhaps, heave a sigh of regret at the thought of the early disappearance of the immemorial methods of communication before the advent of the instruments of a less picturesque, if superior, civilisation.

CHAPTER VI

THE PROBLEM OF THE FRONTIER

THE historic importance of the North-West Frontier has been explained; its rugged nature has been described. That the problems to which it has necessarily given rise should have taxed to the utmost the statesmanship of those charged with the duty of safeguarding India from external aggression, may well have been inferred from what has been written in the preceding chapters.

There are, indeed, few questions which have demanded so large a share of the time and thought of successive viceroys as those concerning the relations of Great Britain with the peoples on and beyond the frontier. And their manner of dealing with them merits, therefore, careful examination.

As has been explained already, the term "frontier" as applied to the North-West of India stands for something which differs in one important respect from the precise meaning ordinarily attaching to the word. The North-West Frontier consists not of a single geographical line, but of two such lines, together with the belt of territory enclosed between them. Such a frontier possesses the possibilities of complications, which cannot arise in the case of a simple frontier consisting of a single boundary-line more or less clearly demarcated between one State and another, for it offers the option of two alternative policies. The paramount Power can adopt a policy of non-interference towards the inhabitants of the intermediate belt of territory, provided, of course, that they in their turn carry out such agreements as it may have been found necessary to make with them—such, for example, as the granting of facilities for transit trade. On the other hand, the existence of a neutral zone, peopled by semi-barbarous tribes, is a standing invitation to a strong and highly civilised Power to push gradually forward to the real frontier, until the neutral zone has been absorbed and the frontier reduced to the more ordinary and simpler type.

No better illustration of this tendency can be found than that of Russia in her advance across Asia towards India; nor could the case for a forward policy under such circumstances have been put with greater cogency than it was by the Russian Chancellor, Prince Gortchakoff, in a circular note to the Powers of Europe in 1864: "Raids and acts of pillage," he wrote, "must be put down. To do this the tribes on the frontier must be reduced to a state of submission. This result once attained, these tribes take to more peaceful habits, but are in turn exposed to the attacks of the more distant tribes against whom the State is bound to protect them. . . . If, the robbers once punished, the expedition is withdrawn, the lesson is soon forgotten. . . . In order to put a stop to this state of permanent disorder, fortified posts are established in the midst of these hostile tribes, and an influence is brought to bear on them which reduces them by degrees to a state of submission. But other more distant tribes beyond this outer line come in turn to threaten the same dangers and necessitate the same measures of repression. The State is thus forced to choose between two alternatives—either to give up this endless labour and to abandon its frontier to perpetual disturbance, or to plunge deeper and deeper into barbarous countries. . . . Such has been the fate of every country which has found itself in a similar position. All have been forced by imperious necessity into this onward march, where the greatest difficulty is to know where to stop."

Great Britain had found herself precisely in this position. Imperious necessity had carried her by degrees across India, and had eventually landed her up against the granite walls that hem in the dusty trans-Indus plains. It was here that she decided to stay her advance. But the invitation to go further was ever present; and that it was not always refused may be seen from the map. British administration has pushed its way up the Kurram Valley as far as the political frontier. It has made considerable inroads into Waziristan. Nor is the policing of the great high-road which runs through the Khyber Pass any longer entrusted to the tribes through whose territory it passes. And there have always been those who have urged that this policy of penetration should be pressed further. There has always been a school of thought, that is to say, which has advocated a forward policy.

How long frontier policy might have remained a shuttlecock between the two contending schools it is impossible to say, had it not been for the action of the tribesmen themselves, which lifted the whole question out of the arena of controversy and forced a decision upon the Government. In June 1897 the Tochi Valley became the scene of a violent outbreak. A month later the Swat Valley rose to the cry of *jihād* at the instigation of one Saidulla, known as the mad fakir. Elsewhere the seeds of disaffection were sown and watered by fanatics, who rose rapidly to temporary power and unenviable notoriety. The delimitation of the boundary, drawn up under the Durand Agreement of 1893, was seized upon by them as a convenient pretext for raising the people. Throughout the frontier the smouldering embers of fanaticism, fanned into flame by the fiery preaching of men like the Adda Mullah, the Fakir of Swat, and the Mullah Sayed Akbar, blazed up with sudden and altogether unexpected fury. The whole rising was officially described as "unprecedented alike in the suddenness with which it broke out at each point, in the large extent of country affected, and in the simultaneous action of distinct tribes or sections of tribes." It called for action on a large scale, and resulted in the expedition known as the Tirah Campaign.

So far as frontier policy was concerned, these happenings were decisive. The military operations were pursued with vigour; and on January 28, 1898, as soon as their success was assured, the guiding principles to be observed in future relations with the frontier tribes were laid down in a comprehensive despatch, penned by Lord George Hamilton, then Secretary of State. Two fundamental ideas ran through the despatch—the avoidance of any extension of administrative control over independent tribal territory, and the concentration of military forces to the best possible advantage to enable the Government to carry out their responsibilities. Thus the policy of non-intervention was firmly established.

Lord Elgin, as Viceroy, had to grapple with the rising: it fell to his successor to give effect to the policy to which the rising had given birth. Lord Curzon threw himself into the task with characteristic vigour. To the onlooker he gave the impression of being completely absorbed in his undertaking. His enthusiasm was infectious and his energy amazing. He was gifted with that brilliant type of imagination which is the indispensable handmaiden of successful statesmanship. Moreover, he possessed extensive first-hand knowledge of the frontier and its inhabitants, acquired in the course of previous travel and study. With a flash of insight he divined the solution of the military problem. British and Indian troops were to be withdrawn from the frontier and their place taken by tribal militia, supported, in case of necessity, by flying columns of regulars posted at convenient bases within, but near, the administrative frontier.

A more delicate problem presented itself in the matter of control. The administered districts on the frontier formed a portion of the Punjab, and as such were under the Lieutenant-Governor. The officials on the frontier were Punjab officials, with the consequence that, while the general direction of frontier affairs was vested in the Government of India, the executive control was in the hands of the Punjab Government. So unsatisfactory a system of dual control was scarcely likely to work smoothly. "Labour without responsibility" was the experience of the local Government; "responsibility without control" that of the Government of India. In a despatch dated August 5, 1898, the Secretary of State had suggested placing the Commissioner of Peshawar directly under the Government of India. This proposal had been submitted to the Punjab Government at the time, and had met with wholehearted condemnation at their hands, the then Lieutenant-Governor, Sir M. Young, declaring that such a change could not be brought about "without introducing chaos into the frontier administration." The arguments and conclusions of the local Government were endorsed by the Government of India in a despatch dated September 13, 1900, in the course of which they advocated a more drastic solution, viz. the creation of a new frontier province, controlled and administered by officials directly under the Government of India.

The whole question was reviewed in all its aspects in a masterly minute by the Viceroy himself. He pointed to the fact that for years past the anomalies of the position had been recognised by a long succession of those best qualified to form an opinion. As far back as 1877 the Secretary of State had declared that the conditions under which the frontier had been given to the Punjab were obsolete. With unerring instinct he placed his finger upon the weak points in previous schemes, which had invariably prevented them from materialising. The grandiose project of Lord Lytton, who aimed at creating a huge frontier province running from Hazara to the Indian Ocean, might still "appeal to the imagination of the enthusiast, but was not practicable in fact." Nevertheless, the time had come when the necessity for placing the actual frontier districts under the direct guidance and control of the Government of India could no longer be ignored. In terse and incisive phrases he summed up the case for change. The existing system "had been reprobated by all the greatest frontier authorities for the last quarter of a century. It attenuated without diminishing the ultimate responsibility of the Government of India. It protracted without strengthening their action. It interposed between the Foreign Minister of India and his subordinate agents, not an ambassador, or a minister, or a consul, but the elaborate mechanism of a local Government, and the necessarily exalted personality of a Lieutenant-Governor. Worked as the system had been with unfailing loyalty and with profound devotion to duty, it had yet been the source of friction, of divided counsels, of vacillation, of exaggerated centralisation, of interminable delay." The whole memorandum was a brilliant example of careful analysis and of unimpeachable argument. The history of the past was probed and laid bare; the facts of the existing situation were sifted and marshalled. The chain of argument was carried with unanswerable logic step by step to its inevitable conclusion. Objections were considered and met. The soundness of its reasoning and of the conclusion arrived at was accepted by the Cabinet, who sanctioned the proposal in December of the same year "as tending to express and enforce the direct responsibility of the Indian Government for frontier affairs, and to free the management of frontier politics from the delay inseparable from the present system." In 1901 the North-West Frontier Province came into being.

It had been an argument of the Punjab Government that, being in closer contact with the frontier than the Government of India, they were usually more impressed with the risks of a forward policy than the more distant authority, and that they consequently acted as a drag upon "the suggestions or proposals of the forward school of frontier politicians, the most strenuous advocates of which will be found in military ranks"; [1] the inference, of course, being that with their removal the Government of India might more easily be led by their military advisers into a policy of adventure. Within three years of the formation of the new Province, this matter was put to the test. In 1903 certain Shiah clans were attacked by neighbouring Sunni tribes, and, though they had put up a successful defence, they straightway appealed to be taken under British protection. The appeal was a strong one. The clans in question had been uniformly friendly, and had remained loyal even during the convulsion leading up to the Tirah Campaign. The correspondence which ensued undoubtedly tended to show that the forebodings of the Punjab Government referred to above were

[1] Sir Mackworth Young, October 19, 1898.

not altogether devoid of justification. Colonel Deane, the Chief Commissioner, declared himself strongly in favour of accepting the invitation of the clans, in spite of the known policy of the Government, which he described rather testily as "a forward one only when necessity compels, and stationary where circumstances permit."

Moreover, the Government of India were themselves divided. Their military advisers, looking beyond the actual question under discussion, considered that the time had arrived when "the essential principles" of the policy of non-intervention should come under reconsideration. Lord Kitchener, who was at the time Commander-in-Chief, was convinced of the advantages of a policy of "peaceful penetration," and endorsed the opinion of the military party that our policy "should contemplate the gradual and peaceful extension of our close control over the tribes as far as the Durand boundary, at any rate where this is necessary on strategical considerations." On the other hand, those members of the Government who were opposed to a forward policy laid stress upon the known predilection of the Pathan tribes for managing their own affairs in their own way, and their intense dislike of paying revenue to any suzerain power. They also pointed out that if we carried our control up to the Durand line we should be brought into direct contact with a large section of the Afghan frontier, "across which raids and counter-raids are of frequent occurrence, for the continuous settlement of which we have not yet found any adequate means."

It must have been with feelings of some satisfaction that the Punjab Government observed the presence at the Council Chamber of the wraith of a former Lieutenant-Governor holding up a warning finger. Ten years earlier an almost identical petition had been made by Shiah clans. On the advice of Sir Dennis Fitzpatrick, the then Lieutenant-Governor, their request had been refused. He had had little doubt as to the genuineness of the request, but he thought that as the Shiahs were regarded with fanatical hatred by the great mass of the people who were Sunnis, "to go in there on their invitation and as their protectors would be about the very worst introduction we could possibly have."

Opinion in the Council Chamber being thus evenly balanced, the Government of India were not in a position to submit any definite recommendation to the Government at home. They thought it best to state all the facts and arguments for the consideration of the Secretary of State, and declared that on the larger question of policy they were content to await the decision at which His Majesty's Government might arrive, "after full consideration of the weighty arguments that our military advisers have now adduced."

The Home Government found no such difficulty in making up their mind. Within two months of the receipt of the despatch, the Secretary of State was able to inform the Government of India that, "after full consideration of both sides of the case," His Majesty's Government saw no sufficient reason "for incurring the risks attaching to the proposed extension of the tribal area under our control."

The non-interventionists were thus able to congratulate themselves on the fact that their policy had successfully stood the first serious test to which it was subjected. It was not, however, to remain long unchallenged. Even while the despatch of the Secretary of State upholding it was being penned, the political agent in the Khyber was drawing up a memorandum on the aggressive behaviour of the Zakka Khel, a turbulent clan of the Afridi tribe. And of the measures suggested, the one which he seemed to think might most probably become necessary was the capture and occupation of the Bazar Valley—an important slice of Zakka Khel territory.

Intractable though the Zakka Khel were, the Government hesitated to take drastic action. A mission was about to be despatched to the Amir of Afghanistan at Kabul, and this had a salutary though temporary effect upon the tribes. Raiding diminished and active aggression gave place to an attitude of interested expectancy. After the first impression caused by the success of the Kabul mission had passed off, the Zakka Khel returned to their old ways, and in December 1906 the Chief Commissioner of Peshawar again represented that nothing short of the occupation of the Bazar Valley would effectually protect British subjects in the adjoining settled districts against the constant depredations from which they suffered.

Thus, although the policy of non-intervention had so recently been reaffirmed, circumstances again conspired to give colour to the contention of the Punjab Government that a frontier administration, freed from the restraining influence of the local Government, would be found among the most powerful partisans of the forward school. It would be a mistake, however, to accuse the Chief Commissioner and his subordinates of any wilful desire to embark lightly upon a policy of adventure. They were the victims of circumstances over which they had no control. They were experiencing the imperious necessity of which Prince Gortchakoff had written in his famous circular of 1864—the almost irresistible tendency of the civilised Power to carry forward its own standards of life, to impose order where confusion prevails, to introduce a reasoned system of justice where disputes are settled by unreasoning force; in a word, to substitute the ideals of civilisation for the crude instincts of barbarism. It is a tendency which may acquire additional driving force from greed or from ambition; but at bottom it is an evolutionary process. It is the working in the domain of sociology of the natural law which demands the survival of the fittest. And where civilisation and barbarism are present, it is the former which is obviously the fittest to survive.

The Government hesitated, and while they did so the need for action grew. By the spring of 1907, the tale of outrage had become a formidable one. During the previous seven years, no less than 32 British subjects had been murdered, 29 wounded, 37 kidnapped and held up to ransom, and a large amount of property carried off or destroyed. The headmen of the well-disposed sections of the Afridis had themselves urged upon the administration the desirability of a British occupation of the Bazar Valley, and there was a steadily growing danger lest the immunity of the Zakka Khel from punishment should have the result of bringing other tribes into their camp against us. It was clear that the limits of forbearance had been reached. All attempts to ameliorate the situation without having recourse to military measures had failed, and the Government of India found themselves compelled by the inexorable logic of events to endorse the proposals of the frontier administration involving the occupation of tribal territory. If after occupation we were to remain and administer the Bazar Valley, they wrote, "we could, by making roads, develop it, protect the law-abiding population, and prevent further intrigues with Afghanistan." The tendency was strongly at work.

Nevertheless, the long-overdue punishment of the contumacious clan was to undergo yet further postponement. The most favourable season for military operations was rapidly drawing to a close. The Commander-in-Chief was of opinion that they might with advantage be put off till the autumn, and the Secretary of State showed a strong disinclination to sanction any advance. Licence received an additional ten months' law. And when the Government of India returned to the charge in January of the following year, and formulated definite proposals for the occupation of tribal territory, the Secretary of State showed symptoms of genuine alarm. "My sense of the fundamental objections to a policy of occupation of Zakka Khel territory," he telegraphed on January 30, "is increased by the definite proposals in your letter of the 9th inst." By the irony of fate his telegram crossed a telegram from the Government of India informing him that Peshawar city had just been raided by a gang of Zakka Khel from the Bazar Valley, sixty to eighty strong; that one police constable had been killed and others wounded, and property valued at a lakh of rupees carried off. This was followed by a further telegram in which the Government of India stated that, however restricted their subsequent action might be, the necessity for immediate punitive measures was so great that action could no longer be delayed.

In this the Secretary of State found himself compelled to acquiesce, though he gave his sanction reluctantly and subject to the condition that a strict time limit should be imposed upon the punitive operations in the Bazar Valley, and that they should entail no occupation or annexation. So fearful was he lest the Government of India were about to commit themselves to a definitely forward policy, that he despatched a further telegram four days later which sounded almost like a cry of despair: "It must be clearly understood, I repeat, that the end in view is limited strictly to the punishment of the Zakka Khel, and not occupation or annexation of tribal territory, either directly or indirectly, immediately or ultimately."

Sir James Willcocks, to whom the expedition was entrusted, struck with exemplary swiftness and complete success. The tribesmen were staggered by the rapidity of his advance, and sustained a crushing defeat. The character of the fighting is sufficiently indicated by their casualties, which amounted between February 15th and 21st to a total exceeding those of all the Afridis throughout the Tirah Campaign. By the end of the month peace was declared, and on March the 3rd the Political Officer, Lieutenant-Colonel (afterwards Sir George) Roos-Keppel, to whose skill and knowledge of the frontier the successful outcome of the expedition was largely due, was able to report that a settlement of the Zakka Khel question had been arrived at which he believed would prove durable, and which would improve our relations not only with the Zakka Khel but with the whole of the Afridi clans.

Not a yard of tribal territory had been annexed, while the Afridis as a whole stood surety for the future good behaviour of the Zakka Khel, holding themselves responsible jointly and severally for the various clans. In face of difficulties of the most formidable nature, the policy of non-intervention had again triumphed.

Lest, however, it be assumed from the repeated successes of this policy that the pressure upon the civilised Power to advance need no longer be treated seriously, it is well to try to assess the magnitude of the obstacles which have had to be overcome. The events referred to above have centred in the main round the block of the frontier populated by Afridis. Further south, in the neighbourhood of the Gomal river, dwells the most troublesome, perhaps, of all the frontier tribes, namely, the Mahsud Waziris. The story of our relations with this tribe during recent times gives a fair measure of the extent of the pressure upon us to advance our frontier which has had to be resisted in the past, and which may in the end compel us to bow before the inexorable logic of the arguments set forth in the famous Russian circular.

CHAPTER VII

THE PROBLEM OF THE FRONTIER (*continued*)

We may take the year 1900 as a convenient one in which to pick up the threads of the story of our dealings with the Mahsud Waziris, for the autumn of that year was indeed a time of crisis in their history.

No very cordial relations are to be expected between a civilised Government with a passion for law and order and a tribe "whose record for all time has been one of thieving and raiding." Relations will necessarily be characterised at all times by an uncomfortable tension never very far removed from breaking point; and for a succession of years the tightly strung thread of forbearance had been subjected to a strain which sooner or later was bound to prove fatal. The more lawless element in the tribe had for long been playing fast and loose with the sixth and eighth commandments, and this with a reckless disregard for the feelings of a people for whom the Decalogue is not only a divine ordinance, but a code by which they have decided that it is both proper and convenient to regulate their lives.

It was pure chance that took me to the borders of Waziristan at the precise moment when the thread snapped; and it was a mere coincidence that I happened to travel along the forty miles of hot and dusty road between Dera Ismael Khan and Tank in the company of the experienced frontier officer representing the Government whose sense of law and order had been so flagrantly outraged. Our objects had nothing in common. His was one of moment—the presentation of an ultimatum to a jirgar of the offending tribe. Mine was one of no interest to any one except myself. I was, in fact, bent merely upon obtaining a specimen of the straight-horned Markhor, and at Tank I and my companion parted. For a long, hot day I pushed south along the edge of the mountains through the dry, brown fog of a sandstorm, and then turned up the valley of the Gomal river. Later I turned south again away from Waziristan and into the mountains of the more friendly Sheranis.

From the point of view of sport my trip was not a success. At the approach of winter the Ghilzais were migrating from the rigours of their own hills to the sunshine and the warmth of the plains, with the result that game was disturbed and everywhere on the move. Moreover, my chances were handicapped by a too faithful observance of duty on the part of my escort, members of the border military police, who dogged my footsteps with patient perseverance from morn to night, and who showed a far more acute interest in the footprints of an occasional Mahsud than in the spoor of the game that I was after.

At nights I retired within the four mud walls of a small blockhouse which enjoyed recognition on large-scale maps under the title of Kashmir Kar, and listened to the keen-eyed Jamadar in charge as he related tales of plunder and sudden death. The Mahsud question was clearly one of burning interest at Kashmir Kar—and not without reason, as subsequent events were to prove. The savage tribesmen had enjoyed impunity too long to prove amenable to the terms demanded at the Tank jirgar, and a blockade of their territory was enforced. For some time they kicked fiercely against the pressure thus brought to bear on them, and Kashmir Kar became the scene of one of those far-off tragedies that embroider the fringes of Indian Empire, and that may, or may not, form the subject of a newspaper paragraph under some such heading as "frontier incident." The Mahsuds came down upon it in force. They breached its defences, carried off its arms, and put some portion at least of its small garrison to the sword.

This, together with other outrages, proved the ineffectiveness of a mere passive blockade, and sterner measures were taken in hand. The blockade was maintained, but to this were added series of sudden and unexpected raids by armed forces into the beleaguered territory. This new method of coercion proved surprisingly effective. It was not adopted until the late autumn of 1901, and by the beginning of January 1902 the recalcitrant tribe gave in. By March 11 all the conditions demanded by Government had been fulfilled, and the blockade was raised.

It is worth while inquiring why it was that the efforts made during many years to come to terms with the Mahsuds were uniformly unsuccessful; because such inquiry will bring out the importance of highly specialised knowledge in dealing with the independent tribes. "If there is a case in which the conclusions of the uninformed are perilous," wrote Lord Curzon, "it is that of tribal policy." Nor is a general knowledge of frontier customs and characteristics sufficient. It is special knowledge of the particular tribe to be dealt with that is required. It cannot be assumed that because one method of dealing with the tribes in one part of the frontier proves successful, it will necessarily prove equally successful when applied to other tribes in other parts of the border. It was in part because this assumption was made that we failed so often in our attempts to negotiate with the Mahsuds. Methods which had succeeded with the Baluchi tribes under the powerful guidance of Sir Robert Sandeman were applied in the case of the Mahsuds, and failed lamentably. The reason was simple, but for long remained unrecognised for want of a little understanding.

In Baluchistan we dealt with the tribes through their chiefs, and this was a method which was eminently suited to their case, for the tribesmen looked up to and rendered implicit obedience to their headmen. Loyalty to constituted authority was bred in their bone and part of their immemorial custom and tradition. We endeavoured to deal with the Mahsuds in the same way, and this was a method which was wholly unsuited to their case, for among the Mahsuds no such thing as reverence for authority was known. Whatever else he might be, the Mahsud Waziri was no respecter of persons. His tribal organisation was intensely democratic. His leading characteristic was a "fierce love of political and municipal independence," and his soul was permeated with a fanatical dislike of the foreigner. Added to this was the highly important circumstance that while we were in occupation of Baluchi territory, far from our being in occupation of Mahsud country we were irrevocably determined, under the policy of non-intervention, not to undertake the responsibilities which annexation would impose upon us.

When, therefore, about the year 1890, without one of the chief conditions necessary to success—namely, occupation—we endeavoured to apply the system in vogue in Baluchistan to the tribes of Waziristan, we were simply asking for trouble. The headmen whom we set up, and whom we proposed to hold responsible for the behaviour of the tribes, were incapable of exercising authority over them. The headmen—or Maliks—were themselves well aware of their own limitations. They pocketed the subsidies which we paid them, and in many instances, no doubt, did their best to carry out their part of the contract—not always without results fatal to themselves. An illuminating but tragic demonstration of the instability of the foundations upon which the system was based was afforded within three years of its introduction, when, in 1893, an Englishman, Mr. Kelly, was murdered by the tribesmen in Zhob. Two of the murderers were eventually handed over by the Maliks, and were sentenced to seven years' imprisonment. The surprising inadequacy of the punishment awarded was explained by the introducer of the system to be due to the fact that "so long as our control over the Waziri country has to be entirely exercised from without and we are forbidden access to it, no matter how well disposed the maliks may be it is impracticable for them to go beyond certain limits." How narrow these limits were, became apparent when three of the leading Maliks who had effected the surrender of the criminals were in their turn murdered by the tribesmen.

The necessity of exacting retribution for this act of insolent defiance seems to have been lost sight of under stress of disorders on a larger scale which led to an expedition in 1894–95. The settlement of 1895 increased the allowances to the Maliks, but left untouched the system which, "worked by enthusiastic supporters who claim for it an ethical superiority, has after a short time landed us in an *impasse* of unavenged bloodshed and rapine," with the result that by the time of my visit in the autumn of 1900 things were as bad as, if not worse than, before. It was laid down, with unanswerable logic, by those who knew the Pathans, that one of two things must be done if any improvement was to be effected. Either the condition essential to the success of the Maliki system must be fulfilled, namely, the occupation of the country—which the Maliks themselves desired, but which the tribesmen emphatically did not; or the system must be changed.

Government had no difficulty in deciding in favour of the latter alternative, and at the jirgar called together on November the 8th, 1900, to which reference has already been made, the Mahsuds were informed of Government's intentions. A fine of 1,00,000 rupees was imposed in punishment of past offences, and, failing payment by a definite date, a blockade of the country was threatened. So far as the future was concerned Government would deal with the tribesmen themselves, and not with their representatives. Similarly, the tribe, or sections of the tribe, would be held responsible for good order, and the allowances paid hitherto to the Maliks would be handed to the tribe to be distributed as they liked.

The jirgar were loud in their protestations of good intentions; but these failing to materialise, the blockade was put into force. How this was succeeded by more aggressive tactics, resulting in the speedy submission of the tribesmen, has already been told. What was of greater interest even than the submission of the tribe was the fact that " the pressure of the offensive blockade rapidly matured what had been silently growing —the authoritative tribal jirgar." Thus an agency which at least possessed the merit of enjoying the confidence of the tribe was firmly established, and the exotic system, which for a decade had rendered abortive every effort of Government to bring about an improvement in a harassing situation, came to a salutary end.

Nevertheless, it is still a question whether in the end the pressure upon the civilised Power to advance will not overcome the most dogged determination to remain where we are. The greatest triumph of the policy of non-intervention was the state of the frontier during the World War. The Amir of Afghanistan had given a pledge of benevolent neutrality to the Government of India at the beginning of the War, and had loyally resisted the various influences which were brought to bear upon him to break it. Throughout these desperate years, when the fate of Great Britain hung in the balance, the tribes had remained surprisingly quiet. "In a world at war it is curious and pleasing to be able to report that the North-West Frontier has no history for the year 1918–19." So wrote Sir George Roos-Keppel. Yet precisely at the time when one would least have expected a recurrence of trouble, namely, at the conclusion of the World War, from which Great Britain had emerged victorious, the frontier was once more thrown into a state of turmoil, and Great Britain engaged for a third time in a war with Afghanistan. "At no period in the history of British rule on this frontier has there been such a record of tribal lawlessness." Thus Sir G. Roos-Keppel's successor a year later.

When, at the conclusion of the second Afghan War in 1880, Great Britain had recognised Abdur Rahman as Amir, she had contracted a treaty with him under which she had undertaken to assist Afghanistan against aggression from without, provided that he followed unreservedly the advice of the British Government in regard to his external relations. On the death of Abdur Rahman and the succession of Habibullah, this agreement was re-enacted by a treaty signed at Kabul on March the 21st, 1905, in words drawn up by the new Amir himself, who, for some reason unknown to me, took exception to the text of the treaty drawn up in the usual form and submitted by the British envoy, Mr. (now Sir Louis) Dane, for his acceptance. The text as finally signed by the two contracting parties, if somewhat lacking in minute precision, at least had the advantage of being both comprehensive and simple. It ran as follows :

> He is God. Extolled be His Perfection.

Then followed the titles of the two signatories, after which :

> His said Majesty does hereby agree to this, that in the principles and in the matters of subsidiary importance of the Treaty regarding internal and external affairs, and of the engagements which His Highness my late father, that is Zia-ul-millat-wa-ud-din, who has found mercy, may God enlighten his tomb ! concluded and acted upon with the Exalted British Government, I also have acted, am acting, and will act upon the same agreement and compact, and I will not contravene them in any dealing or in any promise.

Next followed a paragraph in which the British Signatory pledged the British Government to observe previous agreements. The final paragraph of this singular document set forth the date according to the Muhammadan and Christian calendars, and was followed by the Persian seal of the Amir and the words :

> This is correct. I have sealed and signed.
>
> Amir Habibullah.

How loyally he acted up to it and in what good stead his loyalty stood Great Britain during the Great War has been stated already.

On February the 20th, 1919, the world was startled by the news that Habibullah Khan, Amir of Afghanistan, had been assassinated. The news was unfortunately true. Returning from an excursion, he had pitched his camp in the Kullah Gosh Pass, and after catching some fish in a neighbouring stream had retired to rest. It has been stated that on landing the fish which he had caught he became pensive, dwelling upon the uncertainty of life, and that he exclaimed, "Thus man, too, ceases to exist when the hand of death suddenly lifts him out of his element of life." The same night the hand of death stole silently and unseen into the King's tent, and lifted him out of the element of life. He was found with a bullet in his left temple; but "the Angel of Death had departed, leaving no trace behind him save the body of Amir Habibullah Khan lying undisturbed in his grim, motionless, and lifeless majesty."[1]

To the outside world the news came as a profound shock. Writing a year later, the official recorder of current events in the service of the Government of India observed that, remarkable though it might seem in an eastern country, where the most jealously guarded secrets have a habit of leaking out, mystery still surrounded both the motives and the authors of the crime.[2]

In Afghanistan itself, if we may believe Dr. Abdul Ghani, no such mystery existed. Opinion hostile to the Amir had long been growing. His love of ease and amusement and his neglect of the

[1] Dr. Abdul Ghani, from whose "Review of the Political Situation in Central Asia" I have derived this account of the Amir's death.

[2] "India in 1919," being a report prepared for presentation to Parliament in accordance with the requirements of the 26th section of the Government of India Act, by L. F. Rushbrook Williams.

affairs of state disgusted the ardent spirits of the Young Afghan party which had come into existence, filled with ideas of the rights of man. His European tastes alienated Moslem sentiment. His lavish expenditure from public revenues upon his personal whims called forth the most adverse comment. And, finally, his emphatic rejection of the request of a Turko-German mission either to call a holy war himself or to permit the tribes of the frontier to harry the British as the enemies of Islam, excited widespread suspicion and animosity against him. A spirit hostile to autocracy had been cleverly fostered by one Sardar Mahmud Beg Tarsi—who had lived much in Turkey, where he had imbibed the sentiments and opinions of the Young Turk party—by means of a newspaper, the "Siraj al Akbar," which he had started with the encouragement of the Amir himself. "His proficiency in the Persian language drew from his pen, under the garb of eulogisms of the Amir, some scathing denunciations of the stagnancy of Afghanistan. He administered sugar-coated quinine, which was swallowed with an expression of pleasure and gratitude."[1] A secret society was formed, and anonymous letters warning him against a life of idleness and pleasure, and adjuring him to give attention to the affairs of state, were despatched to the Amir, who, however, turned a deaf ear to all such entreaties. It became a current saying in the bazaars of Kabul that he was lucky, for he had long since given up the kingdom, yet the kingdom did not jettison him. During the usual celebrations of the Amir's birthday in Kabul at the end of 1918, a shot was heard in the town, and the bullet of a revolver fell in Habibullah's car as he passed through Shore bazaar. It was but a few weeks later that he became the target of a second shot, with the tragic result

[1] Dr. Abdul Ghani.

above described. When all that has been said above is borne in mind, subsequent events, and particularly the outbreak of the third Afghan War, so puzzling at the time, become intelligible.

Plate 7.

MOGHUL ARCHITECTURE: THE ENTRANCE TO THE GARDEN OF THE TAJ MAHAL.

CHAPTER VIII

THE THIRD AFGHAN WAR AND ITS AFTERMATH

WITH the death of Habibullah the customary struggle for the throne ensued. Sardar Nasrullah Khan, brother of the dead king, proclaimed himself Amir in Jelalabad; Prince Amanullah Khan, son of the late Amir, did the same thing in Kabul. And it was Amanullah who carried the country, and, what was of supreme importance, the army, with him. He had, however, to secure the support of the Young Afghan party, and in a proclamation issued soon after his accession he declared that he accepted the crown only on condition that all co-operated with him in his policy, which he summarised as freedom for the individual, subject to his obedience to "the sacred law of Muhammad and civil and military laws," and, most important of all, independence and freedom both internal and external for Afghanistan. In his official letter to the Viceroy, informing him of his accession, he likewise wrote of the "independent and free Government of Afghanistan" being ready to conclude "such agreements and treaties with the mighty Government of England" as might be useful in the way of commercial advantages to the two Governments.

Nevertheless, his position was by no means an easy one. The disturbances which broke out in the Punjab in the spring of 1919 reacted upon Afghanistan. To many it seemed that a golden opportunity of recovering from what was regarded as Habibullah's criminal mistake in refusing to raise the standard of jihad had been vouchsafed by Providence to a faithful people. The Young Afghan party and the army clamoured for action. How great was the pressure from the former was tacitly admitted by Dr. Abdul Ghani, himself a member of the Afghan delegation which discussed the terms of peace at Rawal Pindi in August 1919, at the conclusion of the third Afghan War, later on. It was to win over the Young Afghan party, he has told us, that the Afghan plenipotentiaries insisted on the absolute independence of Afghanistan, both internal and external, as a cardinal condition of peace. While the Amir hesitated a reaction against him set in. What, then, was he to do ? Afghan agents in India were plying him with wildly exaggerated accounts of the situation in the Punjab, and it is easy to understand that, relying upon these reports, he seized the opportunity of consolidating his position at home by focussing attention upon a popular adventure across the frontier.

Early in May the British officials on the frontier received information of a special Durbar, at which the Amir launched his enterprise. Weeping bitterly, it was said, he read aloud letters from India, and said, " See the tyranny exercised upon our brethren in India ; and more, tyranny has seized Baghdad and the Holy Places. I ask you : Are you prepared for Holy War ? If so, gird up your loins, for the time has come." Later a proclamation was read in the Hadda Mulla Mosque, on which the mullahs all voted for jihad, and emissaries were sent forth to raise the tribes.

Actual hostilities began with acts of aggression on the Khyber border, in the course of which the water-supply at Landi Kotal was interfered with, and five coolies employed on the water-works were killed. It was only in the central section of the frontier, however, that the enterprise met with any appreciable success. An advance from Khost by a force under General Nadir Khan compelled the evacuation of a number of our militia posts in Waziristan, with most unfortunate results, for Wana was occupied by an Afghan force, and the Mahsuds and Wazirs rose. Elsewhere the adventure met with speedy disillusionment. The fort of Spin Baldak, six miles across the border from New Chaman, the British railhead in Baluchistan, reputed the strongest in all Afghanistan, was blown to pieces with high-explosive shell. In the neighbourhood of the Khyber the Afghan forces were rapidly driven back, their advance base at Dakka taken, and bombs dropped by aircraft on Jalalabad and Kabul. By the third week in May suggestions for an armistice were already being put forward by the Afghan Commander-in-Chief, and following a ding-dong correspondence between the two Governments a truce was arranged and representatives of the two countries met at Rawal Pindi on July the 26th. On August the 8th a treaty of peace was signed. Afghanistan retained her independence—internal and external—and lost her subsidy; Great Britain obtained the frontier which she claimed and the agreement of Afghanistan to its demarcation west of the Khyber Pass. It was further arranged that another Afghan mission would be received by Great Britain in six months' time, "for the discussion and settlement of matters of common interest to the two Governments and the re-establishment of the old friendship on a satisfactory basis."

In pursuance of this arrangement an Afghan delegation, under the leadership of Sardar Mahmud Beg Tarsi, spent the summer of 1920 on the cool hill-tops at Mussurie discussing a number of matters discursively with the urbane and amazingly patient representative of Great Britain, Mr., now Sir Henry, Dobbs. And, later, a British delegation under Sir H. Dobbs proceeded to Kabul, where a year was spent in long drawn-out negotiations, resulting in a treaty signed on November the 22nd, 1921, under which the independence of Afghanistan was definitely recognised, and the appointment of an Afghan Minister to the Court of St. James, in addition to consular officers in various cities in India, agreed to. An agreement between Afghanistan and Russia for the appointment of Russian consuls at Kandahar and Jàlalabad was revoked and British consuls accepted in their stead. Each contracting party agreed to give the other notice of any major operations which it might feel called upon to take for the preservation of order among the tribes on its frontier.

Such was the outcome of the third Afghan War. It pleased both belligerents to regard themselves as the victors. The claim made by Afghanistan that she had fought for and won her independence was discounted by Great Britain letting it be known that this concession would have been made in any case, as a reward for the great services of the Amir Habibullah. Such considerations were not permitted to disturb the atmosphere of complacency through which Afghans viewed the result, and a monument to victory, at the foot of which reposes the British Lion with one leg chained, adds to the picturesqueness of the streets of Kabul.[1]

Some space has been devoted to the third Afghan War because of its effect upon the frontier. If the tribes were slow to rise, they became a serious menace to peace long after hostilities with Afghanistan had ceased. And what was of grave import was the fact that under stress

[1] According to Mr. A. Moore, who visited Kabul in 1922.

of these events the props upon which the policy of non-intervention rested, one by one crumpled and gave way. A number of small posts held by tribal militia, upon which the security of the frontier depended, had to be abandoned, with disastrous effects upon the tribesmen's *moral.* The tribal levies themselves, including the famous Khyber Rifles, proved unequal to the strain, and either deserted in large numbers or had to be disbanded. Moreover, our training of these men proved a double-edged weapon, as we soon realised when we had to send an expedition into their country. That the frontier was well armed was only too well known. Even as far back as the Tirah Campaign of 1897 it had been noticed that the tribes were better armed than in the past, and inquiry established the fact that an arms traffic of formidable dimensions was being carried on between the tribesmen of Afghanistan and a cosmopolitan group of traders operating on the shores of the Persian Gulf. The receiving depot was Muscat, whence the arms found their way to the shores of Makran and across desert routes to the mountains of Afghanistan. The traffic steadily increased until 1907, when the value of the imports of arms into Muscat was returned at over £250,000. Thereafter stern measures were taken to smash the traffic; but by then the frontier was liberally armed. It was not only the quantity and character of the arms which they possessed, however, that now rendered the Mahsuds so formidable a foe. They displayed a comprehensive knowledge of fire discipline and minor tactics—the fire discipline and tactics which we had taught the levies. In a single engagement on January the 14th, 1920, our casualties amounted to 9 British officers killed and 6 wounded and 10 Indian officers and 365 Indian other ranks killed or wounded. The Tirah Campaign of 1897–98 had been responsible for a little over 2000 casualties, 558 killed and 1705 wounded. The operations of 1919–21 resulted in the loss of over 5000 lives, and a total casualty list—dead, wounded, and missing—of nearly 10,000. Such figures are significant.

No better evidence of the increasing pressure upon the civilised Power to advance can be adduced than that provided by statistics of the raids and the resulting casualties during the days following the third Afghan War. During the year 1919–20, no fewer than 611 raids took place in the Peshawar, Kohat, Bannu, and Dera Ismail Khan districts, resulting in the killing of 298, the wounding of 392, and the kidnapping of 463 British subjects; and the looting of property of an estimated value of 30 lakhs of rupees. During the same period 41 raids were repelled, 119 raiders were killed, 80 wounded, and 41 captured.[1] It is significant that the author of the official publication from which the above figures have been taken draws a contrast between the state of affairs north and south of the Gomal, "where our sphere of administration extends right up to the Durand line."

Some modification of the policy of non-interference was indicated by the Viceroy in the course of a speech to the Legislature on August the 20th, 1920, when he said that "the continual and gratuitous provocation" could no longer be suffered, and that it had been decided, therefore, that troops should remain in occupation of Central Waziristan, that mechanical transport roads should be constructed throughout the country, and a broad-gauge railway extended from Jamrud through the Khyber Pass to the Afghan frontier.

For the benefit of the Mahsuds a jirgar was held

[1] "India in 1920," by L. F. Rushbrook Williams.

at Tank on November the 5th, 1921, which was taken advantage of by Major-General Matheson, G.O.C., Waziristan Force, to dot the *i*'s and cross the *t*'s of the Viceroy's statement. The Government would remain in occupation of Mahsud territory as long as it pleased, but there was no intention of introducing the regular administration of an Indian district. No land revenue would be demanded, at any rate for the next twenty years, nor for the next five years would any court fees be levied nor any toll in kind. At the conclusion of that period a light toll in kind and an eight-anna court fee would be charged. No forced enlistment would take place, and, generally speaking, the occupied territory would be administered on tribal lines and in accordance with tribal usage. Allowances would be paid for services rendered in the restoration and maintenance of law and order.

All these changes certainly constituted some departure from a policy of strict non-intervention. Will they eventually lead to an advance to the political frontier ? Such an advance will not be made if it can possibly be avoided. It would be excessively costly, which is in itself a grave objection in view of the very exiguous resources at the disposal of the Indian Government. It will be avoided if it is found possible to remove the main cause of frontier unrest without it. The root cause of frontier trouble is economic. A man who was intimately acquainted with China once said that the problem of that country was the problem of filling three stomachs with one bowl of rice.[1] The problem of the frontier is much the same. The hardy tribesman looks down from the hungry fastnesses of his own highland home upon the rich abundance of the plains spread temptingly at his feet. His reason-

[1] Mr. J. O. P. Bland.

ing is simple and is not complicated by ethical considerations. He swoops down and gathers in the fruit so plainly intended by Providence—so it appears to him—for his consumption. It is difficult to gauge the relative value of life and the rupee on the frontier—the discount at which the former stands and the premium which is placed upon the latter—until one has gathered it from the people themselves. Let one of them speak.

Muhammad Khan was a typical tribesman. He was arrested by a constable at whom he fired two shots from a revolver for no other reason than that the constable, seeing him loitering in the neighbourhood of the city gate, asked him his business. He was a young man; but his life, brief as it was, had been full of episode. What seemed to rankle in his mind was the fact that, though he had always been of a religious turn of mind, trouble had seldom passed him by. At the age of twenty he had experienced a bitter domestic misfortune, his wife having been seduced by a neighbour. "I intended to murder him," he declared; "but fearing that I might be accountable for it before God, I put it off until I had sought the opinion of a mullah." The mullah was apparently of an accommodating disposition, for he was advised that if he left his country he was at liberty to murder any one. Later he drifted to Asmas, well known to the wardens of the marches as the centre of a colony of intractable folk, known as the Hindustani Fanatics. Here he became the disciple of one, Moulvie Abdullah, to whom he swore implicit obedience. It was not long before his fortitude was put to the test, for he was bidden to go forth and shoot one Nasrullah Khan, after which he was to return or die in the attempt. It is typical of the frontier temperament that he accepted this order as a matter of course. He sallied forth to do as bidden, and it was through no fault of his that the enterprise miscarried.

His next errand was to British territory, where he was instructed to commit dacoities. "I inquired whether we should commit dacoities for rifles or for money?" To which query he received the reply—"For both." More interesting still, he was not to refrain from committing dacoities against Hindus or Mussalmans, since being British subjects they were all infidels.

Muhammad Khan made casual mention of a tragic frontier episode which had come his way—the murder while asleep of an Englishman for his money. He told how the murderers had been given up to the British authorities, and he commented laconically upon this betrayal, "For this also those who handed them over got some money from the British." The murderers, it appears, were shot by the British; but what was apparently of greater interest to Muhammad Khan was a pleasing little intrigue which followed upon this calamity. "The deceased had a very beautiful sister, and both Salimullah and Obeidullah wanted her." The latter, being already possessed of a full quota of wives, succeeded in wresting her from Salimullah by getting her married to a relative of his own. This man was, according to Muhammad Khan, only a nominal husband, and Obeidullah was satisfied of his desire.

Two of his accomplices in a dacoity were captured, and the subsequent happenings emphasise the value of the rupee. "One was released in exchange for one rupee, the other for five." He himself fell into the hands of a canal guard. The matter proved susceptible of arrangement—"I gave him two rupees, and he released me." Other exploits, in one of which he killed two men while in pursuit of a comparatively paltry sum of money, led to his becoming a proclaimed offender in British territory, for which reason he objected to orders which he received to convey a message from a mullah in tribal territory to a mullah over the border. "I said that some other man should go; but I was told that martyrdom had to come some day, and that it was right that I should become a martyr."[1]

Muhammad Khan was one tribesman of many thousands, all of whom make similar estimates of the relative value of life and the rupee. Can Great Britain, then, without being driven to occupy and administer tribal territory up to the frontier of Afghanistan, remove the root cause of this attitude of the frontier mind towards these fundamentals? Experiments have from time to time been made. The enlistment of tribesmen in various bodies of militia gave employment and sustenance to a certain number of the younger men. In 1910 the ranks of the army were thrown open to the Mahsud Waziris, and a year later employment was found for an additional 2000 men of the same tribe on the construction of railways and other public works. These experiments were not without promise; but confidence in them was rudely shaken, for the time at any rate, by the effects of the European and Afghan Wars. It was found necessary to close the ranks of the army to all trans-frontier tribesmen; and with some honourable exceptions, notably the Kurram and Mohmand corps and the Chitral scouts, the militias failed to stand the supreme test of a religious war championed by the Amir of Afghanistan.

With the conclusion of the short-lived Afghan War, efforts were made once more to find suitable employment for the tribesmen. The militias were

[1] I have given the narrator of these events the name of Muhammad Khan. Except for making similar changes in the names of other persons mentioned, I have summarised his story from the account which he himself gave of his career.

reorganised. It was realised that they had tended to become too regular. Into bodies of men intended originally to play the part of police, had crept by degrees the training, the discipline, the drill, and the uniform of the soldier. And when the crisis came, the men whose proper function was the policing of roads and the escorting of caravans were called upon to play the much more desperate part of a military screen covering the mobilisation of the regular army. It is arguable that if the militias failed at this supreme test, it was because it was one to which they ought never to have been subjected. With the re-forming of the tribal levies, all tendency towards regularising them was thrust sedulously out of sight. Attention was concentrated upon creating organisations irregular in fact as well as in name, bodies of men, as one authority put it, "incapable of forming fours, but thoroughly acquainted with the country and the people, able to move as rapidly and silently as the raiders they are out to catch." Out of this reaction against the regularising of the levy corps and the enthusiasm for the essentially irregular, emerged the Khassadar, a tribesman undrilled, undisciplined, and ununiformed, the bearer of his own and not of the Government's rifle, distinguishable from the freebooter by reason only of the fact that in return for Government pay he agreed to suppress instead of fostering raiding. With the tribesmen themselves the Khassadar idea caught on; and it has certainly made an admirable start. With the formation of the Khyber Khassadars, raids in a single district —that of Peshawar—dropped in a single year from 145 in 1919–20, to 57 in 1920–21. In Waziristan certain clans went so far in 1922 as to request the British authorities to construct a metalled road from Tochi to Razmak and to establish a permanent fort at the latter place, provided that in place of a regular police force there was set up a body of Khassadars enlisted from amongst themselves. Foiling raiders for regular pay possesses attractions superior, evidently, to those attaching to raiding for uncertain reward; and the fall in the number of raids in the Dera Ismael Khan district since the occupation of Waziristan is as remarkable as in the neighbourhood of Peshawar. From 198 in 1919–20, they fell to 51 in 1921–22; the number of British subjects kidnapped from 127 to 17; and the property looted from Rs. 12,00,000 to Rs. 55,000.

The construction of the Khyber railway will also do much to relieve the economic pressure on the tribesmen of the Afridi section of the frontier. It is a costly undertaking and will in all probability run into a sum of two crores of rupees, or well over £50,000, for every one of its twenty-six miles. Here again the prospect of economic relief has overcome the natural hostility of the tribesmen to such incursions into their country; and competition for contracts in connection with its construction has been brisk. But the railway, unlike the Khassadars, will merely increase the natural pressure upon the civilised Power to advance. Its construction is in itself a big step forward—as is also the occupation of Waziristan, the avowed object of which is the construction of block-houses and roads.

There will be strong forces pulling in the opposite direction—the financial stringency of the Government of India and the natural aversion of the increasing popular element in the Government of the country to accept responsibility for any policy that can be described as extravagant, imperialistic, or adventurous. But the pressure upon the civilised Power is fundamental and will remain while the forces operating in an opposite direction are susceptible of change. An impartial examination of the financial aspect of the question tends to show even now, that in the long run a policy of peaceful penetration would probably prove far less costly than the policy of withdrawal punctuated by punitive expeditions, of which there have been more than sixty during the past three-quarters of a century. The whole aspect of the matter has been completely altered in recent times by two factors of paramount importance—the arming of the tribes with modern rifles and the knowledge of fire discipline and modern tactics which they have acquired. It is only necessary to compare the statistics of recent expeditions with those of earlier ones to realise how formidable an undertaking a punitive expedition has now become. Up to the close of the nineteenth century the actual cost of campaigns across the administrative frontier was not great. Expenditure under this head during the closing twenty years of the century amounted to approximately £300,000, and this sum included the cost of the Chitral campaign of 1895, namely, £112,000, and that of the Tirah campaign of 1897, namely, £124,000.[1] Compare with these figures the expenditure under the same head during the first twenty years of the present century, namely, £19,500,000, and the nature of the change becomes apparent. Still more significant is the sudden leap in cost during the past few years. The blockade of the Mahsuds during the years 1900–1902 of which I have written, cost roughly £250,000; the operations against the tribes in 1915–16 alone cost little short of £300,000—almost exactly the cost of the whole of the expeditions across the border during the last twenty years of the nineteenth century. It is from this year that the

[1] For these figures and those which follow, I am indebted to an interesting series of articles which appeared in the "Englishman" of Calcutta during the summer of 1922, over the initials J. A. S.

cost ascends with such alarming steepness. In 1916–17 we spent £475,000 under this head; in 1917–18, £1,134,000; in 1918–19, only a little less, and in 1919–20, approximately £16,000,000. This last figure includes the cost of the third Afghan war.

Such figures are sufficient in themselves to make it clear that the frontier campaign of to-day is a very serious military operation requiring very large numbers of troops and equipment of a very high standard. In the old days a force of a few thousand men sufficed—the first punitive expedition against the Umarzai Wazirs in 1852 consisted of 1500 men; in 1919–20 it required a force of 45,000 fighting men, or, with the necessary complement of non-combatants, an army of 80,000 men in all, to deal adequately with Waziristan. It was at the beginning of these operations that the extent of the change which has taken place in the character of frontier warfare was brought home with stunning effect. At the beginning of our advance from Jandola in December 1919 we met with a serious reverse, losing in two days 113 killed, including 5 British officers, and 200 wounded, with nothing to set against the loss. Thereafter hard fighting, during which the small gains had to be carefully consolidated and held by permanent pickets as they were made, marked a slow advance. On January the 14th, 1920, another fierce battle took place in a stony river bed overlooked by barren hills. Our casualties on this day amounted to 9 British officers killed and 6 wounded, 2 Indian officers and 365 Indian other ranks killed and wounded. Not the wildest jingo amongst soldiers, hankering for martial glory, would choose a frontier campaign to-day for the satisfaction of his aspirations. A constant repetition of punitive expeditions of this character would become intolerable. Moreover, if the tribes once became convinced that penetration of the kind which has now begun results in an easing of their economic burden without any violent departure from the existing order, under which what passes for public affairs are handled in accordance with tribal custom, the process of introducing civilisation, and by degrees some form of administration, may be accomplished much more easily than has hitherto been thought possible. If the belief that oil exists in appreciable quantity in tribal territory proves well founded, this will prove yet another incentive to a further step forward which may well be accepted by the tribes for the same reason that the Khyber railway has been accepted, namely, that it will pay.

So much for the North-West Frontier. Because of the determining influence which it has exercised upon India itself; because it still provides the Government of India with one of its most constant and insistent problems, and because the general reader is not usually familiar with its story, have I devoted so much space to it. Before returning to the lands which it has served both as a rampart and a gateway, and to the peoples whose ancestors streamed century after century through its rugged portals, a brief reference seems called for to the coming by another highway—that of the ocean—of the most recent of the incursions to which India has been subject —that of the peoples of the West.

CHAPTER IX

THE INCURSION OF THE WEST

It was only in recent historical times, after the human reservoirs of Asia had ceased spilling over into the far-stretching plains of Hindustan, that the Indian seas were opened up to commerce and adventure on a large scale, and became a broad highway running from Europe to Asia. It was, in fact, on July the 8th, 1497, that the famous Portuguese mariner, Vasco da Gama, sailed from Lisbon on the adventurous voyage of discovery which carried him round the Cape of Good Hope and landed him at Calicut on May the 20th of the following year. And it was nigh upon a century later, in 1591, that the first commercial venture from England was embarked upon. Portugal, Holland, France, each in turn played a part in the spirited drama of merchant adventure between Europe and India, which followed upon the voyage of Vasco da Gama. But it was Great Britain that was destined to prevail against all rivals, and if the rounding of the Cape in 1497 is to be regarded as the opening of a momentous chapter in human history, the incorporation of the "London East India Company" by Queen Elizabeth on December the 31st, 1600, under the title of "The Governour and Company of Merchants of London trading into the East Indies," must equally be regarded as its most pregnant episode. It was by the amalgamation of this Company with another trading corporation which received its charter from William III. in 1698, that the "United Company of Merchants of England trading to the East Indies," more generally known as "the Honourable East India Company," came into existence in 1708.

In 1746 began the state of war between Great Britain and France in India, from which the former eventually emerged as the paramount power in Asia. And it was in 1765, after a series of hard-fought battles, waged sometimes against the French and sometimes against the armies of India over a number of years, that the Company, under the imperious guidance of Lord Clive, became the receivers of the revenue of Bengal, Bihar, and Orissa, and thus acquired for Great Britain the virtual sovereignty of these countries. Amongst the battlefields of this period whose names have deservedly become historic are Plassey, where in 1757 Clive broke the power of Muhammadan rule in Bengal; Wandewash, where in 1760 Sir Eyre Coote defeated the French under the hitherto victorious Lally, and Buxar where in 1764 Sir Hector Monro destroyed the army of the King of Oude.

The times were ripe for the advent of a strong power capable of piecing together the fragments into which the splendid edifice raised up by the Moghul dynasty had fallen. Cracks had already made their appearance in it during the reign of Aurungzeb, who dethroned his father, Shah Jehan, and waded to the throne through the blood of his murdered brothers in 1658. For during the third quarter of the seventeenth century there had arisen a new and formidable confederacy, that of the Mahrattas, under their national hero Sivaji, which challenged the hegemony of the Muhammadan kings. In 1723 the Nizam of the Deccan acquired independence. In 1739 Northern India was scourged by Nadir Shah, who swooped down upon Delhi from Persia, massacring there 150,000 people and carrying away treasure of an estimated value of 125,000,000 sterling. And with the death of Muhammad Shah in 1748, the empire of the Moghuls lost all cohesion, and broke up finally into a number of scattered principalities.

It is not history that I am writing, and it is no part of my purpose to attempt anything in the nature of a narrative of the dramatic series of events which culminated in the overlordship of India falling to Great Britain. A description of a single episode must be taken as typical of the manner in which the foundations of British India were laid; and I have little hesitation in taking the Battle of Plassey as my example.

* * * * *

In August the sacred Bhagirathi rolls with rich voluptuousness across the fertile plains of the Bengal delta. On either side it is fringed with continuous stretches of standing crops of vivid green, broken here and there by collections of dust-brown houses, clustering amid thick clumps of shady trees. Chocolate figures, clothed only in exiguous loin-cloths and huge circular hats of plaited bamboo, are to be seen dotted among the crops, giving a touch of life to a scene otherwise characterised chiefly by a languorous repose. The fierce heat of the sun is tempered only by intermittent storm-clouds fitfully spitting forth rain, as they pass on their journey northwards to the mountain walls beyond the plains.

On such an August day I had been floating down the current on a river-flat through the historic plains of Murshidabad, occupied with such thoughts as the proximity of Plassey inevitably conjured up. In 1917 the war which was shaking civilisation to its foundations was never long

Plate 8.

A GROUP OF TEMPLES AT BHUBANESWAR IN ORISSA.

absent from one's thoughts, and it was with a mind prepared to draw comparisons that I stepped ashore on the left bank of the river in the comparative cool of early morning. The famous field of Plassey, whereon between 8 A.M. and 5 P.M., on a burning day in June just one hundred and sixty years before, issues of such vast import had been decided by the military genius of Clive, presented an appearance of extreme peace. The rolling crops which covered the ground in all directions spoke of the peaceful and uneventful pursuit of husbandry, rather than of the stir and clash of great events. They also did much to screen from view such features of the land as might assist in the reconstruction, in a mental picture, of the scenes of a hundred and sixty years ago. Fortunately this difficulty had been provided against, and from the backs of elephants thoughtfully supplied, we obtained a view of much which would otherwise have remained hidden from our gaze.

With the stupendous panorama of the European conflict ever before one's eyes and its monstrous din ever ringing in one's ears, the thought uppermost in one's mind was the absurd insufficiency alike of stage and *dramatis personae* for the enactment of such momentous events. Small pillars marked the positions of the opposing forces, so that the strategical plan lay open to one's gaze. Taking a stand midway between the positions first occupied by the opposing armies, we could see, little more than a stone's throw to the east of the battle, the spot whence Mir Jaffer and his troops, drawn up on the left of the semicircular line occupied by the army of the Nawab, played the part of interested spectators. The danger of envelopment which they threatened, posted as they were at so short a distance on the right flank of Clive's meagre line, was plainly apparent; and it is difficult to estimate the effect of the inactivity which they displayed upon the course of history.

Apart from the restricted area over which the battle was fought, nothing pointed so forcibly to the futility of the mechanism of war then as contrasted with the terrible efficacy of its machinery now, as the unpretentious little pillars from which we learned that the artillery took up positions in front rather than in rear of the companies of infantry. With the appliances of war playing only a minor part, one imagined that numbers must have possessed a proportionately greater value, and, standing on the actual ground on which the battle was waged, it was easy enough to picture the feelings of uncertainty with which Clive and his little band of officers must have been assailed. Facing him and his small force of 3200 European and Indian troops, at a distance of a few hundred yards only, was the notorious Surajah Dowla with a vast concourse of horse, foot, and elephants, numbering in all over 50,000 souls.

The success of the desperate enterprise which lay before him depended on the outcome of the intrigues for the overthrow of Surajah Dowla which had been in progress for some time before. A secret treaty had been negotiated between the representatives of the East India Company and Mir Jaffer, general in the service of the Nawab, based on the assumption that Surajah Dowla would be deposed and Mir Jaffer set up as Nawab in his place. Could the latter be relied upon to play the part assigned to him? There was every reason to suppose that the enterprise would meet with a large measure of public support for Surajah Dowla, "whose character of ferocity and thoughtlessness," in the words of a contemporary Indian writer, Ghulam Husain Khan,[1] kept his

[1] Quoted by Sir George Forrest, C.I.E., in his "Life of Lord Clive," a volume to which I am indebted for the main facts upon which this brief account of the Battle of Plassey is based.

Muhammadan chiefs and the principal citizens of Murshidabad "in continual alarms, and whose fickleness of temper made them tremble," was himself the real, if unwitting author of the conspiracy for his own overthrow. The plot was, in fact, not of Clive's making; he merely took advantage of the situation which Surajah Dowla himself had created. Moreover, elaborate precautions had been taken to ensure constancy on Mir Jaffer's part. Mr. Watts, the Company's agent at Murshidabad, had outwitted Surajah Dowla's spies, and gained admission to Mir Jaffer's house in a closed palanquin such as was used by Muhammadan women. Thus hidden, he had been carried into one of the apartments in the seraglio, where he had been received by Mir Jaffer and his son, Miran. The former had given his full assent to the terms of the treaty, and with a volume of the Koran on his own head and his hand on the head of his son, had sworn with great solemnity that he would faithfully perform all that he had promised.[1]

Nevertheless Clive had doubts. He had expected daily letters from Mir Jaffer, keeping him informed of events at Murshidabad, and Mir Jaffer had maintained a disconcerting silence. From other sources he had received information that the plot had been discovered and that Mir Jaffer and Surajah Dowla had come to terms. On June the 19th he had expressed his fears in a letter to the Company at Calcutta, in which he said that he felt the greatest anxiety at Mir Jaffer's silence, and that he feared even if he was not treacherous, that his vacillation would ruin the enterprise. On the following evening he had received a letter from Mir Jaffer sewn up in a slipper, the language of which was so ambiguous as only to increase his apprehensions. Two days of intense anxiety had

[1] "The Life of Lord Clive," vol. i. p. 433.

followed, and it had not been until 3 P.M. on June the 22nd that he had received a message from Mir Jaffer which had seemed to him to be sufficiently encouraging to justify an advance. He had crossed the river at five in the afternoon, and marching on through a downpour of rain, had reached a wood near Plassey at midnight.

Neither the mango grove known as the Laksha Bagh or orchard of one hundred thousand trees, nor the adjacent brick building—a shooting lodge of the Nawab—which Clive occupied and used as his headquarters, are to be seen to-day. But from the back of an elephant and with the aid of the memorial pillars, one experiences little difficulty in picking out the salient features of the battle-ground. Sir George Forrest has brought together the accounts of a number of those who actually took part in the events of the day, from which a vivid picture of the battle is obtained. Marching out of their entrenchments on the morning of the 23rd, the vast concourse of the Nawab's following formed up in a semicircle facing and enveloping the right of the position which Clive had occupied; "and what with the number of elephants all covered with scarlet cloth and embroidery, their horse with their drawn swords glittering in the sun, their heavy cannon drawn by vast trains of oxen, and their standards flying, they made a most pompous and formidable appearance." [1] A portion of his artillery was drawn up 200 yards only from the British, and it was a ball from one of these which "bounding along and carrying off the arm of one of the King's grenadiers," opened the battle at 8 A.M.[2] An artillery duel at short range continued until the afternoon, when the Nawab's troops, with the exception of a large

[1] Account by Scrafton quoted by Sir George Forrest.

[2] "A Narrative of the Battle near Muxidavad," dated "Cossimbazar, 29th June, 1757," quoted by Sir George Forrest.

corps on the extreme left of the line, moved slowly back to their entrenchments. This latter body was seen to be moving in such a manner as to cause doubt whether its aim was to gain possession of the village of Plassey in the rear of the British position, or whether it was desirous of coming over to join forces with Clive. It was not then known that this was Mir Jaffer's corps and it was kept at a distance by the British guns.

Subsequent events were described by Clive in a note despatched to Calcutta the same evening, which, if somewhat lacking in descriptive detail, at least had the merit of being explicit. "About noon," he wrote, "the Nabob's army returned to a very strong camp in sight, upon which we advanced and stormed the Nabob's camp which we have taken with all his cannon and pursued him six miles. . . . Meer Jaffeir, Roydoolub, and Luttee Cawn gave us no other assistance than standing neuter."

This last statement is scarcely calculated to give an accurate impression of what actually took place. When Surajah Dowla first learned of the approach of the English, he realised the danger that he was in from Mir Jaffer's disaffection and made a supreme endeavour to win back his allegiance. "Taking out the cotton of recklessness from his ear," we are told by the author of the "Riyazu-s-salatin," a Muhammadan historian who completed his history in 1788, and who was writing, consequently, of events only thirty years after their actual occurrence, "he displayed towards the aforesaid Khan flattery and endearment, and sending the Begam of Mahābat Jang to Mir Jaffer, opened the gates of apology for his past shortcomings." Mir Jaffer remained silent, and two days before the Battle of Plassey Mir Madan, the Superintendent of the Nawab's artillery, assured his master that it was at Mir

Jaffer's instigation that the English were coming, and urged him to kill him. The historian records in picturesque language the Nawab's omission to act upon this advice. "In that the arrow of Fate cannot be parried by the shield of Effort, and in that God's decree had already been passed another way—

> To the advice of that wise sage
> That light-hearted man was deaf."

Surajah Dowla made a final effort to win back Mir Jaffer after the Battle of Plassey had actually begun. Sending for him in the midst of the battle when the issue was still in doubt, he appealed to him on the strength of consanguinity and the past friendship of their families. Mir Jaffer advised him to recall his troops from the attack since the day was drawing to a close, and added that he would then arrange for an engagement on the morrow. Surajah Dowla, dissatisfied with this reply, appealed to Rai Dulab, another of his chiefs, from whom he received the same traitorous advice. And it was the demoralising uncertainty created by the orders issued on the strength of this advice, that enabled Clive with his small but gallant and aggressive force, to drive home his impetuous attack.

From Plassey the scene shifted to Murshidabad, thirty miles to the north, which was entered by Clive on June the 29th, and which, a few days later, saw the assassination of Surajah Dowla by one Muhammad Beg at the instigation of Mir Jaffer's son, and the elevation of Mir Jaffer himself to the Musnud of Murshidabad.

* * * * *

The epitaph of Muhammadan rule in Bengal is written in staring letters over the city of Murshidabad. On all sides of one are signs of decay. The jungle has eaten into the heart of the city; its buildings, where not in actual ruin, are frequently crumbling. Even the river—the sacred Bhagirathi—once the main channel of the Ganges and a great and famous trade route, dwindled seriously in volume when the main stream above Murshidabad forced its way eastwards to form what is now known as the Padma river. And the reduced stream itself left its own bed a century ago, pushing its way west of its former channel, which can now be traced by a series of miasmic swamps, notable among them the Motijheel, the haunts of the malaria-bearing mosquito. The result is to be seen in the enlarged spleens of the children, in the falling birth-rate, and in the pallor and general inertia of the people.

Clive's description of the city in 1759, two years after the Battle of Plassey, is almost startling in its unexpectedness. The picture he paints is that of a vast metropolis "as extensive, populous and rich as the city of London," with palaces immeasurably greater than the palaces of Europe; and Mr. P. C. Mazumdar, who has written an excellent synopsis of the history of Murshidabad since its rise to fame under a great Dewan of Bengal, Murshed Kuli Khan, at the beginning of the eighteenth century, gives a glowing account of its former greatness. Its population then ran into hundreds of thousands; to-day it has shrunk to a few thousands only. The mint duties levied at the rate of 2 per cent on the bullion coined amounted, he tells us, to over three lakhs of rupees; and the municipal taxes and duties on trade brought in an even larger sum. Compared with this revenue of more than six lakhs of rupees a year, the municipal income to-day comes to a paltry total of a few thousand rupees; and I was informed by the municipal commissioners on the occasion of my last visit to the town in 1921, that unless financial assistance could be rendered to them by the Provincial Government, this once great city was doomed, in view of "the ever-decreasing taxable capacity of the rapidly decaying population," to fall into a state of chronic and penurious insignificance. Clive had declared that there were individuals in the Murshidabad of his day "possessing infinitely greater property" than any individual in London; and in his statement before the House of Commons he made mention of "Hindu millionaires and other men of property." In 1921 the Municipal Commissioners complained to me that the mere repairing of the roads, few though they now are—for the remnant of the city covers a site of a mere half-dozen miles in circumference—had become a burden which, without financial assistance, they were no longer able to bear. Mr. Mazumdar has given an even more graphic example of the way in which the glory has departed from this erstwhile capital of a great satrapy. "From the pinnacles of the turrets of seven hundred mosques, the voices of seven hundred shouters of the *azan* simultaneously rent the atmosphere of the crowded city." Thus was it in the eighteenth century. At the dawn of the twentieth century hardly seventy places of worship remained, and of these seventy hardly seven were in proper repair.[1]

The most imposing building in the Murshidabad of the present day is the palace of the present Nawab, the foundation stone of which was laid by the Nawab Nazim Hamayun Jah—Shuja-ul-Mulk, hero of the country; Ihtishamuddowla, dignifier of the State; Hamayan Jah, of auspicious rank; Feroze Jang, victor in war—in 1829. A huge pile of buildings in the Italian style, it stands on the left bank of the present channel of the Bhagirathi, and contains among other

[1] "The Musnud of Murshidabad," by P. C. Mazumdar.

things of historic interest, a splendid armoury with a fine collection of weapons, largely of the sixteenth century; picture galleries containing examples of the work of Dutch, Flemish, French, and Italian artists; a record room in which are stored documents of considerable historical interest; a library of many volumes, and a treasure house, the repository of a valuable collection of famous jewels. But the present Nawab finds it impossible on account of the unhealthiness of the place to spend much time at Murshidabad, and even the palace is beginning to take on the dead and silent atmosphere which broods over buildings no longer tenanted.

And not far from this, the most prominent symbol of past greatness, is to be seen the most striking example of present decay, in the artillery park of the Nawabs. The site is now a jungle-covered wilderness, in which a solitary cannon is all that is left of a great armoury bristling with the guns of a powerful line of Oriental rulers. The gun itself is of considerable interest, having been made in Dacca in the year 1637 and christened Jahan Kosha or "Destroyer of the World." It was probably brought to its present site by Murshed Kuli Khan when he raised up the city of Murshidabad upon the site of an older town called Makhsusabad. And with the city he founded also the line of the Nawabs which Clive encountered and defeated on the field of Plassey in the person of Surajah Dowla, and whose representative to-day is the senior nobleman of Bengal. For after having been given the title of Motamul-ul Mulk, Alanddowla, Noser Jang, Noseri —Guardian of the Country, Promoter of the State, Helper in War, the Defender—and appointed Subadar of Bengal, Bihar, and Orissa, by the Emperor Aurungzeb, he obtained patents from the Emperor Farrukh-Sir confirming him in his occupation of the two offices of Nizamat and Dewani which he had succeeded in combining in his own person; an unwise departure, as the translator of the "Riyazu-s-salatin" has pointed out, from the old Moghul policy of keeping the two offices distinct, in that it led to intrigues against the central authority at Delhi. What attracts the attention of the visitor, however, is not so much the gun itself as its strange position. For this huge cannon, 17½ feet in length and 5 feet in circumference, weighing 7½ tons, hangs suspended horizontally some feet above the ground, embedded in the trunk of a pipal tree which has wrapped itself about it and now holds it aloft in an iron grip. No spectacle could better bring home to one the fate of Murshidabad as the graveyard of vanished greatness than this amazing example of the assertiveness of the Bengal jungle.

CHAPTER X

THE IMPRINT OF GREAT BRITAIN

THE results of the commercial adventures of the sixteenth and following centuries, culminating in the acquisition of India by Great Britain, which have been touched on in the last chapter, are not easy to assess. Two results, indeed, of great magnitude will be discerned by the traveller who takes the trouble to reflect upon the matter, namely, the existence throughout the continent of an administrative system of a Western type and the introduction into a country essentially agricultural of the industrialism of Europe. A further result, namely, that arising out of the impact between two civilisations of distinct types, is far less easy to compute. What the ultimate outcome of this impact will be is of incalculable importance to mankind. Its study is of absorbing interest and is too large a subject to be undertaken here. It must be reserved for a separate volume. Consideration of the first two, however, falls properly into these pages.

There is often a disposition amongst visitors to India to take these things too much for granted. We are so used to thinking of India as a British Dependency that the real nature of our achievement fails to impress itself upon us. Here familiarity breeds not contempt but loss of perspective. We travel from one end of India to the other, passing through all the gradations of climate, landscape, and race that the continent contains, as comfortably and as securely as we do in Great Britain, and we find in this nothing to excite surprise. Everywhere there is a smooth uniformity so far as the mechanism of travel is concerned, and it never occurs to us that it might well be otherwise. The scenes through which we pass are rich in contrast. The differences between the peoples amongst whom we travel are obvious and striking; their customs are varied, their languages bewildering. We immediately recognise them as separate and distinct by their mere outward appearance. No one could possibly mistake a Sikh from the Punjab for a Tamil of Madras, or a man of Baluchistan for an inhabitant of Burma. Yet it does not strike us as strange that, in the influences which determine the attitude of all these peoples in the matter of the social economy of the continent, there should be a quite palpable uniformity. We are, perhaps, vaguely conscious that uniformity exists, in other words that the order which we find in one part of India is the same in kind as the order which we find in any other part; but we rest content with the fact and do not trouble ourselves as to its cause.

If we were sufficiently interested we should find little difficulty in putting the matter to the test. We might take, for example, for the purpose of our investigation the most ubiquitous agency with which the public comes in contact, namely, the police. We should find that in physiognomy and dress the policeman of Madras differed widely from the policeman of the United Province or Bombay; but that in the discharge of their respective duties they were inspired quite obviously by a common code. Further observation would go to show that all the wheels of the complicated machine which regulates the public life of the continent revolve in rhythm and are subject to some common control.

There is nothing like travel in Asiatic lands which are beyond the reach of British rule for bringing home to the Englishman the immense advantages which he enjoys in India, such as employment of the English language as the *lingua franca* of the continent, and the working of all such institutions as railways in accordance with English custom and tradition. It is not until he has had personal experience of all the difficulties and inconveniences of travel elsewhere, that all those small things which smooth the path of his progress in India assume their true significance, and that he begins to realise that it is due to something more than chance that he finds himself so much at home amid surroundings so diversified in themselves and differing so widely from those which prevail in his own land. When he has thus ceased taking things for granted and has begun to think, he will find a good deal in the circumstances of British India to excite astonishment.

What we actually exercise control over is, as has already been pointed out, a continent the size of all Europe, excluding only Russia, with a population of 320 million people. Rather less than two-fifths of this area, and rather less than one-fourth of the total population, is administered and governed under British suzerainty by the rulers of 700 different Native States; the remainder is administered directly by us. And the whole of the vast machinery necessary for this stupendous task is directed, controlled, and kept in motion by a body of officials of all kinds—civilians, judges, engineers, doctors, educationalists, forest officers, and so on, of whom the number of Englishmen has at all times been less than 5000, and is likely in the near future still further to diminish.

In the United Provinces a single civilian was until quite recently responsible for the good government of a country larger than New Zealand with a population of 47 million souls. In Burma another civilian exercises supreme authority over a country twice the size of the British Isles.

The achievement is all the more remarkable when it is remembered what it is that is done through the agency of the public services. India is a huge going concern run by the State. The State does not merely carry on the work of government and the administration of justice; it does many other things besides. It constructs and runs railways; it undertakes huge irrigation works; it organises famine relief; it fights pestilence and plague; it doctors and it sanitates; it undertakes the exploitation and scientific treatment of the immense forests scattered broadcast over the land; it monopolises the manufacture of salt; it runs schools and colleges; it makes its influence felt, in other words, in every department of the people's life.

So long as one is travelling on beaten tracks —along the railways and from town to town— one scarcely notices the working of the administrative machine. One meets officials, but they carry on their business in offices very much as officials do elsewhere; and one does not find it necessary to invoke their aid to enable one to pursue one's programme of business or of pleasure. The influence of the government is there but it is latent. It is only when one leaves the railways and towns behind one that one discovers how far-reaching is the arm of authority and how important is the part played by personality in the personnel that is responsible for the working of the system. When one travels for mile after mile over some of the less densely populated tracts of Northern or Central India, passing in

Plate 9.

THE PALACE AT KOTAH.

"Rather less than two-fifths of the area and rather less than one-fourth of the total population is governed under British suzerainty by the rulers of 700 different native states."

the course of a few hours from one epoch of civilisation to another, from a land of large and prosperous villages and of intense cultivation to less trodden areas not yet won from the dominion of the jungle, where man is represented by primitive aboriginal tribes, the works of man by simple collections of wattle huts, and the fears and hopes of man—wherewith are circumscribed the sum total of his spiritual and intellectual aspirations—by crude graven images of wood and stone; then one begins to realise something of the extent and character of British rule.

One's first inclination is to suppose that these more primitive parts of India must lie beyond the fine-spun network of administration; but if one is fortunate enough to accompany the district officer on one of his cold-weather tours through such a region, one finds that this early assumption needs revision. When one has seen these denizens of the jungle gathered round his camp, laying their affairs before him, requesting this for their welfare and that for the righting of some wrong, pleading (with the faith that removes mountains in its efficacy) for medicine for all their ills, one realises that, very far from their being beyond the scope of British rule, they find in the representative of British rule something altogether transcending the idea suggested by the word "official," and approximating far more nearly to some benign Providence in the flesh.

There was only one way in which the vast and varied continent of India could be brought in its entirety within the embrace of the administration, and that way was, in the words of the official documents, by "the repeated subdivision of territory, each administrative area being in the responsible charge of an officer who is subordinate to the officer next in rank above him." In the administrative vocabulary, the word "district" has a technical meaning. It is the most important administrative unit, the districts into which the different provinces are divided forming the base of a pyramid, as it were, of which the Provincial Government is the apex. This is merely a paraphrase of the official text which informs us that "a Province may be regarded as a collection of districts," though the added information is here given that the district "is usually split up into subdivisions, and these again into smaller circles."

I have already called attention to the limitations of statistics; yet it is difficult to draw things in India in true perspective without calling in their aid. Thus it helps towards a correct idea of what is meant by a "district," in terms of superficial area, to be told that there are in British India 267 districts with an average area of 4000 square miles (the average size of an English county is 1000 square miles) and an average population of over 900,000. The extremes, as is only to be expected when dealing with a continent the size of India, have a wide variation from the average. The district of Vizagapatam, in Madras, for instance, has an area of 17,223 square miles, or, to compare it with the corresponding unit in Great Britain, is nearly three times the size of Yorkshire, and has a population of over 3,000,000. In Burma the Upper Chindwin district is five times the size of the average district, but has a population of only 170,000; while the Mymensingh district in Eastern Bengal, which is only half as large again as the average district, has a population of more than 4,500,000.

The district officer, who is known as the "collector" in some provinces and as the "deputy-commissioner" in others, is the principal revenue official and the chief magistrate. The functions which he has to discharge in these two capacities are sufficiently onerous ; but he has in addition a great many other miscellaneous duties. After casually observing that " he has to interest himself in all matters affecting the well-being of the people," an official document feels it necessary to add that " for the proper discharge of his many duties, the collector-magistrate must be accessible to, and intimately acquainted with, the inhabitants of his district." The collector of Mymensingh would probably think this an excellent joke.

I once had occasion to visit the collector of a large district during the camping season, and I learned by personal experience the meaning of the statistics dealing with superficial area. According to the official return, the size of the district was rather more than 5000 square miles. The Royal Commission on the Public Services, of which I was a member, was carrying on its rather laborious inquiries in Calcutta, and a long week-end was all the time that I could spare. My host's note of invitation was cordial, and his instructions for the journey concise and commonplace. I was to leave by the 5 P.M. train, which was due at 9 P.M. He would send to meet me at the station. I complied. At 9 P.M. I alighted on the platform of a small wayside station and looked round for the promised conveyance. Nothing answering to my expectations was to be seen—nothing, in fact, was to be seen at all, except a small group of dusky figures squatting outside the station, dimly visible in the flickering light of the station lamp. As I was debating what to do next, one of the group arose and came towards me. Was I not the sahib who was going to the Collector Sahib's camp ? I was ; then, if it pleased me, we would start. Whereupon I was conducted towards the group, whom I found on closer acquaintance were gathered round an object about the shape and size of a large coffin, with poles projecting at each end. Here was my conveyance. I put in my blankets, clambered in, and was hoist on to the shoulders of two or three stalwart bearers. I was well enough accustomed to the sedan-chair of China. But the chair of that country has a seat, and my present conveyance had not; and the hard, unyielding plank floor upon which I lay seemed to me to be attended with disadvantages over and above those which are in any case sufficiently in evidence even in the seated type. I consoled myself with the reflection that the distance to be covered would probably not be great, and I inquired how soon we might expect to reach camp. "By daylight," was the laconic reply. "But how far is it?" I asked incredulously. "Twenty-four miles," I was told. We did arrive at 6 A.M., and on consideration I felt bound to admit that this was not bad going in the dark, over rough tracks and across unbridged rivers, through a wild and jungle-covered land.

It is casual experiences of this kind that help one towards an understanding of what is meant by British rule in India, and in particular of the task of the district official who, to quote the official document once more, is expected to be "accessible to and intimately acquainted with the inhabitants of his district." Travel in these rural areas also discloses other features of the administration for which we are responsible, namely, the system of local self-government, which one finds at work side by side with the district administration. Investigation goes to show that in theory, at any rate, the system corresponds closely to that which has been evolved in the West, and it is with no small interest that one inquires how a system, which is essentially a product of the democratic West, fits the circumstances of the immemorial East. The inquiry is well worth making, and in the course of it one finds oneself being presented with a more spacious and more detailed picture of rural India than, from the actual nature of the subject-matter, one would expect.

CHAPTER XI

LOCAL SELF-GOVERNMENT

By an act of the legislature passed in 1850, municipal boards were conferred upon a large number of towns all over India ; and the powers and responsibilities thus bestowed upon them were extended by further legislation in the eighties of last century. The inauguration and gradual extension of local self-government in rural areas followed somewhat behind the parallel effort in the case of the towns. There are now about 730 municipalities in British India and 200 district boards, corresponding roughly to county councils in Great Britain. Subordinate to the district boards are some 550 subdivisional boards, known usually as local boards, *i.e.* bodies exercising jurisdiction, under the general supervision of the district boards, over the administrative subdivisions of the district. By the establishment of these bodies we sought to familiarise the vast and varied population of India with those shibboleths of the enlightened constitutionalism of the West—" the elective principle " and " popular control."

In opening the new London County Council Hall on July the 17th, 1922, His Majesty King George declared that opinions differed as to the machinery of local administration and the best methods of obtaining the best results, but added : " It is universally recognised that the root of all good government is a live and active civic spirit."

If we may accept the conclusions of foreign observers, we may congratulate ourselves upon possessing this spirit in a special degree. One such observer has written with enthusiasm of the way in which in Great Britain "the country towns, boroughs, and districts and parishes, and all the machinery of their government are entirely managed by the voluntary labours of those with wealth, leisure, and ability to do so." He has asserted that "no country in the world receives so much and such valuable service from its leisured classes," and finally, that the fact that these classes "undertake all these duties, that they do them so well, and with so little—almost no—friction, and with so little dissatisfaction to those whom they thus govern, is the most impressive feature of English life." [1]

There is no reason to suppose that the peoples of India do not likewise possess in generous measure these civic virtues. Indeed, if we accept the conclusions of Dr. Radhakumud Mookerji, not long since made public in an interesting volume,[2] they possessed in ancient times a system of local self-government predicating capacity for corporate action in a high degree. But the system of communal activity prevalent in ancient India differed in kind from that evolved by the democracy of Great Britain; and it was at least conceivable, therefore, that the latter might not be the one best suited to the soil of India. There is, however, much truth in the comment of another observer of the English and their ways to the effect that they have an immense and ineradicable admiration for their own institutions. The Englishman, as he put it, "sticks to his traditions and usages, and, so help him God!

[1] "England and the English," by Price Collier.
[2] "Local Government in Ancient India," by Radhakumud Mookerji, M.A., Ph.D.

he will force his island by-laws down the throat of great countries like India, China, Canada, Australia . . .,"[1] and it must be admitted that in deciding upon the type of local government to be established in India the authorities of the day went a long way towards justifying this somewhat caustic accusation. In Great Britain the people elected representatives to manage the affairs of the borough or the county, and in India, therefore, the inhabitants of the towns should likewise elect representatives to construct, maintain, and light their streets, provide and maintain their municipal buildings, arrange for conservancy, look after the public health and make provision for elementary education; while the rural population should have roads, markets, rest-houses, pounds, ferries, and dispensaries constructed and maintained; a veterinary staff provided, and sanitation, vaccination, and education arranged for by a body corresponding as closely as circumstances would permit to an English county council.

The result was not altogether happy, and a people with a less robust belief in the excellence of their own institutions might, indeed, have found cause for discouragement at the manner in which, in the useful if somewhat unambitious sphere of municipal administration at any rate, the great principle of "government by the people for the people" was given application. To begin with, whatever may have been the reason, the elective principle did not excite in India the enthusiasm which was hoped for it. Instances of its failure were constantly being brought to my notice during my residence in Bengal. In one ward in a municipality in that Presidency, in which no less than twelve candidates stood for two vacancies, only thirty-seven voters went to the poll. In another contested election ten votes

[1] R. W. Emerson.

only were recorded by an electorate of 259 persons. In a ward-election in an important town, seven out of eight candidates withdrew at the polling booth because the other was a man of low caste with whom they declined to compete. In another case the nominated members of a board objected to sitting with elected members on the ground that the latter might be persons who, according to the social customs of the country, should stand in their presence. An Indian-owned newspaper complained on the eve of the elections in one of the largest and most important towns in Bengal that a first offer of Rs. 1200 had been made for the seventy-nine votes in a particular locality in the city, that the votes in question had actually been secured by a cash payment of Rs. 1300, and that in another area an offer of Rs. 10 per vote was being made.

Official reports of the working of the system in quite recent times are strewn with examples of a similar kind. A report from the United Provinces, while noting a growing interest in elections, struck a somewhat ominous note by adding that this "was not always attributable to an intelligent concern for the welfare of the locality." From the Punjab came an intimation that while a keen interest in elections was evinced in some municipalities, in others "apathy was the rule," and "nomination was more sought after than election." It was also said that in many places "the sectarian spirit showed itself a great obstacle to progress." A report from the Central Provinces declared that during the decade 1902–12 "some improvement in municipal administration was recorded, but in many cases very little interest was shown in elections." In Burma, "elections, generally speaking, aroused very little interest, and it was frequently necessary to nominate members to seats for which candidates were not forthcoming." The same province was successful in giving these rather dull matters a distinctly humorous touch. The municipal committee of Bassein, fired with a sudden and unexpected desire to plunge deep into the most advanced expedients of democracy, took a referendum on the question of undertaking a water-supply scheme. The verdict was against the enterprise; but the committee, undismayed by this rebuff, decided that the people did not understand the proposal put before them and proceeded with the undertaking.

In the case of the rural boards, the great size of many of the districts and the lack of means of rapid travel to which I have alluded are sometimes formidable obstacles in the way of regular attendance on the part of members. I came across a case in the United Provinces where one member had fifty and another a hundred miles of unmetalled road to travel over when attending meetings of the board, and I was told of another case of a member being waylaid and robbed *en route* to the scene of his labours. Away from the beaten tracks this is not an altogether unknown experience. An Indian official stated in evidence before the Royal Commission on the Public Services in India, that even for an official it was sometimes "a very difficult task to pass through wild and dangerous tracts like Chota Nagpur"; and he added, in explanation of a certain falling off in the number of inspections carried out in those parts, that "two inspectors breathed their last from the bad effects of a long and tedious journey."

Another cause of shortcoming is a certain lack of appreciation of the importance of modern ideas on the subject of sanitation. "The usual attitude of a municipal body towards the government sanitary authorities," declared an eminent medical officer in evidence before the Public

Services Commission, "is one of patient toleration. They look upon the department as one of the inflictions of a beneficent Government. An officer of the department reports on the sanitary condition of a certain town; makes, perhaps, five or six recommendations. These are either frankly opposed because the commissioners consider they know better than sanitary experts, or the time-honoured excuse of want of money finally disposes of the recommendations." This last difficulty—lack of resources—is, as a matter of fact, one of the chief obstacles in the way of advance. If the special cases of Calcutta, Bombay, Madras, Rangoon, and Bangalore be excluded, the remaining 726 municipalities have a total income of under £5,000,000, or, on the average, well under £7000 each per annum, while the total income of the whole of the rural boards of the continent, district, subdivisional, and, in the case of Madras, union panchayats as well, amounts only to £6,250,000 a year. Small wonder that the time-honoured excuse of want of money is frequently forthcoming.

Another cause of lack of enthusiasm was undoubtedly to be found in the measure of official control which it was thought necessary to impose upon the newly created bodies, and which was retained long after the period when really healthy self-governing institutions might have been expected to have outgrown the necessity for such tutelage. The importance of having on the boards various officials as well as representatives of races or classes which might fail to secure election, made it necessary to retain a considerable proportion of the seats on all these bodies to be filled by nomination. There was a natural tendency, too, for the actual work of administration to devolve largely upon the official members, whose ordinary duties brought them into much closer touch with the administrative requirements of town or district than was the case with the average non-official member. In the case of the district boards the work devolved mainly upon the district officer, who in most cases was *ex-officio* chairman of the board.

This cause of indifference on the part of the people came into sudden prominence when, in August 1917, Parliament announced its intention of giving wide application to the principles of election and popular control in the higher spheres of government in India; and the Government of India stated their policy in the matter of local self-government consequent upon this announcement in May 1918. Stress was laid upon the part which local self-government was designed to play as a training ground for those who would undertake greater responsibilities and wield more extensive powers in a higher sphere. Political education, it was declared, must take precedence over departmental efficiency; and the measure of official guidance and control which had hitherto been maintained was, as far as possible, to be dispensed with.

To-day—in Bengal, at any rate—district boards elect their own non-official chairmen, and relaxation of official control has, undoubtedly, given a much-needed stimulus to interest in local government.

But the fundamental cause of the disappointing results of nigh on three-quarters of a century of endeavour is to be found in the incorrigible belief of the English as a race in the superiority of their own institutions over those of all other people, however different the conditions may be. This is meeting with tardy recognition to-day. In the official report presented to Parliament for the year 1920, it is admitted that in no other branch of civic activity as in that of local self-government is " the contrast between India and progressive countries at present so marked." But it is explained that " the institutions of local self-government in their present form are a creation of British rule, artificially implanted " upon Indian soil; and that the submerged foundations " of indigenous institutions framed for ends not dissimilar," which were in large measure destroyed during the anarchy of the eighteenth century, " were not utilised to the best possible advantage by British administrators," so that " the existing institutions of local self-government are to a considerable degree alien from the spirit of the people." Some years earlier a Royal Commission, inquiring into the possibilities of a greater measure of decentralisation in the administration, had expressed very similar views. They did not think it possible, even if it were expedient, to restore the ancient village system under which the community was responsible for each of its members, and in turn claimed the right to regulate his actions; but they did hold that it was " most desirable, alike in the interests of decentralisation and in order to associate the people with the tasks of the administration, that an attempt should be made to constitute and develop village panchayats for the administration of local affairs."[1] They added that the foundation of any stable edifice must be the village, " as being an area of much greater antiquity than administrative creations such as tahsils "; and they expressed the opinion that the scant success of the efforts which had been made to introduce a system of rural self-government was largely due to the fact that we had not built up from the bottom. This view at last met with acceptance in the highest quarters, for the Secretary of State, Lord Morley, wrote in

[1] Report of the Royal Commission on Decentralisation, issued in 1909.

his despatch on the reform scheme of 1909, that the village in India had been the fundamental and indestructible unit of the social system, surviving the downfall of dynasty after dynasty. "I desire your Excellency in Council," he continued, "to consider the best way of carrying out a policy that would make the village a starting-point in public life."

That India evolved many centuries ago a highly developed system of local self-government is undoubted; that it differed in kind from the system which we have imported into India from the West is equally certain. Corporate life in ancient India took the form of guilds, notably of crafts guilds and merchant guilds. Such organisations came into being spontaneously, and themselves evolved the laws by which their activities were governed. Such laws, according to the ancient law-books of the country, commanded recognition at the hands of the king (*i.e.* the central government), who was further charged with the duty of seeing that they were respected. That "cultivators, traders, herdsmen, money-lenders, and artisans have authority to lay down laws for their respective classes," is asserted by Gautama some centuries B.C., and that "the king must discipline and establish again on the path of duty all such as have erred from their own laws, whether families, castes, guilds, associations, or people of certain districts," is emphasised by Yajñavalkya. These bodies, therefore, were independent of the central government; they were not its offspring, nor were their functions the product of devolution, as in the case of such bodies as the borough and county councils of Great Britain. On the contrary, they were social organisations with authority which was not derived from but which compelled the recognition of the central government. Side by side with, or out of, these early guilds came into being village assemblies modelled on similar lines and possessing an equivalent status, which seem to have exercised judicial and municipal powers, and to have administered endowments for secular and religious purposes. Dr. Radhakumud Mookerji gives a most interesting account of the constitution and working of such a body, derived from two inscriptions in the Vaikuntha Perumal temple at Uttaramallur in Southern India, probably of the tenth century A.D.

The picture of village government which he draws as a result of his study of these and other inscriptions is as follows. The controlling body was the village assembly, consisting of all persons possessing a certain property qualification, together with moral fitness and a definite standard of proficiency in legal and religious literature. The actual work of the village was entrusted to a number of committees, membership of which was open only to persons possessing certain qualifications, amongst which were the ownership of a specified amount of tax-paying land, residence on his own property, knowledge of the Mantras and the Brahmanas, a capacity for business, and an age qualification of between thirty-five and seventy years. The village was divided into a number of wards — in the case of Uttaramallur thirty — and at the time of the appointment of committees the residents of each ward assembled, and each wrote down on a ticket the name of the person whom he desired to represent his ward. The tickets from each ward were made up in packets and placed in an empty pot, which, in the presence of the village assembly, was held aloft by the oldest priest present. A packet was then drawn by a young boy, and the tickets undone and shaken up in another pot. The process of drawing from this pot then took place, and the name on the ticket was read out and accepted. In the Uttaramallur inscriptions mention is made of an "annual committee," consisting only of persons who had already served on the "garden committee" and "tank (water-supply) committee," or who were advanced in learning or in age, a body clearly exercising general powers of supervision. Other committees were the "garden committee," the "tank committee," the "gold committee"—probably a body charged with the administration of finance—a "*Panchavara* committee," the functions of which are not at present known with certainty, and a committee for "supervision of justice," whose duty it was to convene meetings of the village assembly and conduct elections to the committees.

Under such a system a village was an autonomous unit managing its own affairs largely on communal principles, and though the central government, in the person of the king, exercised ultimate authority over his people, as the symbol of the State he appeared to them "like a remote abstraction, with no direct touch with their daily life, which was governed by the social organisation. The points of contact between the State and the ordinary interests of the daily life of the people were, indeed, very few."[1]

Much new light has been thrown upon this aspect of the organisation of society in ancient India by the discovery at Tanjore, early in the present century, of a work on political science compiled by Kautilya, the chief minister of the Emperor Chandragupta, about the year 300 B.C. In still earlier days political science—in Sanskrit Arthashastra—seems to have been a favourite subject with scholars, but to have fallen into neglect at the time of Kautilya, for his Arthashastra is a compilation made after study of

[1] Dr. R. Mookerji.

numerous earlier works which he rescued from oblivion. Amongst topics of great interest dealt with by these early thinkers is that of the origin of monarchy and the powers and functions of the king. The question is admirably treated by Professor D. R. Bhandarkar in a series of lectures delivered at the University of Calcutta in 1918, and it is to these that I am indebted for the material upon which the brief sketch which follows is based.

Prominent amongst the theories of the origin of kingship which were prevalent in these very early days was that of the social contract. It is certainly surprising to find that a theory commonly supposed to have originated with Western thinkers of the seventeenth century A.D.—Hobbes, Locke, and Rousseau—was a commonplace of Hindu political thinkers six centuries before Christ. Yet a study of the Arthashastras leaves no doubt that this was so. Kautilya states that the people, in order to quell disorders amongst themselves and to ensure the scales of justice being held even between the strong and the weak, the high and the low, the rich and the poor, elected a king to discharge this duty, allotting him " one-sixth of their grains and one-tenth of their merchandise as his share." The main respect in which the Hindu theory seems to have differed from that of its European sponsors of the seventeenth century A.D. was as to the extent of the power thus transferred to the king. Hobbes' view that absolute power was irrevocably transferred to the ruler differs materially from that of the Hindus. Kautilya makes it clear that the king was regarded as the servant of the people, the share of grain and merchandise awarded to him being held to be a wage paid for services rendered. So much so, indeed, that if the king failed to recover stolen property, he was expected to compensate the sufferer from his own purse. "Whatever of the property of citizens robbed by thieves the king cannot recover shall be made good from his own pocket." [1]

The theory of the social contract is also set forth in the Buddhist scriptures, wherein an account of the origin of kingship is put into the mouth of Buddha himself. In the course of a conversation with a young Brahman, Vasettha, he speaks of the confusion caused in past ages by the increase of crime amongst the people, and he goes on to tell of the measures concerted by them for dealing with the state of affairs which had arisen. "What if we were to select a certain being," they are represented as arguing, "who should be wrathful when indignation is right, who should censure that which should rightly be censured, and should banish him who deserves to be banished?" This proposal is acted upon. "Then, Vasettha," declares Buddha, "those beings went to the being among them who was the handsomest, the best favoured, the most attractive, the most capable, and said to him: 'Come now, good being, be indignant at that whereat one should rightly be indignant, censure that which should rightly be censured, banish him who deserves to be banished. And we will contribute to thee a portion of our rice.' And he consented, and did so, and they gave him a proportion of their rice." [2]

Emphasis is repeatedly laid upon the status of the king as being that of a servant of the public, and any assumption of arrogance on his part was apt to call forth caustic reminders of his true position. "What superciliousness is thine, O king!" exclaims Aryadeva, a Buddhist monk,

[1] Kautilya's "Arthashastra," quoted by Professor Bhandarkar.

[2] "The Aggañña Suttanta of the Digha Nikaya," translated by T. W. and C. A. F. Rhys Davids.

Plate 10.

CAVE CHAPTER-HALLS OF THE BUDDHISTS AT ELLORA.

"who art a mere servant of the body politic, and who receivest the sixth part of the produce as thine wages?"[1]

There is another theory of the origin of kingship in the Arthashastras, namely, that the king was ordained by God to quell the social disorders that broke out among men, and that he was, indeed, an incarnation of the divine. This theory is held in reverence to this day, as I can vouch from personal knowledge. But Professor Bhandarkar argues that even those holding it did not associate the idea of absolute despotism with the institution of monarchy, and he quotes from a Sanskrit law-book, the Sukra-niti, in illustration of the position of those who accepted the theory of the divine origin of kingship: "The king who is virtuous is a part of the gods. He who is otherwise is a part of the demons."

The king, then, according to Hindu theory, was the servant of the public charged with certain specified duties in the interests of the common weal, and with powers which were subject to definite limitations. Professor Bhandarkar gives an effective illustration of this in the shape of a story culled from the rich store of Indian folk-lore which the Buddhists collected and edited to suit their purpose—its incorporation in their scriptures under the title of the Jataka tales, or stories of the previous births of Buddha. A king of Takshasila, who had fallen under the spell of an ogress disguised as a beautiful woman, is requested by the object of his infatuation to grant her authority over his kingdom. His reply provides remarkable confirmation of the limitations on the power of a king set forth above. "My love," he objects, "I have no power over the subjects of my kingdom; I am not their lord and master. I have only jurisdiction over those who revolt and

[1] Quoted from the Vinaya by Professor Bhandarkar.

do wrong. So I cannot give you power and authority over the whole kingdom." That over which he had control, namely, his own palace, he did place at her disposal.

The conclusion to be drawn, then, from the works on political science current amongst the Hindus some centuries B.C. is that stated by Dr. Mookerji in the quotation from his "Local Government in Ancient India" which I have given above. Later on, as life became more complex and a greater elaboration of the administration became necessary, the power of the king increased, and the control of the central government over the lives of the people tended to become more exacting. But enough is now known of early Hindu theory and practice in the sphere of administration to make it tolerably certain that it was based on the existence of innumerable semi-independent self-governing bodies, and that "the conception of the king as the servant of the state," to quote another Indian authority of the present day, "was one of the basic principles of political thought in Ancient India."[1]

And it is the exaltation of the past in his history that appeals most forcibly to the sentiment of the Indian nationalist of to-day. The only suggestions of a constructive character in the sphere of government so far made by the extreme wing of the Indian Nationalist party are those recently put forward by Mr. C. R. Das as President of the Indian National Congress which met at the close of 1922. After stating that in his belief the parliamentary form of government introduced from the West is not a government "by the people and for the people," he declares that no scheme of government which does not conform to this description can ever be regarded

[1] Professor Pramatha Nath Banerji, in his "Public Administration in Ancient India."

as the true foundation of Swaraj. The outline of the scheme which he then advocates as the ideal system for India, follows so faithfully in its main outlines the system of two thousand and more years ago which has been sketched above, that his words are worth quoting in full. "To me the organisation of village life and the practical autonomy of small local centres are more important than either provincial autonomy or central responsibility; and if the choice lay between the two I would unhesitatingly accept the autonomy of the local centres. I must not be understood as implying that the village centres will be disconnected units. They must be held together by a system of co-operation and integration. For the present there must be power in the hands of the provincial and Indian Governments; but the ideal should be accepted once for all, that the proper function of the central authority, whether in the provincial or in the Indian Government, is to advise, having a residuary power of control only in case of need, and to be exercised under proper safeguards. I maintain that real Swaraj can only be attained by vesting the power of government in these local centres."

I have devoted some space to a consideration of the system of administration in force in ancient India because of the obvious bearing which it has upon the question which I have been discussing, namely, the unsuitability of the particular type of local self-government which we have instituted to the genius of the Indian people. It is, I think, a not unreasonable deduction from the knowledge which we now possess of the theory and practice of government in ancient India that if, instead of creating municipal and district boards of the Western type, we had begun by re-creating the village organisations which were congenial to the people, local self-government would have made more satisfactory progress than has actually been the case. The steps which have been taken in various parts of India in recent years to establish village self-governing bodies have been handicapped by the prior existence of district and local boards. Instead of being the foundation of the whole edifice, they have had to be tacked on to the already existing institutions, and difficulty has, consequently, been experienced in fitting them into the general scheme. It had been the intention of those who framed the Bengal Local Self-government Bill in 1883 to make the village the basis of local self-government. Union Committees, covering on the average an area of twelve square miles each, were to be established for the management of affairs of immediate interest to the villagers. The Secretary of State, however, insisted upon the district being made the unit, and when the Local Self-government Act of 1885 was passed it was the district, consequently, and not the village, which constituted the administrative unit of local self-government. An expert Committee—the Bengal District Administration Committee—expressed the opinion thirty years later that "this was to begin local self-government at the wrong end," with the result that smaller bodies were left "dependent on the charity" of the district board and "with no clearly-defined position in the general scheme." It was not until 1919 that a special Act known as the Bengal Village Self-government Act was passed with the object of placing union boards as far as possible upon a sound statutory basis, and of providing for the creation of village courts and benches. This salutary return in the direction of the ancient indigenous system is breathing new life into local self-government. Let me conduct the reader to a Bengal village, the scene of the activities of a newly founded union board.

CHAPTER XII

THE INDIAN VILLAGE

In the rainy season—June to October—the vast alluvial plains of Bengal present a wonderful spectacle. In Eastern Bengal the whole land is under water—but water from which spring amazing crops of jute and rice tinting the whole world with vivid green. Villages appear as small islands in an emerald sea, the houses, buried in dense clumps of shady trees—tamarind, nīm, mango, pipal, jack, banana, palm, and bamboo—being built on sites raised artificially a foot or two above the normal level of the monsoon floods. The great expanses of the rivers are covered with flotillas of boats with sails of white, brown, and blue. Creeks, on the placid surfaces of which children may often be seen paddling themselves about in circular pots of black clay, eat their way into the village sites. Often a curious phenomenon may be witnessed, a boat sailing across what appears to be a field of jute or rice. Both crops grow in varying depths of water, usually a few feet. But there are parts of the land where shallow depressions in the surface give the flood a greater depth—up to fifteen feet and more. The existence of these deeps is only to be detected by the particular variety of rice showing above the surface of the water. One would hardly expect to find crops growing in fifteen feet of water. Nevertheless there they are, thick crops of a curious long-stemmed paddy which has so adapted itself to environment that on a rising flood it is capable of growing as much as a foot in twelve hours. In the Ain-i-Akbari, Abu Fazl Allami has recorded that "as fast as the water rises the stalks grow, so that the ear is never immersed, inasmuch as those experienced in such matters have taken the measure of a single night's growth at sixty cubits." I do not know the size of Abu Fazl Allami's cubit; but the figure which I have given above would be vouched for by the agricultural department.

Such crops are reaped from boats; but ordinarily the man of Eastern Bengal spends the day waist deep or more in water. In a world in which the cultivated land is under water for as much as five months in the year, and that at the time of the growing, and in the case of jute the harvesting of the chief crops, man necessarily becomes an amphibian. Yet, oddly enough, he seems to dislike getting his head wet, and it is a common sight to see a man clad only in a modest loin cloth, standing up to his armpits in water and wearing a large circular hat of plaited bamboo to keep off the rain.

The waters, however, do not have things all their own way. They carry with them large quantities of fine silt in suspension, which sooner or later they are bound to deposit. So it comes about that in the great estuary through which the combined waters of the Ganges, the Brahmaputra, and the Megna—finely named "the river of storms"—pour themselves into the Bay of Bengal, a fight between land and water is in constant progress. The mainland may be washed away; but a little farther out, where the silt-laden water of the rivers mingles with the water of the bay, silt is dropped and islands make their appearance above the surface. I know of no better description of this curious battle-ground between land and sea than that given by Mr. Thompson in his final report on the survey and settlement operations in the district of Noakhali. "Seen from the mainland across a few miles of smooth water the coast of North Hatia or any of the other islands within sight appears like a pencil line drawn along the indistinct horizon between water and sky which, as they meet, take both of them the same silver-grey shades. They are thicker lines when the tide is out, and even on approaching near, the effect is the same —a level line with the tones of a charcoal sketch." The battle is a long-drawn one. At times during the past two centuries the mainland has bitten into the bay but has again retreated, and is now, according to Mr. Thompson, much where it was two centuries ago. Nevertheless it continues to lay a broad foundation beneath the waters of the ocean upon which some day, surely, there will be built up dry land. For immediately opposite the Megna the five-fathom line has been pushed out appreciably during the last few decades, and off the Ganges delta is thirty-five miles away. This becomes significant when compared with the deltas of the Mississippi and the Nile, in neither of which cases is the five-fathom line more than a few hundred yards from the nearest land.

In Eastern Bengal the rivers are the highways, and in the monsoon season smaller channels innumerable take the place of country lanes. This is the most convenient season for travel. The heat and moisture are oppressive, and the intrusion of an insect life vast in numbers and bewildering in variety is a source of exasperation; but one can then move freely where one wills, for water, the medium of travel, is universal. And the scene through which one passes, though in a sense monotonous, has an undoubted attraction, for seldom will one see elsewhere so glorious a mingling of so many differing shades of green. The lighter or darker tones predominate according to the extent of cultivation. Where crops are extensive the jungle of palms, plantains, and other trees resembles a series of small islands in a vast bright green sea of rice and jute. Where the jungle is more aggressive and widespread the tables are turned, and the stretches of rice and jute resemble bays and fiords pushing their way into a sombre shore.

Little is to be seen at first sight of the dwellings of man, the jungle that surrounds them is so thick. But as one pushes one's way along narrow openings through it in an atmosphere close and heavy almost beyond belief, one comes upon unexpectedly large numbers of houses, frail and unimpressive certainly, so far as appearance goes, but surprisingly commodious and clean. A cultivator's house—or *bari*—consists often enough of a number of semi-detached sheds of wattle built round and opening on to a courtyard. The big man of the village may have a more substantial residence of brick.

To such a village in the Dacca district I came not long after the passing of the Village Self-government Act of 1919, to meet the members of the union board; and was conducted to a *pandal* erected in a small open space, the counterpart of the English village green. All round the *pandal* in perspiring groups stood the sparsely clad population of the village, interested spectators of what was going forward. In front of me in the centre of the *pandal* stood a table on which were placed the books of the union board; and round me were seated the members of the board, bearded and reverend *seigneurs*, men who carried the confidence of their fellow-villagers. One or two spoke English tolerably well—the schoolmaster of the nearest secondary school, a retired Government servant spending the evening of his days in the quiet of his ancestral home after thirty years of useful and strenuous service as a subordinate judicial officer, and a lawyer practising at the nearest subdivisional headquarters town. The remaining half-dozen—the union boards consist of nine members, of whom six are elected and three nominated—were typical villagers with no knowledge of English and engaged in various occupations besides the cultivation of the land: one a shopkeeper, another a boatman, and so on.

A small tax known as the chaukidari tax for the upkeep of the village police is a compulsory levy; but under the Village Self-government Act a union board may impose additional taxation to enable it to undertake various works for the benefit of the villages. I was shown the accounts. The board, though of recent creation, had imposed additional taxation amounting to a quarter of the chaukidari tax. Did the villagers object? I asked. At first, yes; but it was explained that the board required the money for the construction of certain wells. Now above all things the villagers wanted wells, for a supply of good drinking water was a long-felt want. They would see what the board could do. The board, it seemed, did very well; and during the coming year the rate of taxation was to be doubled for further improvements. Presently I saw the wells, excellent circular shafts lined with brick, some feet in diameter, and with a neat coping round the top. The cost had been Rs. 300—£20—per well, and neither the district board nor any other agency, I was told, could construct such wells for less than double the sum, for the village had done the work itself; the chairman of the board had kept the accounts and done all the clerical work, a member of the board had supervised construction, the labour had come from the village itself. There had been, in fact, no middleman charges, and the village had got the full value of every rupee spent. The year before twenty-five of the boards in the district had raised no revenue by taxation other than that of the chaukidari tax; this year all but fourteen of the one hundred and thirty union boards which had been established within the area had levied additional rates.

After the inspection of the wells we returned to the *pandal* for further talk, and I was told of a scheme upon which the villagers and board alike had set their hearts, the excavation of a large tank or reservoir. But the project, they said, was a big one which, even with additional taxation, must remain for long beyond their means. The scene during the discussion which followed is one which remains deeply impressed upon my memory—the members of the board seated round me, quiet, dignified men, speaking seldom, and always with deliberation; behind me one or two of the young men of the village producing with the aid of large palm-leaf fans a faint but none the less welcome stir in the hot, suffocating air; outside the *pandal* in the fierce glare of the sun naked, dark-skinned children playing on the water's edge, and in the middle distance, against a green background of tropical vegetation, the close ranks of stolid but interested onlookers. During a pause in the conversation an elderly man of good presence rose and asked permission to speak. His words were translated to me sentence by sentence. The tank would benefit the whole people of the village where he had been born and amongst whom he had been

Plate 11.

VILLAGE CRAFTSMEN: THE POTTER.

brought up. Throughout his life he had toiled upon the waters of his motherland and was now a *serang* (river pilot), well known to and trusted by the river steamer companies. For the measure of prosperity which he had been vouchsafed he desired to show his gratitude to Providence. How better could he do so than by contributing to a work of benefit to the people of his village? And he laid before me there and then an appreciable sum in currency notes to be given in trust to the board for the carrying out of the needed work. The whole scene recalled vividly a mental picture of ancient India in the days when the indigenous irrigation system consisted of tanks and channels "which were built partly by individual benefactions and partly by communal enterprise."[1]

It is worth recalling that under the old Indian system of village assemblies this practice of making gifts for public purposes was carried far. It was not unusual for a private individual to vest in the assembly a capital sum the income from which was to provide some service of a religious or secular character. There are inscriptions which tell us, for example, of a number of endowments made by private individuals for the proper maintenance of a tank at Uttaramallur in the district of Chingleput in Southern India; one a gift of land, and others gifts of gold duly accepted by the Assembly to defray the annual cost of clearing the tank of silt. One such endowment is referred to in detail as a gift of 200 *kalañju* of gold, the interest from which, amounting to 30 *kalañju* a year, was to be spent by the Assembly on this particular service. It is added that in gratitude the Assembly exempted the donor from certain taxes.[2] There are many such records of

[1] "Local Self-government in Ancient India," by R. Mookerji.
[2] *Ibid.*

endowments to be administered by village assemblies, a notable type being those for religious ministrations; such, for example, as the provision of lamps to be maintained perpetually burning before the altar of some temple. I am not aware of endowments of this latter kind having yet been made to the village boards which have come into existence under recent legislation; but it is noteworthy that, during the year of which I am writing, gifts for secular purposes aggregating Rs. 10,000 were entrusted to various village boards in the Dacca district.

The trial of petty criminal cases and civil suits was a function of the guilds of ancient India, and the experimental establishment of village courts and benches under the Act of 1919 met with immediate success. In the year 1921, 652 criminal cases and 2218 civil suits were instituted before fourteen such courts and benches, a single village court disposing of 260 civil suits and 66 criminal cases.

It would seem, therefore, that the village is still the fundamental unit in the communal life of India; and it is worth noting in passing, as significant of the feelings of the village population, that at a recent conference of representatives of union boards in the Dacca district, a proposal was put forward for discussion for the abolition of district boards. More significant still, the proposal was carried.

* * * * *

I have said that, in addition to the existence throughout the continent of an administrative system of a Western type, the visitor will notice, as a further striking result of the coming of Great Britain to India, the introduction into a country essentially agricultural of the industrialism of Europe. It is, of course, to the towns that he must turn if he would ascertain how this twig of the Western tree is faring as a result of the experiment of grafting it on to the ancient tree-trunk of the East. And to the towns of modern India, therefore, we must now journey.

CHAPTER XIII

THE INDUSTRIALISM OF THE WEST

Ten or twelve years ago Sir Theodore Morison published a book under the title of "The Economic Transition in India," in which he painted a picture of the growing industrialisation of the country; and he took Bombay, where "the industrial revolution has already been accomplished," as illustrative of the India of the future. Rural India, "with its brown villages and never-ending fields," he spoke of as "the India which is passing away; Bombay," he declared, "is the presage of the future."

The great industrial concerns of Bombay are, it is true, almost entirely in the hands of Indians; and there are doubtless not a few amongst her public men who view with pride and satisfaction the growing industries of their country. Sir T. Morison, indeed, was able to quote such opinions from the public utterances of men like the late Mr. Justice Ranade and Professor V. G. Kale. Nevertheless there are others who view not only with grave concern, but with intense dislike, the coming of this particular form of Western civilisation. Quite recently an Indian nationalist scoffed at the suggestion that the conditions under which the labouring population lived and worked in Bombay might be improved. "What is the good of trying to improve Bombay?" he asked. "It is a foreign wen on the face of India. There is only one thing to do with it: abolish it."[1] And Mr. Gandhi's campaign against machine-made goods of all kinds and his amazing endeavour to introduce the ancient spinning-wheel into every Indian household is of too recent date to need further elaboration. Moreover, this is a subject upon which I may have something to say in a final volume of these impressions. For the present I am merely concerned to give a general idea of the nature and extent of the inroad which modern industrialism has made.

Two great textile industries flourish in India—the cotton industry in Bombay, Madras, and certain up-country centres, such as Ahmedabad, Nagpur, and Cawnpore, and the jute industry in Calcutta. They possess this characteristic in common, that their successive periods of prosperity have been the outcome of war. In the course of a year 2,800,000 bales of raw cotton pour into Bombay. Of these 1,100,000 are required to feed the mills of the city. And amongst the schemes now being carried out for its improvement is the provision of a new cotton green in the northern area, having 200 go-downs with a storage capacity of 1,500,000 bales, and an equal number of open-air storage plots with accommodation for 800,000 bales. This great industry—taking the whole of India—boasts of nearly 7,000,000 spindles and 124,000 looms. It produces every year from 600,000,000 to 700,000,000 pounds of yarn and over 1,580,000,000 yards of woven goods, and it employs from 300,000 to 350,000 persons. It was first planted in Bombay city in 1854, and of the 260 cotton mills in India, more than 180 are located in that presidency to-day. An analysis of the dividends paid by fifty-eight leading Bombay mills in the year following

[1] See the "Manchester Guardian" of July 1, 1922.

the close of the Great War shows an average rate of distribution of 44 per cent.[1] There is, indeed, no need to quarrel with Sir T. Morison's assertion that "in Bombay the industrial revolution has already been accomplished."

But it would be a mistake to assume that Bombay is typical of India. The lines of its development have been determined largely by geographical conditions, and are exceptional rather than typical. The city is the proud possessor not merely of a harbour which can be described without exaggeration as magnificent, but of the only haven of any importance in an immense coast-line running from Karachi in the north to Cape Comorin in the south. Another geographical feature, the importance of which has been realised only in recent years, is its proximity to the Ghāts Mountains, which rise like a vast rampart at no great distance from the coast-line, with which they run parallel, and against which the western monsoon inevitably breaks.

Meteorological statistics in India are always interesting, as has been shown in the opening chapter. The statistics of the annual rainfall on the Ghāts Mountains behind Bombay proved of peculiar interest to the manufacturers of the city. This can be seen by the most cursory examination of the returns of the rainfall. For example, at Igatpuri, a station on the main line of railway a little short of the summit over which the line climbs, the annual rainfall is as much as 130 inches; whereas at Goti, only six miles further east, only 60 inches are registered. From which it is a simple deduction that the monsoon bursting against the wall of mountains precipitates vast quantities of water which simply run to waste.

[1] See "A General Review of the Conditions and Prospects of British Trade in India during the Years 1919–21," by Mr. T. M. Ainscough, O.B.E.

Why, then, should not this volume of potential energy be caught and harnessed? The immense possibilities suggested by these meteorological statistics were insistently pressed upon certain wealthy and capable citizens of Bombay by a well-known character of that city, Mr. David Gostling, with the result that in due course steps were taken to exploit them. The Tata Hydro-Electric Power Supply Company came into existence in 1910, with an authorised capital of two crores of rupees,[1] and the works constructed by the company were formally opened in February 1915. The water is drawn from three lakes to a receiving reservoir, whence it is carried in pipes to the power-house at Khopoli at the foot of the Ghāts, 1725 feet below, developing a pressure of 750 lb. per square inch in the course of its descent. This project, originally designed to supply the city with 30,000 electrical horse-power, underwent expansion during construction, the capital of the company being raised to three crores and the power provided to over 40,000 horse-power.

When once the advantage of this method of developing energy was realised, a ready demand for current arose. It was estimated that the cotton mills of Bombay alone would require 100,000 horse-power, and that the total demands of the city would amount to 160,000 horse-power. A new company accordingly came into existence some eighteen months after the opening of the Khopoli station, for the purpose of carrying out a further project designed when completed to supply 100,000 horse-power. In this case the water is drawn from the Andhra river and the power-station is at Bhivpuri, about seventeen miles to the north of Khopoli.

In 1919 a third company was formed, entitled

[1] One crore = 10,000,000.

the Tata Power Company, Ltd., for the purpose of carrying through another scheme known as the Nila-Mula, which when in full operation will be capable of generating 150,000 horse-power.

Even this does not complete the list of hydro-electric projects associated with the name of the Tatas. The most ambitious scheme of all, known as the Koyna river project, has for its object the creation of a chemical industrial town at or near Jaigarh, a small inlet on the coast a hundred miles or so south of Bombay. Among the chief industries to be undertaken will be the electro-chemical production of aluminium from bauxite, of which there are large deposits scattered over the Indian continent. The Koyna river, after rising near Mahabaleshwar, runs south for some distance parallel to the scarp of the Ghāts chain before it turns east to flow into the Kistna. It has during this part of its course a catchment area of 350 square miles, with an average annual rainfall of from 150 to 250 inches within two or three miles of a natural fall of 1700 feet. The reservoir, which will be formed by the construction of a dam, will have a gross storage capacity of 132,100 million cubic feet, and the energy generated will amount to from 300,000 to 350,000 horse-power. When this great scheme is in operation there will be a prospect of there springing up at or near Jaigarh one of the largest combinations of electro-chemical industries in the world; and with these figures before one it is unnecessary to labour the importance to Bombay and its neighbourhood of the peculiar geographical position which it occupies. "What city in the world is there like Bombay," exclaimed an enthusiastic resident, "with its magnificent twenty miles of littoral, with a gravity water-supply scheme delivering 90,000,000 gallons of water daily, and with the certainty of some 250,000 horse-power hydro-electrically generated being available in the near future ?"[1]

Mention must be made, however, of a disadvantage of some importance which is likewise due to her geographical position. Being situate on a very narrow island only twelve miles in length, the area of the city is inconveniently restricted. It necessarily followed that with the influx of a vast industrial population it became seriously overcrowded. A stroll through the industrial quarters of the town is all that is required to show that within its walls its inhabitants jostle one another uncomfortably. Even before the War, pressure upon its space was so great that its citizens lived crushed together at the rate of over 42,500 to the square mile—a figure exceeded in the case of one city only in the whole of India, that of the capital of the native state of Jeypore, which has a population of over 45,500 to the square mile. And with the boom in the cotton industry which arose out of the War, a large additional population streamed into the city, increasing the number of its inhabitants, according to conservative estimates, by as much as 25 per cent. Land in certain areas of the city sold not long ago at £37 : 10s. per square yard.[2]

Such congestion called for drastic action, and the Government of Bombay took the lead in formulating a programme for the expansion of the city. A scheme was drawn up for the construction by Government of 50,000 tenements at a cost of £5,000,000, and a programme of land reclamation and of building expansion, not only in the city and the port areas, but in the neighbouring island of Salsette, destined to become the site of a Greater Bombay, was framed in co-

[1] Sir George Curtis, K.C.S.I., in a paper published in the "Journal of the Royal Society of Arts" of July 15, 1921.
[2] *Ibid.*

operation with the municipality and the Improvement and Port Trusts at an estimated cost in all of £30,000,000. From which it will be seen that what man can do to overcome the one serious disadvantage with which Nature has penalised Bombay, will certainly be done.

To the advantages conferred by its geographical situation upon this great entrepôt of commerce must be added the advantage which it derives from the composition of its inhabitants. Its population is essentially cosmopolitan, and is made up largely of the keenest trading races of Asia. The foreign-born element is higher here than in any other city in India, no less than 804 per thousand. Amongst its great captains of industry the Parsis are prominent—refugees in days gone by from the hosts of Islam that overran Persia, and never handicapped, as has been so large a portion of the people of India proper, by caste restrictions. Jews there are, too, from Baghdad, Khojas from Cutch, and Banias and Bhattias from Gugerat.

The situation in Calcutta is a very different one. Here, too, there is a large and flourishing textile industry. Congregated on the banks of the Hughli river are innumerable jute mills with something like 850,000 spindles and 40,000 looms, employing in all about 275,000 persons. It has been estimated that the total capital, including shares, debentures, reserve and other funds invested in the mills on the banks of the river, amounts to £30,000,000. But with scarcely an exception the mills are in the hands of Europeans. The fibre is grown nowhere else in the world—it is a practical monopoly of Bengal and Assam; and for many generations the people of these countries had spun and woven it by hand. Yet the industry in its present form, apart from being carried on upon the soil of India and by means of Indian labour, has no claim to Indian nationality. It is palpably an exotic. It is, nevertheless, an enterprise of great interest which merits description.

The credit for first calling the attention of the Western world to this particular fibre rests with a Dr. Roxburgh, who in 1795 sent home to the Directors of the East India Company a bale of what he described as "the jute of the natives." This seems to be the first recorded use of the word jute, which is probably in origin an Anglicised rendering of the word *pat* of Eastern Bengal, sometimes pronounced *jhat*. Its preparation by hand appears to have been an almost universal occupation in the cottages of Eastern Bengal. According to a Calcutta merchant of those days, it pervaded all classes and penetrated into every household. Men, women, and children found occupation therein. "Boatmen in their spare moments, husbandmen, palankeen carriers, and domestic servants; everybody, in fact, being Hindus, pass their leisure moments, distaff in hand, spinning gunny twist." It enabled even the Hindu widow to pay her way instead of becoming a charge upon her family, for its preparation formed "the never-failing resource of that most humble, patient, and despised of created beings, saved by law from the pyre but condemned by opinion and custom for the remainder of her days, literally to sackcloth and ashes." [1]

It was not until 1829, however, that jute made its appearance in the Customs returns. In that year a consignment of 18 tons was exported, valued at £62. Its value was still doubtful, however, and up to the year 1838 the flax and hemp spinners of Dundee found it advisable in their

[1] The merchant's name was Henley. I am indebted to Mr. D. R. Wallace's monograph, entitled "The Romance of Jute," for the quotation.

market quotations to guarantee their products free from Indian jute.[1] In that year experiments met with some success, and exports were made in small quantities averaging by the middle of the century about 12,000 tons a year.

With the outbreak of the Crimean War the supplies of flax and hemp from Russia were cut off, and jute was at once sought after as a substitute, the amount exported annually during the years 1854–58 averaging over 35,500 tons. In 1855 the first yarn spun by machine in India was turned out on the site of the present Wellington mills near Serampore, and four years later the first jute cloth woven on a power-loom made its appearance on the market. The next great impetus which the jute industry was to receive came from another war, the American War of Secession, in 1861. Cotton was at that time still used widely for packing and wrapping purposes. At the outbreak of war in 1861 the price of "middling Orleans" cotton was 9¼d. per lb.; by the middle of 1864 it was 2s. 7¾d. per lb. The effect upon jute was immediate. For the five years ending 1868 the exports of raw jute from India averaged 131,405 tons a year, a figure which rose during the next five years to nearly 243,000 tons. Still the industry in India developed slowly, and up to the year 1870 comprised less than a thousand looms. It was the manufacturer in Dundee who shared with the cultivator in Bengal the benefits of the rapidly increasing demand.

Successive wars, however, during the past fifty years—the Franco-German War of 1870, the South African War of 1899, the Russo-Japanese War of 1904, and finally the European War of 1914—have given to the industry in Bengal the position of predominance which it occupies to-day. On the eve of the outbreak of war in 1914 the

[1] D. R. Wallace, "The Romance of Jute."

mills in India were exporting every year not far short of 370,000,000 bags and 1,061,000,000 yards of cloth, having a total value of nearly £19,000,000. Three years later, when the War was at its height, these figures had jumped to 805,000,000 bags and 1,230,000,000 yards of cloth, with a value of £27,750,000. Sand-bags were made in hundreds of millions. The Calcutta mills turned them out at the rate of 80,000,000 a month as long as they were required to do so. At one moment an order for 136,000,000 was received. I asked if this would embarrass the mills. Not at all; it would merely require the use of one-fifth of the looms of the city for a couple of months. The number of these bags supplied by the Calcutta mills to the allied armies between the autumn of 1915 and the same season in 1917 would have sufficed, allowing thirty-four bags filled with sand to the yard, to girdle the earth with a solid rampart six feet in height. The consumption of the Calcutta mills now averages over a million tons of raw jute and over a million tons of coal a year.

And this activity in the jute industry gave a fillip to a number of subsidiary industries. The supply from abroad of such things as bobbins, plane tree-rollers, pickers, roller-skins, belting, and porcelain thread-guides was cut off, and their production in India became an imperious necessity. For example, the consumption of raw hide-pickers in the Bengal jute mills is approximately 45,000 a month. Had their manufacture not been extemporised in India, the whirr and crash of 40,000 looms and 800,000 spindles would have died down; over a quarter of a million people would have been thrown out of work, and mills worth millions of pounds sterling would have lain idle.

Other industries—notably the tea industry—found themselves cut off from their normal source of supply. Over 300,000,000 lb. of tea are made in India every year ; the value of the tea exported during the year before the War was little short of £10,000,000. Its consumption of Venesta tea-chests amounted to from 1,000,000 to 1,500,000 a year, and they came chiefly from Russia and Japan. Their manufacture was, therefore, organised in Bengal and Assam. And this new industry in its turn called for subsidiary industries such as lead mills and nail and rivet factories. Even here the end of the industrial chain had not been reached, for nails cannot be made without wire, and hitherto there had been no wire-drawing plant in India.

Pruning knives and kindred implements are another essential requirement of the tea industry. In the year 1918 the first Indian pruning knife was made from Indian steel, the product of the Tata works. The consumption of such knives is estimated at 150,000 a year.

These are but examples of some of the smaller industries brought into existence out of imperious necessity due to the War. Another major industry that underwent rapid expansion was the production of iron and steel. The great Tata Iron and Steel Company had been formed in 1907, and the entire plant of the company had come into operation at Jamshedpur, on the borders of Bengal and Orissa, in 1912. It had scarcely more than started on its career, consequently, when its resources were subjected to a tremendous strain occasioned by the demands of war. Large extensions were undertaken. New blast furnaces were put in hand and others planned. The future output of the company is expected to be 1,000,000 tons of steel a year. An earlier enterprise was that of the Bengal Iron Company at Kulti, founded in 1875; and a number of newcomers are now entering the field. The Indian

Iron and Steel Company are erecting works at Hirapur on a scale comparable with those of the Tata Company. At Ondal in the Raniganj district, a company entitled Indian Steels, Limited, is laying down electric furnaces for the production of steel suitable for tool and machine construction; and at Rupnarainpur, the Kirtyanand Iron and Steel Company have erected plant for the production of steel castings on a large scale. And on a par with these are projects for the manufacture of jute-mill machinery, agricultural implements, tinplates, and, last but not least, sulphuric acid on a large scale in the environs of the existing Tata works at Jamshedpur. By the roadside, too, running from Calcutta to Barrackpore may be seen newly erected buildings for the manufacture of machine tools for the Indian market.

No greater impetus, then, could conceivably have been given to the industrial revolution of which Sir T. Morison wrote, than that which was quite unexpectedly given to it by the European War. Yet the industrialism of the West still remains to a large extent an exotic upon Indian soil. I am not likely easily to forget my first inspection of a Calcutta jute mill, for it was a fascinating experience. Twenty thousand spindles whirred unceasingly; a thousand looms crashed inexorably. The thrumming of the engines, the whirr of the spindles, the crash of the looms, all these things denoted a gigantic and sleepless activity. The whole thing was a dramatic manifestation of power. But its ownership and its organisation were not Indian but British. And the same thing applies to practically every jute mill in the country; and the statistics show that of the whole value of manufactured goods exported from India every year, jute manufactures are responsible for more than half. The figures for 1920–21 are: jute manufactures, £35,300,000; all other manufactures, £22,500,000.

Other facts concerning the industrial revolution point in the same direction. The works for the production of machine tools on the Barrackpore road are not Indian works: they are being put up by Messrs. Alfred Herbert. The great iron and steel works at Jamshedpur are the offspring of the great Parsi firm of Bombay—and Bombay, as already explained, is not typical of India proper in this respect. Similarly, the other large iron and steel works to which reference has been made are in the main European and not Indian enterprises. Indian indifference to modern industrialism could hardly be better illustrated than by her apathy in the case of the leather industry. It would be difficult to imagine a country better situated for the production of leather than India. She possesses in almost unlimited quantities the two necessary ingredients, namely, hides and skins on the one hand and tanning materials on the other. By applying the one to the other she had it in her power to increase the value of each hide she sold by from four to five rupees. Yet with a prodigality which cannot be attributed to altruism, and which must, therefore, be set down to indifference, she exported them side by side in shiploads to other countries. In the year before the War she exported 1,632,000 cwt. of raw hides and skins, and 1,467,000 cwt. of dyeing and tanning stuffs. Comment upon these figures is altogether superfluous. Under the influence of war conditions a change came about. A research tannery subsidised by the State came into existence, to be followed by the appearance of new tanneries and the reconstruction of others that were in existence. But the War was in a sense an artificial stimulant, and no development due to

Plate 12.

MARBLE CEILING OF A JAIN TEMPLE AT MOUNT ABU.

"The industrialism of the West still remains to a large extent an exotic upon Indian soil."

it can alter the significance of the state of affairs set forth above.

With all these things in mind, I find it difficult to escape from the conclusion that the organisation of industries on the lines evolved by Western nations—industries, that is to say, which require a huge array of machinery driven by mechanical power, steam, hydraulic, or electric, and which necessitate the aggregation of vast numbers of human beings to perform for a fixed wage so much of the operation as cannot be performed by the machine itself—is something which is altogether alien to the genius of the Indian people. Of course, there are modern industrial undertakings which are exclusively Indian, and I would not have it supposed that there are not Indians outside Bombay who possess the initiative, the technical skill, and the organising ability necessary for the successful running of such businesses. I recall half a dozen such enterprises which I have myself visited, and of which I can speak in the highest terms. But these are exceptional rather than typical, and their existence does not invalidate the general conclusion arrived at above—a conclusion which finds striking confirmation in the verdict of the Indian Industrial Commission of 1916–18 that "the industrial system is unevenly and in most cases inadequately developed; and the capitalists of the country, with a few notable exceptions, have till now left to other nations the work and the profit of manufacturing her valuable raw materials, or have allowed them to remain unutilised." Western industrialism is, indeed, regarded by a not inappreciable section of educated public opinion not merely with indifference but with deep-rooted aversion. "This one thing," said Mr. C. R. Das, long before Mr. Gandhi launched his campaign against the civilisation of the West, "we must remember for ever, that this industrialism never was and never will be art and part of our nature. . . . If we seek to establish industrialism in our land, we shall be laying down with our hands the road to our destruction. Mills and factories—like some gigantic monster—will crush out the little life that still feebly pulsates in our veins, and we shall whirl round with their huge wheels and be like some dead and soulless machine ourselves."

And the modern factory is as uncongenial to the Indian workman as is the industrial system to the educated Indian idealist. It sounds almost a paradox to say that in a country with a population of 320,000,000 the demand for factory labour is always in excess of the supply. Nevertheless, such is the case. And the key to the puzzle is provided by the census statistics, which show that 90 per cent of the vast population of the continent is classed as rural. The significance of this figure becomes apparent when compared with the corresponding figure in a modern industrial State like England and Wales, where the census of 1921 showed that nearly 80 per cent of the people live in towns. This overwhelming preponderance of the rural population is not apparent to the visitor, who usually passes from town to town. But as one's opportunities of travelling in country districts extend, one discovers the paramount part played by agriculture in the economy of the country. One soon realises that like Cain the Indian is a tiller of the ground, and one has little hesitation in deciding that he labours under the curse called forth by the behaviour of Adam. He eats of the herb of the field, and if appearances go for anything he does so in sorrow all the days of his life. Most assuredly does he eat bread in the sweat of his brow. Not that one should judge hastily by appearances. As has already been pointed out, the Indian is seldom given to displays of hilarity, but is disposed by temperament towards solemnity. On the whole, he is probably far happier as a peasant than he will be as a member of an industrial proletariat if ever the hand-loom is completely ousted by the power-loom, and the factory casts its net wide over the countryside and sweeps its inhabitants into crowded towns as it has done in the West.

At any rate, the worker in the factory and the mill is still a villager at heart. He does not settle down and make his home near the scene of his labour. He stays and works as long as necessity compels him, and then he departs—back to his village. In Bengal the workpeople are almost exclusively immigrants from other provinces, who retain their foreign domicile and reside in bachelor messes in the immediate neighbourhood of their work. The workman's heart is not amidst the restless and tireless machinery alongside of which he toils, but away in the village where stands, however humble be the actual building, his deeply loved ancestral home. I have vivid recollections of travelling across the cotton country of the Central Provinces at the time of the gathering of the crop. The landscape wore the untidy appearance which is so marked a characteristic of the Indian countryside. In places the land was flat, in others crumpled. One crop straggled carelessly into the ground of its neighbour, and trees were scattered over the whole promiscuously and in disorder. What particularly attracted my attention, however, was the behaviour of the people. They were, if the employers of labour with whom I discussed the matter were to be believed, as inconsequent as their landscape. The call of the land at such a time became irresistible. Every one who could possibly do so migrated to the fields. A man ordinarily employed on the railway would return suddenly to his natural occupation—that of agriculture—and until the crop was garnered the railway knew him no more. On all sides of me I saw collections of flimsy sheds of brushwood more preposterously untidy even than the rest—the temporary homes of those carried along on the tide of this strange migration from the workshop to the land.

Some years later I had occasion to study a variety of official documents dealing with the question of the efficiency of Indian labour. "The most serious defect of Indian industrial labour," I learned from one of them, "is that it is intermittent." And as I read on further that the worker was at heart an agriculturist, that he only worked at the factory in order to save sufficient money for some family festival or to tide over bad farming seasons, and that he almost always returned to his village at harvest time, the untidy landscape of the cotton country of the Central Provinces rose before my mind. The report which I was studying contained more details than I had picked up on the dusty landscape. It averred that 10 per cent was a very low estimate of the number of absentees at any one time in any particular industry, and that during the harvest season staffs were sometimes reduced by as much as one-third.[1]

The Indian peasant is not, consequently, an efficient workman. Mills have now been in existence in Calcutta for nigh on seventy years; but the number of hands required per loom is still much greater than in similar mills in Europe. The contrast is most marked, perhaps, in the mining industry. The coal seams in India and in the United States of America are of approximately the same thickness. In the latter country

[1] Report on the conditions and prospects of British trade in India at the close of the War, by Mr. T. M. Ainscough, O.B.E.

the amount of coal produced per person employed above and below ground is roughly 800 tons a year. In India in 1920 it was just 100 tons. Some part of the difference is no doubt attributable to the greater use of labour-saving machinery in America; but much is accountable to the inefficiency of Indian labour. The Indian miner has eccentricities of his own which would scarcely be tolerated in Western lands. The Sonthali miner, for example, when he goes below ground takes with him not merely his pick and shovel, but his wife as well. He makes this, in fact, a condition of his going below ground at all.

India has still a long way to go before the industrial revolution is accomplished, and many obstacles to overcome, not the least of which is the unwillingness of the greater number of her people to tread the industrial road.

CHAPTER XIV

WEALTH, ACTUAL AND POTENTIAL

INDIA is actually a poor country according to Western standards, because her wealth is undeveloped—because, in other words, the industrial revolution referred to in the last chapter has not yet taken place. A rough estimate of the average income per head of the population of India at the close of the nineteenth century was £3 a year. Calculations based on recent figures in the Presidency of Madras give a higher figure to-day, namely, £10; but this increase is discounted to a great extent by the heavy fall in the purchasing power of the rupee. Taxation has increased appreciably in recent years, yet at the close of the War (1918–19) its incidence amounted only to a fraction more than 3s. 2½d. per head, or, if land revenue be included, to a trifle more than 4s. 9½d. The meaning of these figures becomes clearer when compared with those of a highly industrialised country such as Great Britain, whose people are credited with an average income of £30 or £40, and who cheerfully pay taxes at the rate of £16 : 12s. per head, or, if local taxation be included, at the rate of £21 per head.[1]

A rapid survey of the two main factors necessary for the production of wealth—man-

[1] Figures for 1922–23.

power and natural resources—will satisfy one that, however poor a country India may appear to be to-day, she is a land of immense latent possibilities. The British flag flies over 13,250,000 square miles of the dry surface of the globe. Of this vast area India claims 1,800,000 square miles, or something approaching one-seventh of the whole. But this seventh part of the British Empire possesses far more than an equivalent share of the Empire's man-power. Of the estimated total population of 440,000,000, India claims no less than 320,000,000, a proportion which exceeds two-thirds of the whole. Figures have been given in Chapter I. which show that this vast human hive of workers is engaged, for the most part, in cultivating the land, and grounds have been given in the preceding chapter for concluding that for many years to come they will continue to be so. Indeed, no greater contrast in occupation than that between the people of Great Britain and those of India could well be found. Whereas the former live in vast aggregations in huge towns, the latter live spread over the countryside in countless villages. In England and Wales, as I have already pointed out, 80 per cent of the population is returned as urban; in India 90 per cent is recorded as rural. Every year some 225,000,000 acres in British India bring forth crops of sugar, tea, and coffee; rice, wheat, barley, and other food grains; linseed, sesamum, rape, and other oil seeds; cotton, jute, and other fibres; indigo, opium, and tobacco. In a single year[1] these spreading acres have yielded 34,750,000 tons of cleaned rice; 10,250,000 tons of wheat; 370,000,000 lb. of tea; 4,500,000 400-lb. bales of cotton; 8,300,000 bales of jute; 500,000 tons of linseed; nearly 1,200,000 tons of rape and

[1] 1916–17, taken at random.

mustard; the same amount of ground-nut; and 2,750,000 tons of raw sugar.

Nor has this immense territory reached anything approaching its full development. The tiller of the soil in India is, to say the least, conservative in his methods. With the aid of modern science the crops upon the land already cultivated can be enormously increased. Take an example. Bengal and Assam hold a practical monopoly in the production of jute, the raw material of the gunny bags in which, year by year, are moved the harvests of the world.

Much painstaking research on the part of the experts of the Agricultural Department, involving the scientific examination on Mendelian lines of innumerable varieties followed by cross-breeding, has resulted in the discovery of varieties of the plant which give a yield much in excess of those hitherto grown by the Indian peasant. A variety known as *Kakya Bombai*, giving on the average 160 lb. of fibre more per acre than the local varieties, has been distributed amongst the villages of Eastern Bengal during the past few years, and by the year 1921 was being grown on an area of 200,000 acres. So successful was the crop, that it was estimated that the eventual increase in the yield of the plant on the jute lands of Bengal might easily amount to 400,000,000 lb. of fibre, worth probably £2,750,000 sterling. Scarcely had this estimate been made when a still more highly productive variety was discovered, giving on the average a yield of 80 lb. an acre more fibre than *Kakya Bombai* itself. A similar story can be told of rice. Research produced not long ago two varieties giving yields greater by some 250 lb. per acre than that of the local variety. In 1919 these two varieties were grown on 250,000 acres, with the result that the food supply on this area was increased by

60,000,000 lb. of grain, worth £200,000. Research on these lines is still proceeding, and further success in this direction is practically assured. Be it remembered that round the head of the Bay of Bengal alone lie 20,000,000 acres of productive rice land, and some idea of the ultimate value of these discoveries can be formed.

These are not the only ways in which the agricultural output is being increased. By means of irrigation vast tracts of land formerly desert are being brought under the plough. The Punjab provides a notable example. Here an arid waste has been transformed into a bounteous granary. Canal colonies have been plotted out, and nearly 9,000,000 acres in the province have been brought under cultivation by irrigation works classed as productive, *i.e.* works capable within ten years of their construction of producing sufficient revenue to cover their working expenses and the interest charges on their capital cost. It was only when these great projects began to bear fruit that the North-Western State Railway—a system with nearly 4000 miles of track—began to pay. In British India as a whole 67,000 miles of canal irrigate 28,000,000 acres of land, the estimated value of the crops irrigated by Government works amounting to over £156,000,000 a year. Existing schemes are constantly being added to, and it is officially estimated that by the time that projects now under construction are in full working order, and assuming that a great scheme in Sind known as the Sukkur Barrage is carried through, the present irrigated area of 28,000,000 acres will have increased to 40,000,000 acres.[1] All these things are sign-posts pointing the roads along which India is travelling

[1] This huge project, the greatest irrigation scheme in the world, was formally inaugurated by Sir George Lloyd, Governor of Bombay, in the autumn of 1923, when he laid the foundation stone of the great barrage at Sukkur which will henceforth bear his name.

towards a vastly increased production of raw material.

Another large potential source of wealth are the forests, which cover over 250,000 square miles of territory. These immense tracts are gradually being taken in hand; but the out-turn of timber and firewood at present amounts to only 2 cubic feet per acre, while the manufacture of paper pulp from such things as bamboo—of which there are vast quantities—has only recently been undertaken. A useful product of the forests is the fruit of certain trees widely distributed over the continent, to which the commercial name of myrobalan has been given. Its value is due to the tannin which it contains, and which renders it an important tanning agent. It is exported at the rate of from 40,000 to 60,000 tons a year. By a happy coincidence, the country which produces a tanning agent on so large a scale likewise possesses in almost unexampled quantity material which, when tanned, becomes a commodity of universal consumption, namely, leather.

No statistics are required to apprise any one who is familiar with the Indian landscape, whether in north or south or east or west, of the part played by the cow in the internal economy of the country. Let him call to memory any rural scene, and he will find it dominated by the bullock or the cow. A vast expanse stretches away in flat monotony to a distant horizon. Overhead, the sun steers its course across space more monotonous in its featureless uniformity even than the dusty plain below. A small cloud of dust rises from the ground. As it approaches it is accompanied by the creaking and groaning of crude wooden wheels upon primitive wooden axles. The procession moves with the slow, unrhythmical motion which is peculiar to the draught bullock. The string of bullock-carts which emerges from

Plate 12.

TEMPLES HEWN OUT OF THE ROCK AT KHANDAGIRI IN ORISSA.

its fog of dust is a thing of immemorial antiquity and of universal distribution. You will see it threading its leisurely way along dusty country lanes, and you will also see it lumbering the streets of great cities—hauling bales of cotton to and from the mills of Bombay, and blocking the riverside streets of Calcutta. There is scarcely an operation in Indian agricultural life in which the cow does not play an essential part. It treads out the grain on countless threshing-floors; it drags, with patient resignation, the archaic plough with which the Indian peasant turns over the soil of the continent; with a similar imperturbable indifference it raises water to be poured over the thirsty land from innumerable wells, plodding out interminable circles as it turns the Persian water-wheel, or stamping out straight lines as it passes up and down the inclined ramp of the simple haulage variety. These things have been recalled in order to clothe the dry bones of statistics with flesh and blood. It was estimated by the Indian Industrial Commission that there were in India 180,000,000 head of cattle and 87,000,000 sheep and goats; and in any case the export of hides and skins is not a matter of computation but of fact. The year before the War, the quantity of hides and skins exported was 1,906,931 cwt., valued at £10,606,000.

The mineral wealth of the continent is still more a matter for future development. The output of coal has increased fairly rapidly during the past few years, from 12,000,000 tons in 1910 to 22,500,000 tons in 1919; and with the introduction of electrical cutting plant should continue to show expansion. In 1919 over 300,000,000 gallons of petroleum were produced, mainly in Burma, and varying quantities of such minerals as manganese, wolfram, mica, saltpetre, and gold. More significant is the fact that recent surveys have disclosed the presence in the hills of Orissa of immense deposits of iron ore of unusually high grade. These discoveries include what appears to be a range of iron ore running almost continuously for forty miles, and rising to heights of from 2000 to 3000 feet above sea-level. It has been asserted that at one place a ravine cutting across the iron-ore range shows a continuous thickness of 700 feet of high-grade hematite containing over 60 per cent of iron; and it has been estimated that in this one field alone there are 2,800,000,000 tons of ore. And it requires but little imagination to perceive that, as time goes on, such deposits of iron must become a first-class imperial concern.

It will be seen, then, that with the two factors of primary importance for the production of wealth—man-power and raw material—India is generously endowed. It has also been shown in the preceding chapter that in the task of converting her potential wealth into actual riches she requires assistance from outside. Is she prepared to welcome the help of Great Britain in this work? It is certainly not unnatural that, in view of the history of Great Britain in India, of the fact that the development of her resources which has so far taken place has been the work of British experts, British administrators, and British merchants, and that her trade has been built up in the main by British enterprise and financed by British capital, there should be a desire on the part of the people of Great Britain to see the commercial ties between the two countries strengthened. On the one hand, India has a surplus of the raw materials which Great Britain requires. On the other hand, the Indian market is even now of paramount importance to the people of Great Britain, for it absorbs nearly one-sixth of her total exports to the world. Its potential value depends upon the future rise in the standard of living and the increase in the wealth of its 320,000,000 consumers; and to its eventual possibilities, therefore, it is difficult to assign a limit. Can the trade between the two countries be fostered to their mutual benefit? In other words, can India be included in any possible scheme for the commercial federation of the British Empire?

The answer to these questions is not an easy one, for the case of India is far more difficult than that of the Dominions. Preferential tariffs in her case are possible, as I have shown elsewhere;[1] but owing to the nature of her external trade, the scope for mutual assistance by this means is limited. Moreover, Indian public opinion is at present very far from accepting the principle enunciated by those who urge the formation of something in the nature of a British Zollverein, that "wherever it is possible, the imports which are required by any part of the Empire from external sources should be obtained from within the Empire."[2] Her public men are profoundly suspicious of any proposals for the manipulation of her tariffs in the interests of imperial trade. And if we are to be quite frank with ourselves, we must admit that they are so not without cause. The story of the Indian cotton duties—first the omission of cotton goods from the general Indian import tariff of 1894, followed by the imposition of an equivalent excise duty upon the Indian cotton industry when, shortly afterwards, as a result of the storm of indignation which broke out in India, it was found expedient to abandon this invidious exception; and the further manipulation of the duties under pressure from Lancashire in 1896—has left behind it a legacy of bitter

[1] In an essay entitled "India and Imperial Reciprocity," included in "An Eastern Miscellany": W. Blackwood & Sons, 1911.

[2] See, for example, an article by Professor Hewins in the "Nineteenth Century and After" for November 1922.

memories. As we have sown, so are we now reaping.

A temperate statement of the Indian attitude is to be found in the "Indian Modern Review" of October 1922, an admirably conducted periodical which voices the views of a large section of educated public opinion in India, which, without necessarily being extremist, is emphatically nationalist. After arguing that while Great Britain has certainly much to gain from preferential relations between herself and India, the latter country stands only to lose by them, the writer touches upon the political aspect of the question. "However striking the idea of an Imperial Zollverein may be to the imagination, it must remain an absurdity so long as the different countries remain separated, not merely by long distances, but by feelings and prejudices based on race, colour, and political status. So far as India is concerned, Imperial Preference is not a practical proposition at the present moment. The question rests largely on sentiment. But to appeal to Indian sentiment in the existing state of things in the country is to misread human nature." And he concludes with this warning: "Imperial Preference forced on the people under present circumstances is likely to make them regard it as another device invented for the further exploitation of the country. It would, indeed, be extremely unwise to take a step which is calculated to embitter feelings and strengthen prejudices, and which may easily lead to disastrous consequences."

These are the words, not of the politician seeking popularity in an appeal to race prejudice, but of Dr. Pramathanath Banerji, Minto Professor of Economics at the Calcutta University. And the views which he expresses are to be found stated with equal emphasis in the report of the

Indian Fiscal Commission of 1922. The Commission as a whole was impressed by "the almost complete unanimity with which Indian witnesses opposed the principle of Imperial Preference"; while the explanation of this attitude on the part of the Indian public, put forward in a minute by the minority, is that it is due to "India's present political status in the Empire. The conclusion is therefore inevitable," they add, "that this question can only become a matter of practical politics when the promised goal of responsible government is reached."[1] Indian opinion is not afraid of tariffs; quite the contrary. The men who are now qualifying in the legislative councils to take over the government of the country in the future—all those, in short, who have accepted the recent reform scheme as an instalment of responsible self-government and are classed compendiously as "Moderates"—are quite frankly Protectionists. They desire to see tariffs employed for the protection of Indian industries; and that means protection against the competition of British goods, since Great Britain is by far the largest salesman in the Indian market. It must be taken, therefore, that a preferential tariff as between Great Britain and India is not, at the present time, a matter of practical politics; and other means of developing trade between India and the rest of the Empire must be sought.

The most effective course will be to see that the capital, the business acumen, and the science which India requires, and for long will continue to require, from outside for the development of her

[1] The Commission consisted of twelve members under the presidentship of Sir Ibrahim Rahimtoola, C.I.E. Of the five European members, one, Mr. J. M. Keynes, M.A., C.B., was unable to attend and took no part in the proceedings. The Minute of Dissent, amounting practically to a minority report, was signed by five of the seven Indian members, including the President.

resources are provided by Great Britain. The direction of the flow of trade is influenced by many things besides tariffs. A notable object-lesson is provided by the trade in Indian hides, which up to August 1914 was dominated by German interests. When war broke out we woke up to find that the export hide market of Calcutta was entirely in the hands of German firms or firms with German affinities, who were bound by trade arrangements to sell to the continent through a ring of German dealers at Hamburg and Bremen. In 1913–14 Germany alone took 35 per cent of India's raw hides, and in the four months before the outbreak of war 39 per cent. As the War progressed, the importance to Great Britain of the rough tanned cow-hides known as East India kips was realised, and from August 1916 the Government of India assumed complete control of the trade in the interests of the War Office, which took the whole available supply for use in the manufacture of boots for the British and allied armies. The quantity required by the Army for the "uppers" of its boots was estimated for the year 1917 to be a *minimum* of 80,000,000 feet; and the quantity of tanned hides shipped from India rose from less than 200,000 cwt., valued at less than two crores of rupees the year before the War, to 365,000 cwt., valued at nearly five crores of rupees, in 1917–18.

Conditions brought about by the War were of course abnormal, and permitted Government action of a kind that would scarcely be tolerated during times of peace. Indeed, with a gradual return to more normal conditions, the sentiment expressed by the phrase, "India for the Indians," has developed with great rapidity. Nor have we any ground of complaint on this score. It is perfectly natural that Indians should desire to develop their trade and their resources primarily in the interests of their own people. And it behoves us to make it clear that in bringing to her aid our capital and our business skill, we are not animated by a selfish desire to exploit her to her own disadvantage. That it is to our own advantage that her resources should be developed by British rather than by foreign enterprise may be frankly admitted; what we have to do is to prove to her, if we can, that it is equally to her advantage that this should be so. And if we are to do this, there must be no more episodes on a par with the Tariff Acts of 1894–96, to which reference has been made.

Our task in this respect is not an easy one. The mere fact that British dominion in India arose out of the trading operations of a commercial corporation leads a certain school of Indian thought to look askance at the development of their resources and their industries by British merchants. There is indeed, as I have shown in the preceding chapter, a not inconsiderable section of Indian nationalists which takes the extreme view that Western industrialism is in itself an accursed thing, which at all costs must be denied access to the sacred soil of India. Mr. Gandhi is the most prominent exponent of this view. But he is not alone, as I have shown by quotations from the writings of Mr. C. R. Das and others.

I have mentioned this because it is important that we should realise the complicated nature of the problem with which we have to deal. It may assist towards an appreciation of the difficulties if I now sum up briefly the conclusions which have to be deduced from what has been written above. Broadly speaking, they may be said to be as follows:

(i.) That India is now a factor of supreme importance in the commerce of the Empire.

(ii.) That as time goes on this importance is likely to increase to an incalculable extent.

(iii.) That her public men are hostile to any tariff concessions to British trade.

(iv.) That the wise course for Great Britain to pursue is to concentrate upon increasing India's wealth by the development of her resources.

(v.) That in seeking to provide India with capital, business skill, and scientific advice with this end in view, she has to take into account two tendencies at present prevalent in India: that of the section of Indian public men which appreciates the advantages of industrial development, but is jealous of outside aid; and that of the idealists, who view with intense dislike the whole system of industrialism, which they regard as one of the worst products of the materialism of the West.

The question of importance, then, is how far are these two tendencies likely to militate effectively against British enterprise in the development of Indian trade and industry? The answer is, I think: not nearly so far as might *prima facie* be supposed. To deal with the former first. The extreme idealism of those who look askance at the civilisation—and particularly at the industrialism—of the West is scarcely likely to prevail against the hard necessities of life. Mr. C. R. Das gave up an exceedingly lucrative practice at the Bar in pursuance of the life of renunciation which he preached. But neither he nor Mr. Gandhi found it practicable to give up the use of railways and motor-cars, against which the latter so fiercely inveighed. And a proposal put forward at the meeting of the Indian National Congress in December 1922 for the boycott of British goods was rejected as impracticable. Then with regard to Indian jealousy of external aid in the development of her resources. The hard facts of the position have been explained in the preceding chapter. And however strong may be the desire of Indian industrial magnates to see Indian resources developed by Indian agency, they know, when it comes to a practical business proposition, the value of outside aid. A visitor to Jamshedpur, the great Tata industrial city on the borders of Bengal and Orissa, noted not long ago that not more than three or four Indians had gained a footing among the upper thirty who formed the management of this vast enterprise. The rest were English, Scotch, and American.[1] It must be for the good of India that her wealth should be increased; and since outside aid is necessary to this end, what has to be done is to make it clear to India that the aid which Great Britain can offer her is given to the mutual advantage of the two countries; that if British business men look to receive a reasonable return themselves, they have no desire to deprive her of her legitimate share of the total profit. In other words, that what they desire to do is not to exploit her to her disadvantage, but to co-operate with her in a business of mutual benefit.

The question is really one in which sentiment plays a paramount part. India has reached a stage of political growth when, having acquired a share in the control of the government of the country, she is thrusting out her hands to grasp the whole. While the dangers of too precipitate a leap from the stage of partial to that of complete indigenous control are staringly apparent to all who are familiar with conditions prevailing in India, no surprise need be felt at the sensitiveness of the intelligentzia of the country in the matter of foreign—which in this case means British—inter-

[1] See the "Manchester Guardian" for January 13, 1923.

ference. India's awakened national consciousness insists that acquiescence on the part of her public men in the continued exercise of control by men of another race, whether in the sphere of administration or in any other field, is tantamount to an admission of their own inferiority. Need it, then, cause us surprise if such acquiescence is, for the most part, not forthcoming? Or that where it is, it is but grudgingly given? And while we may be convinced in all sincerity that in the interests of India herself the guiding hand of Great Britain must remain for some time yet, we may at least try to banish from the mind of a proud and sensitive people the idea that on this account we harbour towards them feelings of contempt.

As a people, we have been all too prone to pass by with insular indifference India's contributions to the progress of the human race, not perhaps because of any deliberately formed conclusion that these were not worthy of our interest or our admiration, but because in India the performance of the task immediately to our hand has absorbed the whole of our energies and attention. Let us lift our gaze from the ground immediately beneath our feet, and at least attempt to pierce through the veil which our own distinctive outlook upon the universe tends to draw across the achievements of another race; and let us pay our tribute to the upward-aspiring spirit which inspires the great masterpieces in her literature and her art. Let us, above all, render homage to the lofty spiritual ideals which have marked her progress as, along with the other civilised races of the world, she has struggled forward up the steep ascent by which humanity, with halting steps, has groped its way from that long and brooding night of barbarism which lies behind the first faint light of civilisation's dawn.

Plate 14.

THE RELIGIOUS LIFE OF INDIA.

"... and let us pay our tribute to the upward aspiring spirit that inspired the great masterpieces of her literature and her art."

It may be that not until India has attained full self-government—as Professor Pramathanath Banerji and the signatories to the minority report of the Indian Fiscal Commission hold—will such a community of interests spring up between her and the other units of the British Empire as will lead her spontaneously to become a contracting party in some scheme of Imperial federation. But much in the meantime may assuredly be done to bridge the yawning gulf which, to the detriment of both, has opened in recent years between the Indian and the British peoples.

CHAPTER XV

THE LURE OF THE PRIMITIVE

NEARLY one-quarter of the whole surface of British India is under forest of one sort or another. Centuries back, when the early Aryan immigrants were making their way from Central Asia into the hospitable tracts of the Ganges valley, the forest may well have been spread over the greater part of the land. There is at any rate a school of thought in India which assigns to it a paramount part in shaping the intellectual outlook of the Indo-Aryan race.

The argument runs in this wise. The physical surroundings of primitive man have played an important part in determining his outlook upon the universe. Thus the sea has exercised a supreme influence upon the races dwelling in Northern Europe. To the men living on the island shores of countries like Great Britain it was the sea that stood for Nature—a thing of rugged power hurling a perpetual challenge to man, a thing to be fought and overcome, subdued and brought under the dominion of man. And man accepted the challenge and fought the elements and prevailed against them. But his very victory was proof of the existence of a gulf between him and Nature—of a spirit of antagonism between them. " He looked upon his place in the world as extorted from a hostile scheme of things, retained in the teeth of opposition." [1]

In the same way, it is argued, the forest exercised an abiding influence upon the people of India. Here Nature manifested herself in a garment of friendship, not in the armour of one girt up for battle. The forest offered no challenge to man; it extended rather an invitation to him. It gave him "shelter and shade, fruit and flower, fodder and fuel." [2] He dwelt in the midst of Nature, and he found his own life in harmony with the life which pulsated rhythmically around him. He became conscious of being an integral part of one great life principle which permeated all things, and such a thought as that of man being hostile to, or even distinct from, the rest of Nature never took shape in his mind.

The different directions thus given by environment to the thought of the progenitors of the peoples of Europe and of India are held responsible for the divergent attitudes of mind of East and West towards the problems of the universe. Man, regarding himself as something distinct from the rest of Nature, conceived of the world either as having been built by a Divine Mechanic or as being the outcome of a chance combination of blind forces. His attitude of mind towards such a world was naturally utilitarian. The world with which he found himself faced was there to be made the most of; to be used, and so far as possible fashioned, to his advantage. And dominated by this conception he devoted his energies to acquiring control over Nature. He became an efficient mechanic, and his outlook necessarily tended to become materialistic.

[1] "The Message of the Forest," by Sir R. Tagore, published in the "Modern Review" for May 1919.

[2] *Ibid.*

On the other hand, man, regarding himself as one with Nature, was not assailed by such ideas as the conquest of Nature. To such an one the universe was not something apart; not the creation of a Divine Master Builder. Rather was the earth, and man himself, as one with Nature, a particular manifestation of the Divine itself. And the attitude of mind of such a man towards the universe was anything but utilitarian; on the contrary, it tended towards extreme idealism. And, in the view of the apostles of this school of thought, this conception of the universe "as the manifestation of the Supreme Soul, whose nature is to realise his unity in the endlessness of the varied," has come to India from the great peace of its ancient forests.[1]

It is undoubtedly the case that the forest forms the background of many a picture of ancient Indian life. An important branch of early Vedic religious literature bears the name of Aranyaka, or "forest treatises," works of an allegorical and mystical character leading up to the philosophical speculations of the Upanishads. These works were to be studied in the forest, in particular, as some modern scholars hold, by the various orders of ascetics that came into existence in early Vedic times. As time went on, the word *vanaprastha*—forest-dweller—came into use as a name for such ascetics; and later still there came into existence the classic division of life applicable to all members of the three higher, or twice-born classes, into four distinct stages, those of studentship, of married life, of retirement in the forest, and, finally, of complete severance from the world. Of these four stages into which the lives of the twice-born were divided according to the institutes of Manu, it was definitely laid down that the third, after the functions of a house-

[1] "The Message of the Forest."

Plate 15.

THE INDIAN FOREST.

"The forest forms the background of many a picture of ancient Indian life.

holder had been duly discharged, was to be spent in the forest. "When a householder sees his skin wrinkled, and his hair white, and the sons of his sons, then he may resort to the forest."[1] Here he was required to live the life of a hermit, "without a house, wholly silent, subsisting on roots and fruit . . . dwelling at the roots of trees." And in order "to attain complete union with the Supreme Soul," the hermit "who dwells in the forest" must study the various sacred texts contained in the Upanishads.[2] The forest likewise provides a frequent setting for the episodes narrated in the great epics; in the forest, too, in the words of Tagore, "the most intense pathos of human life found its background in the greatest of our romantic dramas."[3]

The theory briefly set forth above is one of much attractiveness. The picture of the forest extending its hospitality to man—its portrayal as an abode of eternal peace, as a welcome haven from the storms of life to which men retired to meditate upon the profound and puzzling problems which forced themselves upon the acutest minds of a highly cultured race—possesses a strong appeal. But it does not accord with conditions at the present day. The forest of the present day is too often the haunt of the beast of prey. The tiger and the panther from their abode in its sombre depths war against man. They harry his cattle, and they prey even upon man himself. The crocodile takes his toll of human life, as also do numerous tribes of poisonous snakes. So disastrous is their onslaught that the State offers rewards for their destruction. In a recent year—1921—over 200,000 rupees were paid in such rewards, the destruction of nearly 25,000 beasts of prey and 57,000 snakes being registered

[1] "The Laws of Manu." [2] *Ibid.*
[3] "The Message of the Forest."

within the confines of British India. The victory was anything but a bloodless one, for man in his turn lost nearly 23,000 lives—over 19,000 from snake-bite and 3360 from the attacks of wild animals.

Nor can it be said that the forest to-day is the hermitage of any cultured section of the people. It is the haunt, rather, of excessively primitive aboriginal tribes, of which the Bhils and the Kohls of Central India and the Central Provinces may be taken as examples. Far from these denizens of the forest occupying themselves with profound metaphysical speculation, they live in constant dread of a shadowy crowd of powerful and malevolent beings, the inhabitants of an unseen world, but one, nevertheless, which is ever present in their midst and whose activities interfere constantly with the lives of men. By such folk the malaria-carrying mosquito which abounds in forest-lands would be regarded, if indeed it was understood that she was the cause of fever, as the agent of some malignant being of this shadowy and generally hostile world.

The normal occupation of such tribes consists of hunting, fishing, the collection of forest products, and a certain measure of shifting cultivation. Their weapon of offence is the bow and arrow. Some reprehensible primitive practices survive among many such aboriginal tribes, while others have only been discarded in comparatively recent times under the civilising influence of Great Britain. Dr. Edgar Thurston, writing of the practice of female infanticide prevalent among the Kondhs of Ganjam and Orissa until the middle of last century, declares that they maintained that the Sun God, in contemplating the deplorable results produced by the creation of feminine nature, charged men to bring up only as many females as they could restrain from producing evil to society.[1] And the same writer, commenting upon the deep-rooted nature of the belief in the efficacy of human sacrifice, reminds us that as recently as 1907 the district magistrate of Ganjam received a petition requesting him to sanction the performance of the rite.

Here, then, is ample material to intrigue the student of ethnology. Not all men, however, are ethnologists, and even for those who are not, the forest possesses a curious charm. If analysed, the appeal which it makes to civilised man would be found, as often as not, to be due to the idea of elemental simplicity for which it stands. It provides so fine a foil to the complexity of life in great cities. And there are times when the burden of civilisation is suddenly felt to be too heavy and the lure of the primitive becomes irresistible. Rousseau and Tolstoy both found it so.

It is easy enough to paint imaginary pictures of the jungle which from this point of view possess a singular attraction. Its exuberance in tropical and semi-tropical zones seems to tell of the large warm-heartedness of Nature. I recall an area of over four hundred square miles in the low hills away on the shadowy borderland beyond Bengal, where immense bamboos grow like weeds in Nature's garden, clustered together ten thousand to the acre. Here, surely, life could expand, away beyond the cramping influence of brick walls and slate roofs. Deep in this untamed wilderness of orchids and bamboos the heart of Nature must pulse joyously. Of its elemental simplicity there is no question. Man is born here, lives here, dies here, knowing nothing of the man-made world of which the twentieth century is so proud—the world of bricks and mortar, and of Nature's

[1] See an article in a collection reprinted from the "Times" of May 24, 1911, under the title of "India and the Durbar."

energy trapped and cunningly harnessed in divers ways to do for man a thousand and one things beyond the comprehension of the forest-man. Where the products of this unfamiliar world have been thrust uninvited into his primitive universe his tendency is to ignore them. Railways, for example. I remember travelling over the hill section of the Assam-Bengal railway. That we might better enjoy the scenery a narrow platform had been rigged up over the cow-catcher on the engine. We were steaming along at twenty miles an hour, winding amongst hills buried in densest jungle of vivid green, our steepest gradient 1 in 37. Suddenly the man on my right shouted. Simultaneously the man on my left burst into a cry and violently waved a small red flag which he carried. We were rounding a curve, and the black mouth of a tunnel loomed up a hundred yards in front of us. But it was an object between us and the tunnel on which I suddenly found my gaze riveted. Sleeping peacefully, his head pillowed on one rail and his feet across the other, lay a man. On we came inexorably. Nothing, it seemed, could prevent his being guillotined, and nothing could make me take my eyes off his prostrate form. In the nick of time, just when it seemed that we must be the reluctant witnesses of a gruesome tragedy, he wakened and flung himself off the line. Some day, I suppose, these folk will learn that the railway embankment was not thrown up for them to sleep on; but that day, as the railway officials know from sad experience, is not yet. Man here is still an elemental being, strangely unsophisticated, amazingly ignorant of the intricate mechanism which other branches of the species have evolved and with which they delight to elaborate life.

Yet the primitiveness of the jungle, so attractive in theory to the city man, jaded in spirit with the artificiality and complexity of modern life, has certain less pleasing features which do not obtrude themselves in the picture which he conjures up. Its emotions are elemental. And dominant amongst elemental emotions is fear. A man who knew the jungle once painted it as it really is, a place dark and brooding, "its shadows full of living things moving silently, themselves like shadows, between the trees, slinking under the bushes and peering through the leaves." Dispassionately he set forth the elemental impulses by which life in the jungle is actuated. "The rule of the jungle is first fear and then hunger and thirst. There is fear everywhere: in the silence and in the shrill and the wild cries; in the stir of the leaves and the grating of branches; in the gloom; in the startled, slinking, peering beasts. And behind the fear is always the hunger and the thirst, and behind the hunger and the thirst fear again." The hard struggle for existence which drives the man of the cities protesting to his daily toil is there in the forest also. It is there in its elemental form—in that form which displays Nature red in tooth and claw. "The herd of deer must come down to drink at the water-hole. They come down driven by their thirst, very silently through the deep shadows of the trees to the water lying white under the moon. They glide like shadows out of the shadows, into the moonlight, hesitating, tiptoeing, throwing up their heads to stare again into the darkness, leaping back only to be goaded on again by their thirst, ears twitching to catch a sound, and nostrils quivering to catch a scent of danger. And when the black muzzles go down into the water it is only for a moment; and then with a rush the herd scatters back again terror-stricken into the darkness. And behind the herd comes the leopard, slinking through the undergrowth. Whom has he to fear? Yet there is fear in his eyes and in his slinking feet, fear in his pricked ears and in the bound with which he vanishes into the shadows at the least suspicious sound."[1] Yes, the burden of existence is not confined to civilised life. It is there in the jungle also—in its most elemental form.

And when men, wearied of the burden of civilisation, succumb too completely to the lure of the primitive, this truth is startlingly revealed. For a return to elemental life means also a return sooner or later to elemental emotions in all their crudity, and a rejection of the checks which civilisation imposes upon them. Those who are incapable of bearing the burden of civilisation will, if they can, wage war against it. That is why men of distorted genius who succumb to the lure of the primitive become a danger to society. It would be easy to write much on this subject, but the story can be read elsewhere—in the history of the French Revolution, the seeds of which were sown by the teaching of Rousseau; more recently still in the history of Russia, traced back to the teaching of Tolstoy. But if man, jaded with the unremitting toil of his days, does not take the lure of the primitive too seriously—as seriously as Rousseau or Tolstoy or Gandhi—he may cast aside the burden of civilisation for a space without harm to himself or others, and may find refreshment for mind and body in the Indian forest. Armed with rod and rifle he may make sport of the elemental emotions which give to the life of the denizens of the jungle alike its savage joys and its poignant bitterness. Let the brief record of a personal experience serve as an illustration.

[1] "The Village in the Jungle," by Mr. L. S. Woolf.

CHAPTER XVI

JUNGLE LIFE

We had travelled all day over the Indian plain in a bone-shaking rattlebox of a motor car, with the brilliant sunshine of the Indian winter beating down upon us and the all-pervasive dust of the dry season heavy in our nostrils. The track which we followed, such as it was, was not always plainly discernible; but our pilot drove with a courage and a sublime faith derived from an unquestioning fatalism, and towards sundown we forged our way into a region of rolling hills and scattered jungle, and from the summit of a long swell of rising ground, looked down upon the waters of a broad river flowing in turbid volume athwart our course. There is, fortunately, a limit to the faith of even the most bigoted fatalist, and the river proved the limit in this case. We pulled up. A more primitive form of conveyance was called for to compete with the conditions prevalent in the more primitive world which we were about to enter, and it was there awaiting us in the shape of two or three elephants, on whose broad backs we passed dry-shod over the river. On the far side, beneath the shelter of some splendid forest trees, we found a comfortable camp ready for us.

We had 900 square miles of forest at our disposal—magnificent, riotous jungle where the tiger roamed at large, the panther preyed, the pretty little cheetul deer browsed, and where at nights the jackal bayed the moon with mournful, blood-curdling yowl. It was December and all was now green—mile upon mile of the big-leafed sāl, ebony, aura, wide-spreading banyans, and clumps of giant bamboo. Later on, when the hot breath of summer began stirring among the branches, the gorgeous "Flame of the Forest" would burst into flower, and the jungle for miles round would become a sea of vivid scarlet.

I happened to revisit the district a year later in the month of April. Famine threatened the land, and those in authority were already speculating on the flowering of the mowha tree, and looking to it to make good in some measure the deficiency in grain. The thermometer rose daily to 100° Fahrenheit in the shade, and the white man perspired and tossed uneasily during the heat of the day beneath the double awning of his tents, and went abroad only during the freshness of early morning and the comparative cool of the evening. The forest in those days was beautiful; but it was also full of discomfort. I have vivid recollections of a long night vigil. A panther had killed a goat on the edge of a small clearing intermittently cultivated by the members of an aboriginal tribe. I rode out from camp twelve miles on a pad-elephant—a journey of incomparable weariness and discomfort—and towards sunset climbed into a tree above the body of the dead goat. Movement was forbidden and cramp inevitable; but the hope of success banished indecision, and I determined to see it out. The sun sank and the short Indian twilight descended with a curious hush upon the land. Out of this silence the strange noises of the jungle gradually emerged. Mosquitoes—clouds of them—buzzed and bit fiercely and relentlessly. Pea-fowl strutted pompously to the water of a neighbouring pool, making an absurd bustle as they went. Parrots swooped from tree to tree. Suddenly, just as dusk was deepening into dark, the blurred outline of a ghostly form appeared for a moment in the undergrowth twenty yards away. Its coming was marked by a death-like silence, and then, altogether unexpectedly, there broke out on all sides a wild chorus of jabbered objurgation. The branches above my head were violently jerked and shaken; heavy bodies seemed to be hurling themselves from tree to tree, and night was made hideous with screechings and splutterings as of inexpressible rage. It was as though some phantom troop of wild cats had been let loose by some malignant being of the unseen world. But of course it was not cats; it was monkeys.

For an hour or more they chattered and danced and jibbered, exhibiting the fierce hatred of their kind for the hereditary enemy that preyed upon them. As for me, I knew that for the time being hope was dead. I stretched my cramped limbs and scratched my bitten hands and neck until I was nearly mad with the irritation. But at last silence came once more, this time the heavy silence of full night. A faint light from the moon trickled through the branches, but not sufficient to give more than a blurred outline to the objects close by. I was at tension once more, and strained my eyes to the farthest visible distance. Yet when the panther did put in an appearance again I never saw him come. His movements were absolutely noiseless, and my first knowledge of his presence was when I became aware of a dim form actually on top of the goat's body. He was so close that it would have been difficult to miss, and I shot him and carried him back in triumph —twelve miles in the dark on my protesting pad-elephant.

This, however, is a digression. During these

golden December days life in the forest was pure joy. We camped where we would, moving through the forest along shady tracks on foot or on the backs of elephants as we pleased, the impedimenta of our camp carried by camels. Our marches through the forest were always full of interest. There was great variety of both plant and animal life. Monkeys grimaced humorously at us, and a flash of brilliant turquoise through the air marked the flight of the beautiful blue jay. Here and there we came across sinister cairns of stone, marking the spot where at some time or other man had fallen a victim to the blood-lust of the tiger, grim reminders that the forest has its hostile moods. Two such monuments we passed during the first day's march. It is on record among the statistical returns issued by the Government of India that during that year 767 persons were killed by tigers. And the cattle upon which man—at any rate, Indian man—depends so greatly suffered even more, over 26,000 head of cattle having been reported slain by tigers during the twelve months. Any one who knows what the cow is to the Indian will understand the tragedy of that. Nor are tigers the only foe. I once found my rifle-bearer busy with a crocodile that I had shot. He was absorbed in what seemed to me to be a somewhat meticulous examination of the contents of its stomach. But his interest was justified. After fishing out a handful of pebbles, he extracted a copper anklet, the erstwhile adornment, it is to be feared, of some unfortunate peasant girl. The figures for the year showed a total mortality due to wild beasts of all kinds, including snakes, of 26,242 people and 102,240 head of cattle. Certainly the forest has its cruel moods.

It was some days before we got to grips with tiger; but in the meantime there was plenty of other game to tempt us into the shady depths of the forest. Panther, pig, black bear, and the lordly sambhur stag, besides other varieties of deer, were brought to bag, and the pot was replenished as often as necessary with teal, peafowl, partridge, quail, and snipe.

Early in January we were back on the banks of the river some miles below our first camp. We were just about to cross one morning to beat the jungle on the other side for deer, when the silver-toned tinkle of a camel bell became audible, and a moment later camel and rider hove into sight. In a moment the camp was all astir. The news passed rapidly from mouth to mouth; a buffalo had been killed by tiger ten miles away to the south. Everything moved like clockwork. A few sharp orders were given; the rifle-bearers were recalled; the elephants were geared up, and by 11.30 we were off, travelling down the right bank of the river. Five miles down we saw a remarkable sight—forty or fifty crocodiles, mostly of huge dimensions, some running to seventeen feet in length, according to the reckoning of the expert of the party, lying on a sand-bank basking in the sun. We had no time to waste on them, however, and we pushed on, turning inland away from the river into thicker jungle. By 2 P.M. we reached the neighbourhood of the "kill," and found an army of tribesmen assembled with gongs and tom-toms and pikes and staves, all thirsting for the fray. Our dispositions were quickly made, and as soon as we were posted the beaters formed line a mile or two away and started driving the jungle towards us.

I was in a tree commanding a narrow ravine. The ground immediately in front of me was partially clear—low scrub jungle with patches of rank grass and trees dotted here and there. Fifty yards away the forest closed in, strictly limiting my field of vision. Posted high up among the branches of large timber trees, I could make out here and there the dusky forms of the "stops" in two lines converging towards me on either side.

It is an exciting thing waiting for a tiger, and one experiences a variety of sensations: depression at one moment at the thought that he may not after all be there; high tension at the next, in anticipation of what at any moment may occur. Those versed in forest lore knew that he was there, for the behaviour of the ravens told them all that they required to know. My swarthy rifle-bearer knew well enough; but he was not by nature communicative, and I spent forty minutes of crowded emotion before my doubts were finally laid to rest by a hoarse roar in the vicinity of some thick clumps of bamboos on my right front. For a moment there was violent commotion. The "stops" broke into volleys of untranslatable invective touching the ancestors of the tiger for many generations back, the bamboos rustled significantly, and then silence again. Five minutes or thereabouts elapsed before the drowsy hush of the jungle at high noon was broken again, this time on my left. Still there was nothing to be seen, and my wrist-watch slowly ticked off another four minutes from eternity. The tension was becoming almost unbearable, when for a third time there came a sullen roar from the dense growth almost immediately in front of me. After this a great many things happened in an infinitely short space of time. A large striped body loped with powerful feline movement across my left front—not a nice, clear-cut target, but a body in rapid motion, partially hidden by long rank grass. I emptied both barrels at it, and it disappeared from view in a thorn thicket. My attendant stuffed cartridges into my hand and pointed at the thorn bushes. I heard, with huge relief, a savage groan, and shifted my position until I caught sight of a writhing mass of striped fur glinting in the sunlight through the obstructing leaves of a sāl tree. Taking chances with wounded tigers does not pay, and I fired another two barrels to make sure. In due course we descended from our leafy perches, the beaters came up singing paeans of victory over the vanquished foe, and the tiger was hoisted on to an elephant and carried in triumph back to camp. There he was measured with much ceremony—9 feet 5 inches from nose to tip of tail.

The forest of which I have been writing lies for the most part south of the Sone river; south, too, therefore, of the rich plain of the sacred Ganges, where dwelt those Aryan settlers of whose life in the forest we read in the Indian epics and sacred books. Forest still bounds this land on the north, cutting off the cultivated plain from the towering parapets of the Himālaya. This forest, too, at the present day is on the whole hostile to man. Under the general name of Terai, it extends for hundreds of miles along the foot of the Himālayas, the haunt of tiger, rhinoceros, elephant, panther and other game, and —more dangerous still—the fever-carrying mosquito. Like the forest elsewhere, it has seasons of great beauty. Its dense greens are lit up in early spring by the crimson and scarlet blossom of numerous flowering trees, the cotton tree, the "Flame of the Forest," and a beautiful tree, the *Erythrina indica*, known locally in parts of the Terai as Mādār, and often called by Europeans the Indian coral tree.

Great tracts thickly overgrown with timber trees alternate with stretches of pampas grass from fifteen to twenty feet in height, through which it is impossible to force one's way except on the back of an elephant. For which reason the tiger and all other forms of game are shot here from an elephant howdah. A line of forty or fifty elephants will beat a tract of jungle up to the guns waiting on other elephants. Thus posted, one may study with interest the life of the jungle as it surges round one. Wild fowl rush to and fro in the undergrowth. A lordly peacock sails overhead. The russet back of a crow-pheasant glints in the sunlight. Pretty green parrots shoot across one's field of vision, and on the branch of a neighbouring cotton tree a small, wise-looking owl blinks knowingly at one. But always is there the suggestion of death lurking in the sombre depths of the foliage. More particularly is this the case where man has reclaimed with fire and plough some small part of the wild for his own advantage. Such, for example, are the plains of Cooch Behar, where the Kochs have bitten into the forest. The landscape here possesses the charm of a certain irregular uniformity. Vast plains dotted with expanses of immense rank grasses and patches of wild cardamom, stretch away as far as the eye can see until they lose themselves in a haze-girt horizon. Wherever one looks there are trees, sometimes singly, sometimes in clumps, and sometimes in large areas. The wattle and thatch houses of the people are half hidden among banana trees and bamboos. The soil is light and sandy, and mustard, tobacco, and sugar-cane are prominent crops. Wild fig and plum trees bring forth a small, hard inedible fruit. Cattle graze on the edges of the forest.

But these men are clearly at war with the forest. A cloud of vultures circling round on the outskirts of a village, tells of the toll taken by the forest from the people's herds. There are few more repulsive sights than that of a crowd of vultures burying their long, gruesome-looking heads and necks into the entrails of a carcase.

Plate 16.

THE FOREST OF THE TERAI.

"Great tracts . . . through which it is impossible to force one's way except on the back of an elephant."

Even the near approach of man drives them off only for a little way. Gorged and bloated-looking, they hover away for a short distance, palpably intoxicated by their heavy meal. And then gaining courage they return, stripping the bones of every vestige of flesh in an incredibly short space of time.

Once only did I hear of a case of friendly intercourse between the denizens of the forest and man. A young child disappeared from a village in Cooch Behar. Some time afterwards a small being, scarcely recognisable as human, was found in the forest, brought up from its earliest years by a bear. It was more animal than human, and, utterly unversed in the ways of men, died not long after its reclamation. But this case was as exceptional as it was pathetic. While I was in camp, the guest of His Highness the Maharaja, news was brought in of the death of a villager in an encounter with a bear. We went out at once, and were successful in tracking her down and shooting her. Near by we located and caught her cub. We brought him back to camp in a sack, and offered him milk and bananas; but he was bad-tempered and spilt the milk and growled at the bananas. He was instinctively averse to entering into any sort of relations with man.

High up on the lovely wooded ranges of the Eastern Himālayas beyond the range of carnivorous animals, the forest offers a more friendly welcome to man. And here man, in the shape of the priesthood of lamaism, has built himself retreats in the heart of kindly Nature. But of this I have written elsewhere.[1]

[1] In "Lands of the Thunderbolt."

CHAPTER XVII

PICTURES FROM AN ETHNIC PAGEANT

THE immense contrasts in the physical characteristics of India impress themselves upon the visitor at a very early date, as do also the obvious differences of race to which reference has been made in the opening chapter.

Later on, as he becomes more familiar with his surroundings, it is borne in upon him that besides differences of race and community there are differences of epoch—that in India at the present day there exist side by side types of at least two complex and highly-developed civilisations—those of modern Europe and of ancient India—and types also of very primitive man. It is as though the evolution of sections of the people—ethical, social, intellectual, and religious—had been arrested centuries back, while that of others had proceeded normally. It would be difficult to imagine a greater contrast than that which is provided by the existence side by side of the primitive animist with his crude superstitions and his rigidly-restricted intellectual outlook, and the cultured Brahman with his lofty conceptions of the Divine, his daring speculations on the nature of things, and his meticulously ordered life as a member of a social organisation which demands of him a strict observance, in all his daily doings, of a highly-elaborated ritual.

The persons classed for census purposes as

animists, of whom there are estimated to be upwards of 10,000,000 scattered over the continent, provide an example of arrested intellectual and religious evolution. The stunted growth of their intellect renders them credulous to a degree which the man from the Western hemisphere finds it difficult to fathom. And credulity, at times, is responsible for tortuous thinking giving rise to action of a startling kind. Here is an example. A number of buildings were in process of erection in the district of Midnapur not long ago, when some temporary difficulty arose in connection with the supply of water. An idea took shape—how or why, who can say ?—among the labourers employed at the works at a neighbouring railway centre, that to overcome this difficulty the contractors were kidnapping children to be buried in the foundations as an offering of appeasement to the malignant unseen power that was interfering with the work. They marched forth *en masse* to deal with the supposed kidnappers, and the district officials found themselves confronted with one of those strange problems with which the records of the administration are strewn.

Another element in the population to which the general appellation of " criminal tribes " has been given, may be taken as an example more particularly of arrested ethical evolution. It is estimated that there are 4,000,000 of these troublesome and unattractive people scattered over the face of the land. It has been said of them that the whole structure of their social habits is conceived upon the basis of crime. Their distinguishing characteristic is, in fact, the practice of burglary or theft as an hereditary occupation. There is on the Indian statute book an enactment for their exclusive benefit known as the Criminal Tribes Act of 1911, under the provisions of which members of such tribes may be concentrated in settlements, where they can be subjected to adequate supervision and assisted to gain a decent livelihood. The care of them, however, is only too often an unsatisfactory and a disheartening labour, and even the Salvation Army, which is co-operating with Government in the discharge of it, finds it a grievously-uphill task.

My first acquaintance with a criminal tribe, as such, was at a settlement organised by the government of the United Provinces and managed by the Salvation Army in the neighbourhood of Moradabad. All previous attempts to deal successfully with these people had failed. Attempts had been made to settle them on the land. They complained that land without cattle was useless; and a paternal Government gave them cattle. This generosity was misplaced, for, instead of rearing cattle, they simply sold those that had been given them. They next demanded seed, and seed was given them. But when the time for sowing came, the seed was not forthcoming, for they had eaten it. The particular settlement which I visited was occupied by a tribe of people called Haburas. Efforts were being made to teach them the various processes in the manufacture of silk, and some progress was being made with the children. The adult part of the population was, for the most part, intractable. They sat in the sun round the courtyard, which formed the centre of the settlement, dozing or feeding on such things as lizards and other equally unappetising dishes. They break the back of a lizard when caught, and then, when they are ready for a meal, toss it alive on to a fire. Mr. Begbie has given a vivid description of this and other settlements which he visited. "If you could look into the faces of these people," he writes, "you would see

Plate 17.

A CRIMINAL TRIBE SETTLEMENT AT MORADABAD.

"They sat in the sun round the courtyard which formed the centre of the settlement dozing or feeding on such things as lizards."

there a bitterness, a hopelessness, and a despair such as would almost terrify your well-being and make you afraid. . . . Nature has brought them to that point where they can experience suffering and exercise reflection, and then has abandoned them."[1]

In Bengal a settlement for the redemption of Kharwal Nuts has been organised at Saidpur under the management of the Salvation Army. Saidpur is a considerable railway centre, and a feature in the plan of redemption was the employment of the Kharwal Nuts, under proper supervision, as gangmen on the line. The intention was frustrated by the Kharwal Nuts themselves, whose incorrigible aversion to steady work baffled the laudable intentions and the ingenuity of Government, the railway officials, and the Salvation Army alike. Their origin is shrouded in obscurity, though they themselves maintain that their ancestors came from Bhojpur, in the district of Arrah in Bihar. They may be classed as animists, though they worship the Hindu goddess Kali and other deities of their own, but have no regular priests. Their moral code is a simple one, consisting of a solitary commandment, "Thou shalt not be found out." They declare that they cannot live without intoxicating drink. They live the life of gypsies, wandering over the countryside, with no ostensible means of livelihood other than begging. Their hereditary profession is, however, thieving. And, despite every endeavour, they are perpetually breaking out of the settlement on thieving expeditions, and as perpetually smuggling intoxicating liquor in. The children are taught a single game for their amusement, the preparation for, commission of, and hiding after theft and dacoity. I have been told that there have even been occasions when the

[1] "Other Sheep," by Harold Begbie.

small children of the manager of the Saidpur settlement have been dragged into this elevating pastime to give an added touch of realism by playing the part of police!

A panchayat has been instituted in the settlement for the disposal of cases among the inmates. Its decisions, which are binding upon the community, are determined solely by expediency. In the early days of the settlement, money was stolen from the manager. On the panchayat being informed the money was repaid, and no further thefts were committed against him. Admirable, no doubt, and much to the credit of the panchayat! The same body heard an inmate of the settlement informing the manager that he knew who were the perpetrators of a recent crime, and they had him up and fined him Rs. 16. Another example of the award of sentences is not without its humorous side. Two men from the settlement had broken out and joined a third man on a dacoity expedition. On their return they were awarded a heavy fine. For breaking out with intent to commit crime? Certainly not; but for carelessness in allowing their accomplice to lose his life while engaged upon the enterprise.

A characteristic which in a better cause might be regarded as meritorious is a baffling *esprit de corps*. In practice it acts as a barrier against redemption. There are inmates of the settlement who have developed an aptitude for weaving, and one such person was ready to cut himself off from the tribe and to become a useful member of society. There were, however, difficulties in the way, and when not long afterwards he died, he was refused burial by his fellows, and this last office had to be performed for him by the manager himself.

It would be difficult, as I have said, to find a

greater contrast between any people than that between the class of which I have been writing—mere flotsam on the fringe of civilisation—and the orthodox high-caste Hindu. However amorphous Hinduism may be as a religious faith—upon which I shall have something to say later on—it possesses an elaborate and rigid code as a social system. What a man may eat, with whom he may eat it, from whom he may take water, from what group of people he may take his wife: all these things are laid down for him by rules which he may break—but at his peril. As every one knows who knows anything at all of India, it is all a matter of caste. What is not so generally known is what precisely is meant by caste. It is often popularly supposed that the term caste refers to the four great divisions into which, as we learn from the ancient Sanskrit texts of a semi-priestly and semi-legal character, the immigrant Aryan people was separated; that is to say, the Brahmans or priesthood, the Kshatriya or military class, the Vaisya or husbandmen, and the Sudra or lower orders, whose function it was to serve the members of the first three. These were certainly more or less definite classes—as they are to this day—which were evolved by a process of elaboration from the two great groups of people who met on the soil of India as a result of the incursions from the north-west, to which reference has been made, namely, the immigrant Aryans and the aboriginal inhabitants whom they found already in possession of the land. The former were sharply divided from the latter in that they alone were admitted to the reading of the Vedas and to participation in the religious ceremonies associated therewith. They were the true Aryans, and to this day the members of the three classes in question are known as the twice-born, from the fact that they are initiated into the ceremonial of the ancient religion and invested with the sacred thread—the outward and visible sign of their second or spiritual birth. In this general classification of the people of India there was a fifth division, to which were assigned all those who could lay no claim to membership of the other classes. These were regarded as "untouchables," and according to the racial theory set forth above, of which the late Sir H. Risley was a prominent exponent, consisted of the pure aboriginal tribes, the intermediate class of Sudras being in all probability the offspring of Aryan fathers and aboriginal mothers.

But these great divisions of the people are not, strictly speaking, the castes of the present day. The castes as they exist to-day consist of innumerable water-tight groups, which are now generally believed to have come into existence quite independently of the classes referred to above, though they claim to belong to one or other of them, the social status of the caste depending upon the class to which it belongs. These castes are very numerous, no less than 180 main castes being recognised in the census returns. These in their turn are split into innumerable sub-castes, and the sub-castes in their turn into smaller groups, to which various terms, such as *gotra*, are applied. Nor have the many castes come into existence as the result of a single influence. The late Sir Herbert Risley distinguished seven different types of caste, the most important being based on tribe, on occupation, on sect, and on race. The feature of the caste system which is most apparent to the visitor to India is the restriction which it imposes on the freedom of its members in the matter of social intercourse. For example, a person with whom one has intimate relations in commercial or public life is prohibited from dining with one. In the south of India he will be struck with the gulf which yawns between the man of high caste and the "untouchable." Amongst the latter there are castes whose members pollute a Brahman if they come within range of sixty-four feet of him. Such persons are prohibited from even entering the high-caste quarter of a village, and must leave the public highway on the approach of a Brahman. There is a large labouring caste in Southern India, named Paraiyan, with a membership of 2,500,000. It is from this caste that our word pariah is derived. But the fundamental test of caste is the restriction which it places upon a man's freedom of choice in the matter of marriage. The sub-caste is endogamous, the gotra exogamous, which means that a man may not marry within his gotra nor outside his sub-caste.

It is, however, as I have said, in connection with caste rules on the subject of purity of food that the visitor is usually made aware of the existence of a rigid socio-religious system governing the lives of all those calling themselves Hindus. And it was a dramatic incident, arising out of a violation of these rules, that apprised me of the sanctity with which the system is still regarded.

During the summer of 1917 it was persistently rumoured in Calcutta that the ghī (clarified butter) sold in the markets was adulterated with animal fat and other substances. Not only is ghī an important article in the Hindu dietary, but it is also an indispensable article in religious ceremonies, which are rendered ineffective by the use of an impure substance. The matter was consequently one of gravity to the orthodox sections of the community, and particularly to the Marwaris, the wealthy trading community hailing from Rajputana in the west of India, which has long been domiciled in Calcutta, where its members constitute a distinct and important section of the population. At the instance of the Marwari Association, samples of ghī were obtained from various markets in the town, an analysis of which showed that by far the greater part of the commodity sold in Calcutta was grossly adulterated. One such sample was found to contain no ghī at all, another only 5 per cent; and of a very large number of samples examined, only seven were reported to consist of pure ghī. These lamentable disclosures very soon became public property, with the result that a deputation of Brahmans demanded of the Marwari Association the excommunication of the offenders. The Association delayed coming to a decision and the Brahmans took action. Learned priests were summoned from Benares, meetings were held, and a decision come to that all Brahmans who had unwittingly made use of adulterated ghī must undergo a ceremony of purification on the banks of the holy river.

In accordance with this decision a crowd of 3000 Brahmans assembled on the riverside at Jaganāth Ghāt on the morning of August the 16th, and began the performance of the ceremony of purification known as *Prayaschita Homa.* The gathering steadily increased until, by the morning of the 19th, the number of those performing penance amounted to close upon 5000. During these long, hot August days and on through the heavy hours of night, these men fasted and repeated the mantras ordained for the purpose; and on the banks of the sacred river, here in the heart of the second city in the British Empire, in the presence of vast assemblages of people numbering many thousands, fires of purification burned with steady flame, fed from time to time with offerings of spices and ghī.

The situation had assumed immense proportions. For the time being it occupied the attention of the Calcutta public to the exclusion of all else. It filled the columns of the daily press, and on the last day of August an influential and representative deputation of about 100 Hindu gentlemen, the spokesmen of a large number of associations, waited upon me and asked that immediate action might be taken to prevent the sale of adulterated ghī in future. A bill to amend certain sections of the Calcutta Municipal Act was immediately drafted, and passed through all its stages at a single sitting of the Bengal Legislative Council three days later.

Greater interest, however, attaches to the action taken by the community chiefly affected. Mention has been made in Chapter XI. of the codes of laws evolved by the various corporations of ancient India, such as crafts and merchant guilds. In a communication to me on the subject of the steps to be taken in the situation which had arisen, the Marwari Association spoke of the powers which " under the unwritten social laws of the country the caste Panchayats have possessed from time immemorial for dealing with offences against society and religion " ; and they added that " the inhabitants of many of the principal villages and towns of Rajputana now living in Calcutta have chosen their own representatives for the constitution of a regular panchayat " to deal with the offenders. This panchayat, which consisted of three different committees charged with dealing with offenders belonging to three different castes—the Agarwallas, the Maheswaris, and the Brahmans—sat from 11 A.M. until 8.30 P.M. on August the 19th, when it announced its decisions. Two Agarwalla firms were fined Rs. 100,000 and Rs. 25,000 respectively, and the proprietors excommunicated for a year ; a number of Maheswaris were excommunicated for life ; and two Brahmans were excommunicated for two years and three months respectively and fined. These decisions were conveyed by representatives of the three committees of the panchayat to the Brahmans still engaged in the ceremony of purification on the river-banks. They were accepted as satisfactory, and on the following day the Prayaschita was brought to a close, the Brahmans returning to their homes.

The interest of the incident lay in the proof which it afforded of the latent strength of the ancient socio-religious structure of the Indian people. An offence had been committed against social tenets and religious practice. At once the priestly caste, the ancient aristocracy of the race emerged as the traditional leaders of the people and dominated the situation. Amid the surroundings of a great Western city of the twentieth century was enacted a scene culled from the drama of Indian life two thousand years or more ago. In this incongruous setting was performed an elaborate ritual reaching far back into Vedic times. The admittedly efficient administrative machinery imported from the West fell into the background of men's minds. It might be called in to assist in guarding against similar trouble in the future, but it was powerless to deal with the situation which had actually arisen. It was to the caste Panchayat, with its laws and its authority rooted in antiquity, that the Indian turned in this emergency which had arisen in matters affecting the most intimate aspects of his life.

It would be a mistake, of course, to suppose that in these days a Brahman is necessarily a scholar or a priest. Brahmans are found in all ranks of life, rich and poor, high and low; he may be a priest or a peasant, a scholar or a dunce, a man of refinement and culture, or one steeped in ignorance and superstition. One of the most tragic and pathetic examples of distorted religious zeal, which came to my notice when in Bengal, was that of a villager who had sacrificed his baby daughter to Kali. The crime was deliberate and cold-blooded, and no grounds existed for the exercise of the prerogative of mercy. He was a Brahman. But broadly speaking, the Brahmans still form an aristocracy of the distinctive culture of India.

CHAPTER XVIII

THE INCURSION OF ISLAM

THE ethnic pageant which passes across one's vision as one travels over India is made up of many tableaux. There is one such tableau which at once arrests attention because of the many points of contrast which it provides with the rest of the procession of which it forms a part. It is the tableau in which we see represented a religion, a civilisation and culture, and an outlook differing profoundly in all material respects from those of Hinduism, but nevertheless an essential component of the India of to-day—that of Islam.

That the gulf which separates the Muhammadan from the Hindu is a wide one becomes apparent from the moment that one begins to understand the nature of the social systems which are the product of Islam and Hinduism respectively. That of the latter, as has been shown, is exclusive: that of the former is communistic. Under the Hindu social system men are graded minutely and segregated in an infinite number of water-tight compartments: under Islam all men are equal. Hinduism is essentially aristocratic: Muhammadanism is as emphatically democratic. The result of these differences is astonishing. Two immense communities live side by side over vast tracts of the Indian continent; yet neither can claim a relative within the ranks of the other, for Hindu caste restrictions make intermarriage an impossibility. Mention has been made earlier of the separate supplies of drinking water provided at the railway stations for Muhammadans and Hindus. And as every Indian administrator knows, the chasm between the religious observances of the two communities is such as to constitute a perpetual potential source of racial rioting. Hindu veneration for the cow as a sacred animal is ingrained and very real, and no orthodox Hindu can think of the slaughter of cattle without experiencing feelings of positive pain. On the other hand, the religious observances of the Muhammadan demand the sacrifice of the cow—hence the ever-present seeds of trouble. And just as the slaughter of cattle is an abomination to the Hindu, so the images in the temples and the idol processions of the Hindus are an offence against the austere monotheism of the Muhammadan. Closer investigation discloses other divisions between the two communities, notably, differences of language. The classical language of the Hindus is Sanskrit, those of the Muhammadans, Arabic and Persian. And just as Hindi may be said to be the spoken language distinctive of the Hindus, so may Urdu be said to be the distinctive tongue of the Muhammadans. Hence the teaching, or its omission, of the one or the other in the schools, is a potential source of communal dissatisfaction.

But the difference between Islam and Hinduism is brought most strikingly to the notice of the visitor by the contrast between Muhammadan and Hindu architecture, to which reference has been made in an earlier chapter. And if one ponders upon the contrast between these two types of self-expression, it is borne in upon one that here one sees but the reflection of a similar contrast in the environment in which their authors were respectively nurtured. I have spoken already of the paramount part played by the forest in the childhood of that branch of the Aryan race, which made its home in the hospitable reaches of the Ganges valley. And if one studies the architecture which it evolved as it grew from childhood to maturer years, one finds little difficulty in seeing in it an exuberance of ornamentation and a complexity of design which mirror faithfully enough the rich luxuriance of tropical vegetation. As one gazes at the shimmering beauty and the wealth of detail upon the walls and pillars of the Dilwara temples on Mount Abu, and gazes up at ceilings "whose workmanship dims the memory of the stairway of Christchurch and the roof of the Divinity School in Oxford, and gives the spectator a new standard of beauty,"[1] one calls to mind instinctively the creeper-clad tree-trunks and the leafy canopy of the Indian forest. One sees this resemblance asserting itself—whether recognised by the writers or not—in Mrs. Stevenson's description of them as "a very fairyland of beauty, the fineness of whose carving is only equalled by the white tracery of hoar-frost";[2] and again in Professor D. R. Bhandarkar's reference to "the mysterious beauty of this long *pradakshina* (pillared corridor) in the mystic play of light accentuated here and there by the gleam of white marble,"[3] which conjures up a vision of a forest glade lit up with flashes of sunlight glinting through the tree-tops. The same thought inevitably comes to mind when one reads his description of the hall of the temple "with its intricate forest of pillars elaborately carved."

In the same way, the spaciousness and purity of line of the great buildings of Islam conjure up

[1] "The Heart of Jainism," by Mrs. Sinclair Stevenson.
[2] *Ibid.*
[3] "Some Temples on Mount Abu," contributed to Rupām, July 1920.

Plate 18.

THE DILWARA TEMPLE ON MOUNT ABU.

"... an exuberance of ornamentation and a complexity of design which mirror faithfully enough the rich luxuriance of tropical vegetation."

visions of vast spaces and uninterrupted horizons; their fountains and water-channels and cool pavilions, the oases which acquire so poignant a significance in a weary and dry land. Their kin with the natural beauty of the land where Islam was born strikes one irresistibly when one has before one a picture of the founder of this great and militant creed and his environment, sketched in strong and vivid outline by some master pen, such, for example, as that of Carlyle. His description of the Arabian desert at once directs attention to its salient features—"Savage, inaccessible rock mountains, great grim deserts alternating with beautiful strips of verdure: wherever water is, there is greenness, beauty: odoriferous balm shrubs, date trees, frankincense trees. Consider that wide, waste horizon of sand, empty, silent like a sand sea, dividing habitable place from habitable. You are all alone there, left alone with the universe; by day a fierce sun blazing down on it with intolerable radiance; by night the great deep heaven with its stars." And then we are given a portrait of the man—"He is alone there, deep down in the bosom of the wilderness, has to grow up so—alone with Nature and his own thoughts. . . . A spontaneous, passionate, yet just, true-meaning man! Full of wild faculty, fire, and light; of wild worth all uncultured, working out his life-task in the depths of the desert there." And these great spaces underfoot and the mystery of the star-studded heavens above made a deep impression upon his inquiring mind—"From of old a thousand thoughts, in his pilgrimings and wanderings, had been in this man: What am I? What is this unfathomable Thing I live in which men name universe? What is Life? What is Death? What am I to believe? What am I to do? The grim rocks of Mount Hara, of Mount Sinai, the stern, sandy solitudes answered not. The great heaven rolling silent overhead, with its blue glancing stars, answered not. There was no answer. The man's own soul, and what of God's inspiration dwelt there, had to answer!"[1]

And as the architecture of these peoples was the embodiment in wood and stone of their ideas, particularly in the realm of religious thought, so may the same divergence which strikes one in the character of their buildings be expected in their conceptions of the spiritual world. If the exuberant variety of a prolific tropical environment is mirrored in the religious buildings of the Hindus, it will be reflected, surely, in their ideas of the unseen powers to whom they are erected. And this is of course the case. The unseen world of the Hindus is peopled with gods infinite in number and kind. In the same way, just as there was no variety in the environment of the Arabs, nothing but an awful aridity, hard in outline and of a stern nature, so was their conception of that which lay beyond their world a monotheistic one. To the Bedouin sheik, Muhammad, as to the Bedouin sheik, Abraham, before him, there was but one God—and He was of like nature with the land of those who worshipped Him, a stern and a jealous God.

The atmosphere of Arabia clings to the world-wide institution which has sprung from the preaching of the Arabian Prophet. No one who has heard the Koran recited by the mullah is likely to forget the curious rhythmic declamation produced by a sing-song modulation of the voice, which is the traditional method of reading the sacred volume. Like so much else appertaining to Islam, it comes from the desert. Thus sang the Arab camel-driver long before the days of Muhammad as he urged on his slow-moving

[1] Carlyle's "Heroes"—Mahomet.

charges across the trackless waste. The words were different, but the way of speaking them was the same. Islam grew up in the desert, and the simplicity and the vigour of life in the desert stamps all its institutions. Later, it is true, pomp and luxury blossomed forth in the Court of the caliphs, notably in that of the Omayyads of Damascus ; but these things were alien from, and not characteristic of, the teaching of the Prophet of Arabia. Abu Bakr, the first caliph, lived during the early months of his tenure of the office under a tent of camel hide in a small village outside Mecca. Later, when he moved his abode to the town itself, he was served by a single slave. The temperament of the early leaders of Islam had in it the grit and hardness of the land in which they were nurtured. They demanded of their disciples an unquestioning obedience.

Discipline was strengthened by an astute employment of their religious fervour. With clockwork regularity, prayer was led by the commander of the forces five times a day. The floor of the mosque resembled a drill-ground, the congregation an army. Ranged in compact order behind their leader, they imitated with military precision his every movement. The call to prayer became a bugle-call sounding the fall in ; the service a drill by which the people were taught to respond *en masse* to the commands of a single man. There are few more impressive sights even at the present day than that presented by the courtyard of a mosque—the great Court of the Juma Masjid at Delhi, for example—at the time of the celebration of the service on one of the great days of the Muhammadan year. The whole vast courtyard is crowded with picturesque, turbaned figures, in long lines, gazing at the Imam. Prayers are intoned and the great congregation falls to its knees, and from time to time bows down as one man to the earth, each man resting on his hands and knees and placing his forehead on the ground. The discipline thus inculcated has gripped the follower of the Prophet so powerfully, that he responds to the call automatically, whether he actually hears it or not. At the prescribed hour the devout Moslem turns towards Mecca and prays, in the mosque, in the street, in the field, wherever he may be. When the reformed legislative council came into existence in Bengal in 1921, the Moslem element in it insisted upon a daily adjournment of a quarter of an hour at the time of the evening prayer.

There is, perhaps, no more moving celebration in the annals of religious observance than the annual celebration of the Mohurrum. A passion-play of intense dramatic content, whereby is kept in perpetual remembrance a shocking tragedy arising out of the fierce personal jealousies and tribal animosities amid which Islam was reared, it is suffused with the atmosphere of the land and the times in which it was originally enacted. Staged upon the Plain of Kerbela, a hungry waste stretching in unbroken monotony from the banks of the Euphrates river towards the setting sun, it went near to rending in twain the edifice which was being raised up on the foundations laid by Muhammad. It did, in fact, split Islam into the two great divisions which have persisted to the present day, those of the Sunnis and Shiahs respectively. Those who have travelled over the great rolling expanses which lie between the Euphrates and Tigris rivers, and who have encountered in their depths roving bands of Arab horsemen, whose attitude has been a matter of anxious speculation, will have little difficulty in picturing the scene.

A caravan of horsemen and foot people is making its way across the dusty expanse. It is

Plate 19.

THE JUMA MASJID AT DELHI.

"Prayers are intoned and the great congregation falls to its knees and from time to time bows down as one man to the earth."

led by a young Arab sheik, Husain, the son of Ali, who had espoused Fatimah, the daughter of the Prophet, whose death had taken place amid the lamentations of his people in Medina some fifty years before. He is making his way with his family and a little band of followers to the town of Kufah, for the theologians of that place, viewing with fanatical dislike the riotous living of the Omayyads of Damascus, whose scion Yazid has claimed the caliphate, have bidden him take upon himself the mantle of the Prophet whose descendant he is. As the caravan toils on its way, the attention of its leader is caught by a little cloud of dust far off on the horizon to the south. As it approaches it increases in size after the manner of a dust storm, blown before the wind. No dust storm, however, this, for there emerges from it, dimly at first, but in clearer outline as it descends upon those watching it, a great host of horsemen. Little doubt as to their mission. They have come, three thousand strong, under the command of the Governor of Basra, and by order of Yazid, to bar the way to Kufah. The sun streams down upon these two hosts drawn up in the middle of the endless plain. Beyond them is silence and the emptiness of space. From the town of Kufah comes no sign. And alone in the wilderness with his little band of followers, the Arab sheik is called upon to take a great decision. Will he submit and, swearing the oath of fealty to Yazid, live? Or will he die? The answer is not long in doubt. One by one they fall, stricken down on the dusty earth until Husain and one small son are all that are left alive of those who had set forth with such high hopes for Kufah. The Arab sheik sinks on the ground clasping the boy in his arms. An arrow loosed at random kills the child, and a little later Husain himself is struck in the mouth as he stoops to moisten his parched lips with water.

Thus died the descendant of the Prophet; and to this day, on the anniversary of the massacre, a thrill passes through the Muhammadan world. It is this grim tragedy which for the Shiah Muhammadans—the followers of Ali and the opponents of the Omayyads—has become the subject of a solemn and moving celebration. Year by year the death and burial of the martyrs is re-enacted with a realism which has to be seen to be believed. In Persia, the stronghold of the Shiahs, I have seen a vast concourse of haggard and wild-eyed mourners cutting themselves with knives in a frenzy of despairing grief, until the blood has flowed forth, bespattering them in their white garments with great splashes of crimson. There is in the case of the Mohurrum, as an Indian writer has observed, " no simulation of grief but the actual passion and exaltation of most poignant sorrow, the heart-rending experience of a loss and bereavement just sustained. These are no play-actors but genuine mourners whose heart-strings are racked and drawn taut by the intensity of grief." [1]

Though the Sunnis often stand aloof from these observances during the greater part of the Mohurrum, they celebrate the Ashura or tenth day, which is an important day for the whole of the Moslem world. And pondering upon this great annual celebration one is struck by a special significance which it possesses. For it knits the Muhammadans of India to something which is not Indian—the great brotherhood of Islam which transcends the bounds of countries, and from which comes a call independent of, and greater than the call of country. The truth of this was demonstrated when, during the

[1] Mr. N. Gupta, in the " Modern Review " for November 1922.

Kilāfat agitation after the War, appreciable numbers of Indian Muhammadans, leaving home and country, went forth to Afghanistan and Central Asia as fugitives, following the example of the Prophet himself when he fled from faithless Mecca to the faithful of Medina.

What, then, was the manner of the coming of this great faith from the stony deserts of Arabia to the plains of Hindustan? The rapidity with which Islam spread after the death of Muhammad in A.D. 632 is one of the most remarkable episodes in the annals of mankind. The religious fervour of the armies of the caliph carried them victoriously north and east over Syria, Mesopotamia, and Persia; and within a century the waves of the rising tide were lapping against the shores of India. From Makran the victorious Arabs pushed on eastward and in A.D. 712 wrested the sceptre from the ruler of Sind, which thenceforward became a Muhammadan State.

It was not, however, until nearly three centuries later that the armies of Islam became a serious menace to India proper; and it was not along the desert highway of Makran but through the historic gateway in the North-West Frontier once more that the incursion came. This fresh influx, which was to mark a new epoch in the history of Hindustan, was heralded towards the close of the tenth century A.D. by a series of border forays between the Rajput ruler of the Punjab and a recently established principality of Turkish race with its capital at Gazni. And in A.D. 1001, a decisive battle fought at the foot of the mountains near Peshawar left the Hindu forces crushed and broken and Peshawar an annex to the Moslem principality. The hero of this exploit was one Mahmūd of Gazni, a fierce and dynamic figure, who opened the gates of India to the on-coming hordes of Islam which swept down through the mountain passes wave upon wave, until India became a vast Muhammadan empire. With the same iconoclastic zeal with which the Prophet of Arabia had smashed the idols set up by the backsliding Meccans in the Kaaba—the holy place dedicated by the Patriarch Abraham to an undeviating monotheism — did Mahmūd determine to lay waste the temples of the idolaters. His most famous and probably his most destructive visitation was to the renowned temple of Somnāth, which he destroyed in A.D. 1024, carrying portions of its sacred lingam to Gazni, there to be trodden underfoot at the threshold of the great mosque of the city.

The incursions of Sultan Mahmūd were the forerunners of others of a more permanent character. The next invader of importance was Sultan Muhammad of Ghor, who began his operations against India within a century and a half of the death of Mahmūd of Gazni, which took place in A.D. 1030; and by the close of the twelfth century, the conquest of Upper India, including Bengal, was all but complete. It was his successful General, Kutb-ud-din, who became the first Muhammadan Emperor of India; and with his accession to the throne at Delhi began the long line of rulers popularly though inaccurately described as the Pathan dynasty, lasting from A.D. 1206 until A.D. 1526. Under the despotic rule of the Sultans at Delhi, and the equally arbitrary sway of the governors of the more distant provinces, Muhammadanism spread. To this end immigration was aided by conversion, often undergone from motives of expediency, so that when the next famous incursion down the historic highway from Afghanistan took place—that of Babur, the founder of the Moghul dynasty—there was already a large Moslem element in the population of India. The splendour of the Moghul dynasty during nearly two centuries under men whose names are famous throughout the world—Babur, Humāyun, Akbar, Jahangir, Shahjahan, and Aurungzeb—is well known, and is testified to by the great buildings with which they beautified the cities of Fatepur Sikri, Agra, and Delhi. The imperishable place which this great line of sovereigns has won for itself in the temple of fame was due in no small degree to the breadth of vision and the religious tolerance of the earlier rulers of the line, just as its eventual break-up was due in large measure to the religious bigotry of Aurungzeb. After the latter's death in A.D. 1707, Moghul sovereigns continued to succeed one another upon a nominally Moghul throne. But this procession was little more than a shadow-show thrown upon a screen dominated by anarchy, from which the country was only freed by the rise to power of Britain.

Muhammadan empire in India has receded into the dusty limbo of the past; but eight centuries of Muhammadan dominion have left an indelible imprint upon its soil, for Islam claims 70,000,000 of the 320,000,000 of the continent's inhabitants. It is in the Punjab and the adjacent North-West Frontier Province, as one would expect, that Muhammadanism is most strongly entrenched at the present day. Of their joint population of 22,000,000, 13,000,000 are returned as Moslems. South of the Punjab the percentage drops rapidly to twenty in the Presidency of Bombay. As one travels east the same falling off is noticeable. The United Provinces, with its vast population of 47,000,000, contains less than 7,000,000 Moslems, and the

Central Provinces, lying to the south, less than 600,000 out of a population of 14,000,000. Farther east still, in the province of Bihar and Orissa, we find little more than 3,500,000 Muhammadans in a population of 34,500,000. It comes as a complete surprise, consequently, to find in Bengal, lying still farther east, an immense Muhammadan population—no less, in fact, than 24,000,000 out of a population of 45,500,000. How is it that in Bengal, with its intimate Hindu associations stretching far back into the dim and distant past, we find an actual preponderance of Muhammadans? It can only be accounted for by the conversion of the people on a vast scale. And a little observation will show one many things which indicate that the bulk of the Moslem population is made up of the descendants of converted Hindus. I am acquainted with a polished Muhammadan gentleman occupying a prominent position as a public man among his co-religionists in the province, who is descended from a well-known Brahman family. Murshed Kuli Khan, the great diwan of Bengal, who moved the capital from Dacca to Murshidabad at the beginning of the eighteenth century, was himself the son of Brahman parents. An assistant inspector of schools in one of the eastern divisions of the Presidency stated officially not many years ago that he found about 50 per cent of Moslem boys in secondary schools holding the essentially Hindu doctrine of the transmigration of the soul; while a so-called Muhammadan sect, with the title of *zazazwas*, which deified their leader and worshipped him as a divinity, quite recently acquired a considerable vogue in the south-eastern districts of the Presidency. Such a practice, while in keeping with Hindu tradition and belief, is of course a rank violation of the tenets of Islam.

The story of the Muhammadan conquest of Bengal has been told in a volume entitled the "Riyazu-s-salatin," a work compiled during the years 1787 and 1788 by one Ghulam Husain Salim, Zaidpuri, a servant of the East India Company, who was persuaded to undertake the work by Mr. George Udny, the Company's representative at Malda. At the request of this gentleman, he tells us, he "placed the finger of consent on the eye, and, girding up the loin of effort and venture, collected sentence after sentence from every source, and for a period of two years devoted himself to the compilation and preparation of this history." In a picturesque passage in his introductory chapter he makes it clear that it is to the Muhammadan period that he proposes to confine his history, for "inasmuch as the object of the author is to chronicle the history of the Musalman sovereigns, therefore, not busying himself with the details of the affairs of the Hindu Rais, he reins back the graceful steed of the black pen of writing from striding this valley, and gives it permission to canter towards relating and reciting the details of the history of the Muhammadan rulers and sovereigns."[1] His account of the Muhammadan conquest of Bengal is short and to the point. He tells us how a soldier of fortune, Muhammad Bakhtiar Khilji, having overrun Bihar, set out for Nadiah, the capital of Lakhmaniya, the aged sovereign of the Sena dynasty, which early in the twelfth century had shorn the still more famous Pala dynasty of much of its territory and power. The Raja was in the inner rooms of his palace, with his food before him, when Bakhtiar Khilji with eighteen followers burst into the building, and, rushing impetuously

[1] "The Riyazu-s-salatin," translated from the original Persian by Maulavi Abdus Salam, with copious and valuable notes by the translator.

upon the king's retainers, "put the harvest of the life of many to his thundering and flashing sword." The aged king, "getting confounded by the tumult of this affaire," bolted by a back-door and sped barefoot to the river, where he escaped by boat. Whereupon "Muhammad Bakhtiar, sweeping the town with the broom of devastation, completely demolished it, and making anew the city of Lakhnauti (Gaur), which from ancient times had been the seat of government of Bengal, his own metropolis, he ruled over Bengal." From that time, adds the historian, "the kingdom of Bengal became subject to the emperors of Delhi."

If one cares to journey to the district of Malda in the north-west of the Presidency of Bengal as it is to-day, one will light upon interesting evidence in support of this statement of the historian. For here, in a tract of country which has been swallowed up to a great extent by the jungle, are to be seen the most imposing ruins of which Bengal can boast, the remains of two considerable cities, those of Gaur and Pandua. From Portuguese sources we learn that the former was a city of stately buildings with broad, straight thoroughfares lined with shady trees, having a population of 1,200,000 souls. Standing amid its ruins to-day, with the jungle creeping up to the buildings themselves, it is difficult to believe that here stood, only a few short centuries ago, a city of such vast proportions. Its inhabitants must have been congested, for De Barrow states: "The population is so great and the streets so thronged with the concourse and traffic of people, especially of such as come to present themselves at the King's court, that they cannot force their way past one another, and thus such as happen to fall among the horsemen or among the elephants, which are ridden by the lords and noblemen, are often killed on the spot and crushed under the feet of those beasts."[1]

It remained the capital of Muhammadan Bengal until the middle of the fourteenth century, twenty-six viceroys from Bakhtiar Khilji ruling from it. In the year A.D. 1338, Malik Fakhru-d-din, an armourer, "meddling in administrative matters, obtained much influence, and resolving in mind to usurp the viceroyalty," slew the viceroy and ruled in his place. He did more, for, finding the empire of Muhammad Shah falling into decay, "he withdrew his hand from submission to the Emperor of Delhi and proclaimed himself king."[2] For the next two centuries, till A.D. 1538, Bengal was ruled by independent Muhammadan kings, and for some part of this period, up to the year A.D. 1414, the capital was transferred to Pandua, a city twenty miles north-east of Gaur. It is here that still stands the finest known example of Muhammadan architecture in this part of India, a vast building known as the Adina Masjid. Built by order of Sikandar Shah in A.D. 1375, it recalls the great mosque of Damascus, which was the glory of the Omayyad caliphs, whose regime of pomp and splendour provided so great a contrast to the rigorous frugality of the caliph patriarchs whom they succeeded. Both ground-plan and dimensions are said to be modelled on this famous building, from whose *mimbar* Muawiah, the founder of the Omayyad dynasty, preached and called for vengeance upon the murderers of the caliph Othman. Even in its decay it is a stupendous pile, a vast quadrilateral more than five hundred feet in length and not far short of three hundred feet in breadth. Its huge walls, of stone for the

[1] I am indebted to M. Abid Ali Khan of the Bengal P.W.D. for this quotation.

[2] "The Riyazu-s-salatin."

first eleven feet and of elaborately carved brickwork for another dozen feet, give an impression of immense solidity and strength. On the inside, opening on to the great central courtyard, are rows of cloisters; and in the centre of this enclosure can still be traced the walls of the great nave of the mosque, sixty-four feet in length and thirty-three feet in breadth. The *kiblah* or prayer-niche still stands in a finely decorated wall, and not far from it is a magnificent *mimbar* or pulpit of black basalt and hornblende richly carved. To the north, looking down upon the pulpit, is an upper chamber, the Badshah-ka-Takht, or king's gallery, containing three *kiblahs* in the west wall, beautifully ornamented with carving and with inscriptions in the picturesque Tughra character. And opening off this is another room, now roofless, known as Sikandar's chamber, in which the king and his family sat, according to tradition, before and after the Friday prayers.

Two centuries of independence were brought to a close in A.D. 1538, when the Afghan Sher Shah, emerging victorious from a welter of civil strife in Bihar and Bengal, became a power in the land, and, driving the Emperor Humāyun into temporary exile, ascended the throne of Delhi in his place. For some years thereafter Bengal was ruled by military governors, and it was not until the year A.D. 1607 that the Moghul emperors, seated once more upon the throne at Delhi, established the system of civil government in Bengal, with a nazim at the head of the executive and a diwan in charge of revenue and finance generally, which Clive found in force when he won his dramatic victory over Surajah Dowla on the field of Plassey.

It was under one of the early nazims, Shaik Allanddin Chrishti Farugi I'tizad-ud-Daulah, Nawab Islam Khan, that the Moslem capital of

Bengal was transferred east to Dacca, where it remained for nigh on a century. This move was made with a view to consolidating the eastern frontier of the Muhammadan Empire. It was accompanied by a forward policy, under which colonies of Moslem feudal barons were planted out in the eastern districts, and a powerful fleet, based on Dacca, patrolled the waters of the Padma and Megna rivers. Hence the Moghul buildings, which still confer upon Dacca an historic interest; hence, too, the predominantly Muhammadan character of Eastern Bengal, which was a not unimportant factor in deciding Lord Curzon's Government to make of it a separate province in 1905—a measure which, to the chagrin of the Muhammadans of the newly created province, was reversed in 1912.

The founding of this new capital is bathed in an atmosphere of romance. In the third year of the reign of Jahangir at Delhi, a notable flotilla might have been seen ploughing its way eastwards through the waters of the Padma river. Great craft, manned by as many as one hundred and fifty oarsmen, escorted a State barge, from whose masthead flew an ensign emblazoned with the famous Lion and Sun. At a spot on the left bank of the Buriganga river the fleet came to anchor, and from the deck of the royal barge stepped ashore Islam Khan, the Viceroy of the Moghul emperor. The spot is known to this day as Islampur, and is a quarter of the modern town. Ere he returned to his barge his ear was caught by the sound of drums—the *dhak* of the Hindu—and a religious procession came into view. The Viceroy was a man of imagination. He recognised the strategic advantages of the site, and, hailing the drummers, formed them up and ordered them to play while he despatched men east, north, and west, with instructions to each to plant a flagstaff as soon as he was out of ear-shot of the drums. Thus with the Buriganga as its southern boundary did he fix the limits of the future capital, and called it Dhaka (Dacca) or the Drum.[1]

A century later the capital of Bengal was moved once more, this time to Maksusabad, by the diwan Murshed Kuli Khan, who re-christened the place Murshidabad after his own name, as related in Chapter IX. But Dacca has outlived Murshidabad, for while the latter is in ruins and has a diminishing population, the former received a new lease of life when it became the capital of Eastern Bengal and Assam in 1905. And though its reign as the capital of a province was short-lived, it is now the second capital of Bengal, and has recently become the seat of a modern university, which opened its doors in 1921. It is therefore an important city, with a great future before it.

[1] See an article in the " Dacca Review " for August-September 1914 by Khan Bahadur Syed Aulad Hasan.

CHAPTER XIX

ISLAM IN INDIA

THE existence of the 70,000,000 Moslems in India is the most formidable obstacle in the way of those whose battle-cry is " India a nation." The startling fact to which attention has already been called, that no Muhammadan can have a Hindu relation, and *vice versa*, is an indication of the nature of the obstacle. The attachment of the Muhammadans to Islam as an institution transcending the bounds of country, illustrated in the preceding chapter by reference to their observance of the Mohurrum, serves as a further indication of the manner in which and the extent to which the claims of nationality are qualified in the case of this large and important section of the inhabitants of India. This attachment to Islam has had a profound influence upon the position of the community in India in recent years, for it has been one of the most powerful factors militating against their adoption of the education given in the schools and colleges established by Great Britain. The backwardness of the Muhammadans in this respect as compared with the Hindus is notorious, and has acted as a serious handicap in the race for political power.

The educational ideal of Islam differs markedly from that of Europe; in India, owing to the attitude of religious neutrality which the Government felt compelled to adopt, the educational courses of the Madrassahs, on the one hand, and of the schools and colleges on the other, are as the poles asunder. The former are almost entirely religious, the latter exclusively secular. The whole curriculum of the Madrassah revolves round the Koran and the literature of Arabia; its main subjects are Arabic poetry and prose, grammar and composition, rhetoric and prosody, logic and Muhammadan law, Koranic exegesis and criticism, the science of apostolic tradition and scholastic theology. It is this course which in Islamic countries turns out statesmen and administrators, and in Bengal, during the period of Muhammadan rule which has been described, not only were there Madrassahs all over the country staffed with distinguished Arabic scholars who devoted their lives to the advancement of Islamic learning and taught the theology, law, and literature of their faith without remuneration, but innumerable mosques which were Madrassahs in miniature.[1] In other words, the learning and culture which had blossomed in the famous universities of Islam, the great Madrassah at Baghdad, and the famous stronghold of orthodoxy, al-Azhar, which still survives in Cairo, flourished on Indian soil. With the break-up of the Muhammadan Empire many of these institutions collapsed; there was, however, for some time yet a demand for the type of education given in the Madrassah, for Persian remained the language of the law courts until 1837; and with the intention of training Muhammadans as officers in the service of the East India Company, Warren Hastings himself established a Madrassah in Calcutta in 1782. With the discontinuance of Persian as the language of the courts in 1837, the Madrassahs ceased to serve any practical

[1] See a memorandum by Maulavi Abdul Karim, submitted to the Calcutta University Commission.

purpose beyond that of turning out Islamic scholars and divines. It is significant of the spell which Islam casts upon its members, that in spite of the heroic efforts of far-sighted leaders of the community such as Sir Syed Ahmad, the founder of the Muhammadan Anglo-Oriental College at Aligarh, which has since become the Muhammadan University, the Rt. Hon. Syed Ameer Ali, Nawab Mohsin-ul-Mulk, and others, the bulk of the Muhammadans of India still held aloof from the schools and colleges which were open to them. Even so recently as 1914, a committee appointed by the Government of Bengal to consider questions connected with Muhammadan education, found that wherever private Moslem initiative was concerned it tended to develop purely Islamic institutions; and the result of this attitude was brought to the notice of the Calcutta University Commission of 1917–19 by the Muhammadans of Calcutta, who pointed to the fact that although more than half the population of the Presidency was Musalman, less than 10 per cent of those who received university education were Muhammadans. The Bengal Government Committee of 1914 attributed this attitude of the Moslem community to a strong feeling that a separate system of education would preserve their social and religious independence. The Calcutta University Commission endorsed the same view, which had been stated even more emphatically by the Indian Education Commission of 1882. A candid Muhammadan, in the opinion of that Commission, would probably admit that the most powerful factors in keeping the majority of Moslems aloof from the educational movement of the day were pride of race, a memory of bygone superiority, religious fears, and a not unnatural attachment to the learning of Islam.

It has been in no small measure their pride in Islam, then, which has kept the Muhammadans from throwing in their lot with the Hindus and taking advantage of the facilities provided by Government for acquiring a liberal education on modern Western lines. It has been the same influence which has led leaders of the community possessing greater political vision to urge upon their co-religionists the importance of emancipating themselves from their rigid conservatism in the matter of education. Yet again it was this same thing which threw the whole weight of Moslem opinion on to the side of Government and cautious progress, when advanced Hindu opinion began to demand rapid progress in the direction of self-government, still more when talk of cutting adrift from Great Britain began to be heard. Finally, it was once more the same factor which was responsible for the dramatic change in the attitude of the community towards Great Britain which took place when the curtain was rung up on a stage whereon was displayed the Turkish Empire, the leading state in the world of Islam, ranged up in battle array against Great Britain. It is, indeed, this deep attachment on the part of the Muhammadans, whether of India or elsewhere, to Islam as an institution transcending all boundaries of race, of language, and of country, that is the dominant factor in determining their attitude in any given circumstances. No one who does not realise this can hope to understand their action at times of crisis, still less to appreciate in advance the course which in any particular circumstances they will be likely to pursue.

The merest sketch of the part played by the Muhammadans in the politics of India during the past three or four decades is sufficient to make this clear. When the Indian National Congress was formed in 1885 to advocate Indian Home Rule, leading Muhammadans of the day took stock of the position, and it was then that a great leader came forward to guide his people. Sir Syed Ahmad Khan viewed with grave anxiety the trend of the new movement. He knew how far his own people had lagged behind in the sphere of education. He was acutely conscious of the dangers of the purely secular education of the schools and colleges which Government had set up. But he realised also the urgent necessity of a break with the rigid educational traditions of Islamic orthodoxy if, without sacrificing its individuality, his community was to play a part in the future of the country worthy of the historic importance of its past. His call to his people was definite and clear. "Concentrate upon fitting yourselves for the task which lies before you; shun the political catch-cries that are ringing in your ears," was the slogan with which he flung himself into the arena. And the first-fruits of his leadership were the Muhammadan Anglo-Oriental College at Aligarh, at which the science of the West was combined with the moral and religious training of Islam, and an annual gathering of the leading men of the community under the title of the All-India Muhammadan Educational Conference. Amongst the broader-minded and more far-seeing leaders of the community the lamp thus lit by Sir Syed Ahmad burned brightly. The Anglo-Oriental College at Aligarh did much to further the hopes which he cherished; and as recently as 1910, when a demand for its expansion into a Moslem university was making itself felt, a great and cultured leader of the community gave expression to aspirations identical with those formulated by Sir Syed Ahmad a quarter of a century before. Pre-eminent among the questions of the day, declared His Highness the Aga Khan, then President of the All-India Moslem League, is the foundation of a Muhammadan university at Aligarh. The picture which he held up before his audience was that of an educational centre and intellectual capital to which all Moslems should turn for light and guidance. They must keep abreast of the knowledge and learning of the day, but this in itself was not enough. "We should lay bare before the rising generation the treasures concealed in ancient Arabic lore with a view to developing the spiritual and emotional side of their nature."[1] The object of such an university should not be to gratify mere sentiment or vanity. "We believe it to be necessary for the truc development of our principles and ultimate spiritual unity of our faith."[2] And the foundation upon which all was to be built up was attachment to the enlightened rule of Great Britain—"our loyalty to the throne must be absolute."

The necessity for some form of political organisation was not lost sight of, and an Anglo-Muhammadan Defence Association came into existence in Upper India early in the closing decade of the nineteenth century. It did not survive the death of Sir Syed Ahmad Khan in 1898; but the need of such an organisation was still felt, and the prospect of an early measure of constitutional reform which arose at the end of 1905 proved to be the stimulus required to bring a definitely political organisation into being. Following upon the reception by the Viceroy, Lord Minto, on October the 1st, 1906, of a representative deputation which placed before him the views of the community with regard to the proposed constitutional reforms, an All-India Moslem League was inaugurated at a gathering

[1] Speech at Delhi, January 1910. [2] *Ibid.*

of Muhammadans from all parts of India held during the latter days of December of the same year. Some little time elapsed before the constitution of the League took final shape; but in March 1908 a final draft was ratified, and His Highness the Aga Khan elected President.

The views which the Muhammadan deputation placed before the Viceroy in 1906 were those of a community acutely conscious of the fact that it differed fundamentally in its religious, social, and ethical ideals from the majority of the inhabitants of the land in which it dwelt; and further, that, faced with a movement in the direction of the democratic constitutionalism of the West, it was in danger of losing that which it desired above all things to maintain, namely, the individuality which it derived from its participation in the world of Islam. The problem which it propounded was, indeed, a sufficiently formidable one. How was a system of government which predicated homogeneity of population to be adjusted to meet the case of a population whose outstanding characteristic was its heterogeneity? It was the imminence of this problem which brought the All-India Moslem League into existence.

As the mouthpiece of the community, the League demanded that Muhammadan interests in the new legislatures which it was proposed to set up should be entrusted to Muhammadan representatives elected by an exclusively Muhammadan electorate; and declared with an emphasis which left no room for ambiguity as to its meaning, that no scheme which did not provide for a specified number of seats in the said legislatures to be filled by Muhammadans so elected would meet the necessities of the case. It demanded more. It asked that in the event of a Hindu gentleman being appointed to the Government of India, a similar honour should be accorded to a Muhammadan; that the proportion of seats to be allotted to the community in the new legislatures should be calculated not merely upon its numerical strength, but upon a consideration of its political and historical importance as well; and finally, that in the case of all public bodies to which the elective principle might apply—municipal, district, and local boards as well as legislative councils—the principles demanded in the case of the legislatures should be given effect to. Nothing could have disclosed more effectively than did the vigour and perseverance with which these demands were pressed, the cleft between the two great sections of the population, or the qualifications with which the Indian nationality of the Moslems of the continent is hedged around.

Loyalty to the British Government was still the keynote of Muhammadan policy, and was loudly proclaimed in the public utterances of its leaders. "Our attitude towards the British Government is not one merely of loyal acquiescence, but of devotion based on a deep-rooted conviction that God has ordained British rule for the welfare of the Indian peoples . . . and on a firm belief that the interests of our community and of the subject races generally are absolutely identical with those of the British Government." Thus Khan Bahadur Sir Mian Muhammad Shafi, who later became a member of the Government, in a speech in October 1909. And in summing up the policy of the Moslem League, he declared, "The maintenance on a permanent basis of British rule in India and a reasonable measure of self-government for the country, with due regard to the rights and interests of the various communities inhabiting the Indian continent, are the two chief aims which the Muhammadan community has had and will continue to have in view." Similar sentiments were expressed by other leaders of the community, stress being laid upon the community of interest between Great Britain and the world of Islam. The Muhammadans of India, declared the Rt. Hon. Syed Amir Ali, "are connected by ties of religion, tradition, and race with the whole of Western Asia and Northern Africa, right away to the Atlantic—countries where the prestige of England stands high, and where England is recognised as the champion of justice and fair play." And it was to their pride in Islam that the President of the League appealed when he urged his co-religionists to take advantage of the facilities offered under British rule for their moral and material advancement. "The community that carried culture to the Pyrenees and to Central Asia, the community that can still recall with emotional pride the greatness of Cordova and Damascus, cannot be dead to its sense of duty. I appeal to you with all the force in my power to imitate the spirit of those who made Toledo and Baghdad, to work day in day out for the noble object of elevating Moslem life so as to hold forth the highest ideals before the younger generation. . . . Let our Pole Star be active and unimpeachable loyalty to the sovereign and the glory of India and of Islam."[1]

Not all the demands of the Moslem League were granted. But the principle of communal representation on the legislatures by means of separate Muhammadan electorates was conceded, and survived the still greater step towards the democratic constitutionalism of the West taken ten years later, when large changes in the size and powers of the legislative councils were made by the Reforms Act of 1919.

[1] Speech by His Highness the Aga Khan at Delhi, January the 29th, 1910.

Nothing short of an open breach between Great Britain and Turkey, the fountain-head of Islam, could have changed so completely, as has been the case, the attitude of the Muhammadans of India towards the British Government, or have driven them into alliance with the extremists among the Hindu politicians. Fear for the future of Islam not only brought into existence a Muhammadan extremist party, pledged to work in political co-operation with the extreme wing of the Indian National Congress, but created a feeling of profound disquiet in the minds of more moderate men, and eventually, as a result of the preaching of the mullahs, stirred the feelings of the illiterate masses as well. How fragile was the texture of the Hindu-Moslem entente was perpetually being demonstrated by the attitude of the masses. For all their professions of friendship, such episodes as the Shahabad riots of the autumn of 1917, when the Hindus, flinging themselves upon the Moslems of Bihar, burst open the flood-gates of fierce racial and religious passions, rankled deep down in the mind of the Muhammadans, leaving a legacy of bitter memories behind. Later, when the Moplah rebellion broke out, carrying fire and sword across huge tracts in the south-west of the continent, the Hindus learned, through the aid of forcible conversions to the faith of their persecutors, something of the proselytising fanaticism of which Islam is capable. Yet, paradoxical though it may seem, the fanaticism of the fierce and uncultured Moplahs and the Hindu-Moslem entente of the politicians were derived from a common source—a fervid attachment to Islam. The action of the former was fanatical and unreasoning, of the latter deliberate and calculated. Amongst the Moslem extremist politicians there were undoubtedly men whose primary motive was hatred of Western domination; but apart from these there was the bulk of the educated men of the community which found itself gradually being forced, through no fault of its own, into a position of extraordinary difficulty. With the conclusion of hostilities men began to take stock of their position, and upon the minds of Indian Muhammadans the fate of Turkey as one of the vanquished nations began to prey. The task of reconciling the claims of secular loyalty to a Christian power with the equally insistent claims of religious loyalty to Turkey became for all a formidable and distracting one, and for some insuperable.

Any detailed narrative of the events leading up to the formation of the Indian Khilāfat party for the protection of Islam, or of the widespread agitation conducted under its auspices, would be beyond the scope of this volume. A single episode will suffice to indicate the strained state of feeling amongst the community, and to illustrate what has been said as to the extent to which the attitude of the Moslems of India is influenced by a consciousness of their organic relationship to Islam.

As the War dragged on, the embers of discontent smouldering in the Muhammadan mind glowed more brightly. The least breath proved capable of fanning them into flame. In the Nakhoda mosque in Calcutta the Imam, Ahmad Musa Misri, an Egyptian known far beyond the confines of India, when he led the faithful in prayer at the weekly Friday service, prayed ostentatiously for the welfare of the Turkish caliph. Many little things went to show that the nerves of Moslem India were on edge, and in the late summer of 1918 a little breeze, which in more normal times would have passed unnoticed, blew upon the embers and kindled them into flame. A descriptive paragraph in a newspaper, which to an impartial reader was wholly innocent of offence, was held by the Muhammadans who read it to contain an implication insulting to the memory of the Prophet. A misleading translation in Urdu was widely circulated, and all true Moslems were called on to rise and avenge this insult to their religion. The editors of the Muhammadan vernacular press ran amok with pens dipped in gall, and day after day lashed the feelings of their readers with column after column of vitriolic writing. Meetings were held at which overwrought speakers gave vent to their pent-up feelings without restraint. Resolutions were passed pledging those who supported them to protect the honour of Islam, and calling upon Government to take action against those who were held to have insulted the memory of the Prophet.

The paragraph complained of had appeared at the end of July. By the end of August the pulse of the Moslem community was throbbing feverishly far beyond the confines of Bengal, and a plan was evolved by the leaders of the agitation for the holding of a great gathering in Calcutta early in September to be addressed by learned Maulanas from all parts of India, and to extend over three days. Leaflets in the vernacular were circulated broadcast, in which it was stated that at different places insults had been offered to Islam and its Prophet; that the time had arrived when it was necessary to state to Government that "the waters had risen too high," and that "the cup of patience was already full," that steps must be taken without delay "to prevent these unholy attacks and accursed occurrences"; and that Ulemas (learned men), Maulavis, Supis (spiritual leaders), and National leaders would attend a meeting which all Brothers of Islam should take part in to consider proposals for the protection of their Holy Religion. On September the 1st the

Secretary of the Committee formed to organise the demonstration stated that 1200 invitations to Ulemas and other leading men had already been sent out.

Below the surface, and notably amongst the huge illiterate labouring population that lives and labours in the mills in the environs of Calcutta, propaganda of a still more sinister character was being carried on. Men were being urged to remember the Shahabad riots of the previous autumn, and amid a storm of angry mutterings the ominous word *jihad* was to be heard being bandied from mouth to mouth. The masses were being shaken by one of those violent spasms of racial and religious excitement which are apt to sweep across the deep waters of Indian life with such disconcerting rapidity. And by an unfortunate coincidence the Bakr-id, the great feast of the Muhammadans, involving on a large scale the sacrifice of the cow, and the Durga Puja, the greatest of all the festivals of the Hindus of Bengal, fell at the same time and were imminent. It required little wisdom to perceive that in such circumstances the holding of a huge demonstration such as was proposed must be attended with the risk of grave consequences. And since the organisers of the movement refused to accept the advice tendered to them to postpone the gathering until after the celebration of the religious festivals, when a calmer atmosphere might be expected to prevail, Government was compelled to step in and prohibit the demonstration.

It was scarcely to be expected that in an atmosphere so highly charged the storm which had gathered should pass altogether harmlessly by. For a day or two there were outbreaks of rioting in the town, and an attempt was made by a fanatical mob of mill hands from one of the adjacent areas to force one of the military pickets which were holding the approaches to the town. Some firing, resulting in some loss of life, was unfortunately unavoidable before normal conditions were restored.

The deeper causes of this threatening outbreak were never in doubt. They were emphasised in the course of a prolonged interview held, owing to the urgency of the times, late at night between myself and some of the Ulemas who had come from other parts of India to take part in the proceedings. My visitors laid stress upon the fact that they were not politicians but religious leaders of the people, concerned only with the safeguarding of the religion whose care was their sacred charge. They said that on such an occasion that which was rankling deep in their hearts should be openly spoken. It had seemed to them that for some time past the attitude of Government towards their community had grown cold. This was all the more galling in that it suggested that their loyalty under circumstances of the greatest difficulty was but lightly valued by Great Britain. The representations of the All-India Ulema deputation on the subject of the impending constitutional changes seemed to them to have been ignored. Did not this point to a cynical indifference on the part of Government towards their views? And at a time when this unfortunate impression was gaining ground in the minds of the leaders of the community a number of incidents had occurred—the Shahabad riots and the alleged insults to Islam were given as examples—which had deeply stirred the feelings of the masses. However strong their attachment to the British throne, loyalty to Islam must always be their first and paramount consideration.

Throughout these pages I have sought to avoid writing of things which are, in essence, ephemeral. In this instance I have made use of a passing episode for purposes of illustration. That which I desired to illustrate was the strength of the call of Islam—a call which rings insistently in the ears of the devout Moslem, whether of India or elsewhere, drowning the call of country and all else. The particular incident of which I have made use is all the more valuable as an illustration, in that it occurred before the uprising in the Punjab which some months later was to give so powerful an impetus to anti-Government agitation throughout the land.

I do not, of course, suggest that the great mass of Muhammadan peasants, if left to themselves, would have known anything of events in Turkey, or, if they had, would have been unduly stirred by the probable fate of that country. As a Muhammadan gentleman once said to me, "As long as the *Khutbah* is recited after the name of the Sultan of Turkey as caliph, the ordinary man will not worry over the fate of that country." But the masses follow blindly the lead of their mullahs, and the mullahs take their cue from those at the top of the religious hierarchy; and those at the top know well enough that the one cry above all others that can be counted on to rally the masses of their people is the cry of "Islam in danger."

CHAPTER XX

THE RELIGIOUS QUEST OF INDIA

On all sides of him the visitor sees evidence of the extent to which religion enters into the daily life of the people. Temples and mosques abound; and the calendar is strewn with festivals and fasts of all kinds—Hindu and Muhammadan—many of which are officially recognised by the days on which they take place being proclaimed as Government holidays. In a chart of the monthly festivals Mr. Underhill mentions over two hundred and sixty Hindu celebrations alone.[1] Something has been said in the preceding chapter of the religious discipline of Islam. But the ritual of Islam does not differ in essentials from that of Christianity. Both, being monotheistic, have evolved a form of worship appropriate to the basic belief on which they rest—differing in detail, certainly, but similar in kind.

It is when one visits the temples raised up to the religions which have been born upon the soil of India itself that one is struck, and at first puzzled, by the nature of the observances which one sees. In the Jain temples on Mount Abu, I have seen ascetics sweeping the ground in front of them as they walked, and ministrants in the same temples carrying through their celebrations with cloths bound over their mouths. Here one is brought

[1] "The Hindu Religious Year," by M. M. Underhill.

into contact with a great principle running through much of the religious thought of India, and exalted in particular by the Buddhists and the Jains—that of *ahiṁsa*, literally harmlessness, but connoting a deep reverence for the life principle and a spirit of extreme loving kindness, consequently, to all animated beings. The binding of a cloth over the mouth during the performance of certain rites is to guard against the destruction of the life principle in the air by inhaling it, and the sweeping of the path is similarly for the purpose of brushing aside any insect upon which the walker might otherwise tread. For the same reason a Jain will care for vermin upon his own person with the greatest punctiliousness.

The number of Jains in India to-day is comparatively small, about 1,250,000 in all. The vast majority of the population—somewhere about 220,000,000—is recorded at each census as Hindu. But if it be asked what constitutes a Hindu, no definite answer can be given. Hinduism as a religion is not comparable with Christianity or Muhammadanism, or even, in this respect, with Jainism or Buddhism, for it claims no founder propounding a faith for the salvation of mankind; and there is no agreement amongst Hindus themselves as to what is essential in a man calling himself a Hindu. The word Hinduism itself finds no place in the ancient Sanskrit texts of the Aryans; and so tolerant has it proved itself of religious beliefs, that it has been admitted to contain "doctrines and modes of worship from the lowest fetishism to the sublimest ideas of the Godhead."[1] Another well-known Hindu has defined the term negatively as applicable to all inhabitants of India who are not Christians or Muhammadans or Parsis or Sikhs or Jains or

[1] By Babu Sarada Charan Mitra.

Buddhists; and he has amplified his definition by stating that it includes in its widest acceptance "the most sublime conceptions of Indian sages with regard to God and the soul, as well as debasing superstitions of half-savage tribes living in the forests."[1] Others have been more definite, and have laid down certain beliefs as essential to any one professing Hinduism—for example, belief in the immortality of the soul, in the doctrine of Karma, in the transmigration of the soul until it attains Moksha (salvation), and in the possibility of attaining Moksha in any of several recognised ways, namely, *Karma* or virtuous action, *Bhakti* or devotion to God, *Jnāna* or the attainment of knowledge of the true nature of things by meditation.[2] Many hold that a belief in the Vedas as inspired writings is essential, but I think that the two fundamental and almost universal beliefs characteristic of Hinduism are the doctrine of Karma and transmigration, or the tenet that as a man sows so he reaps here and hereafter through countless incarnations—of which more later; and the possibility of release from re-birth, the achievement of which may be said, indeed, to be the supreme object of the Hindu religion. Certain it is that most Hindu practices are based upon the theory of successive lives conditioned by acts in the present and the past; and for this reason another prominent Hindu, the late Mr. V. Krishnaswami Iyer, has asserted that he could not conceive of a follower of Hinduism who repudiated Karma and reincarnation. Every educated Hindu would likewise subscribe, I think, to the existence of the three roads along which it is open to a man to travel on his quest of the supreme goal: *Karma-mārga*, the path of works, which in its religious aspect amounts to a strict

[1] Rao Bahadur K. Ramanujachari.
[2] The late Mr. Justice P. R. Sundara Aiyar.

observance of ritual; *Bhakti-mārga*, the way of complete devotion to God, when a man, having trodden the *Karma-mārga*, devotes himself to an ecstatic adoration of the deity; and finally, *Jnāna-mārga*, the path of knowledge, when, having finished with the things of this world, he becomes a Sannyasi, his mind thenceforward cut off entirely from all sensuous things and from all desire—even for his own future—and fixed solely upon the Absolute Brahman.

The visitor will see numberless persons in the guise of Sannyasis, but for the most part these will not be true ascetics treading the real road of knowledge, but caricatures of the genuine Sannyasi engaged, as often as not, in living a life of idleness at the expense of a long-suffering public. It is in the nature of things that the particular aspect of the religious life of India which is most apparent on the surface is that of the *Karma-mārga*—the rites and practices of the masses: that which, in a word, may be described as popular Hinduism. The Hinduism which occupies so large a part of the daily life of millions of people may be seen in practice almost anywhere—at the great melas (religious fairs) which take place all over the country, in any one of the thousands of temples to Vishnu or Shiva which dot the land, or at some great centre of pilgrimage such as Benares in the north, Madura or Conjeeveram, or, indeed, at any of a number of famous religious centres in the south of India or at Puri in Orissa. It is at this latter place that there rise, not far from the blue waters of the Bay of Bengal, the spires of the great temple of Jaganāth to which pilgrims flock from all quarters of India, and notably at midsummer, when the famous car of Jaganāth is drawn by thousands of devotees along the broad highway which runs for over a mile from the temple in the town to the garden retreat in which, for a space of eight days, the image of the god reposes.

Of the surrounding country it might well be said—to the Hindu, at any rate—"Put off the shoes from off thy feet, for the ground whereon thou standest is holy ground." Within a day's journey of the great pilgrim city are to be seen outstanding milestones marking out, over a period of more than two millenniums, the road along which India has travelled in her diligent and unceasing quest of the unknown. In the ruins of ancient temples which cover the land, one sees stretching across the centuries stage after stage of the journey pursued by her with dogged persistence in her search after God. Great figures of the past have left their mark upon the land. The hermitages of ancient monastic orders cluster in the hillsides; immense temples raise their spires towards heaven; the commands of famous kings, deep graven in the enduring rocks, ring down the corridors of time to arrest the attention of the passer-by to-day.

If from Puri one travels thirty miles north to Bhubaneswar, a city of great temples, and on from there another four miles in a south-western direction, one comes, near the village of Dhauli, to two parallel ridges thrown up like folds in the plain, and at a spot on the north face of the southernmost of the two, one finds one's gaze attracted to the head of an elephant hewn out of one end of an outcrop of rock four or five feet in height. Closer inspection discloses the fact that the elephant stands guardian over a polished slab of rock some fifteen feet in length, on which is graven an inscription in three columns. The historic interest of this message from the distant past was made known by the genius of one

Plate 20

A HINDU ASCETIC.

"The visitor will see numberless persons in the guise of *sannyasis*, but for the most part these will not be true ascetics treading the road of knowledge but caricatures . . ."

James Prinsep, who succeeded in deciphering it in 1838. We are in the presence here of the famous edicts of Asoka, the great missionary emperor of the Maurya dynasty, who made of Buddhism a world religion. We are gazing upon the commands of a great monarch graven by his orders upon this same rock more than two thousand one hundred and seventy years ago. I have recalled elsewhere the fact that it was remorse at the misery caused during his conquest of the kingdom of Kalinga—which embraced the modern district of Puri—that turned the heart of Asoka towards the teaching of Buddha.[1] The awful loss of life and the king's remorse are referred to in Edict XIII. of the general edicts, and it is interesting to find that this edict is omitted from the Dhauli inscription. Edict XIV. contains the statement that "this set of *dhamma* edicts has been written by command of the King Piyadasi (Asoka), beloved of the gods, in a form sometimes condensed, sometimes of medium length, sometimes expanded, for everything is not suitable in every place, and my dominions are extensive." It was evidently not considered suitable that the devastating war by which Kalinga had been brought under subjection of the Maurya empire should be referred to in an inscription of the edicts within that territory. On the other hand, the Dhauli rock contains the special edicts addressed not to the public but to the king's officers, which are not found inscribed with the general edicts elsewhere except at Jangada in the adjoining district. Briefly, they are an instruction to his officers to see that the people of the newly conquered territory are not oppressed. The date of the Kalinga edicts is believed to be 256 B.C. Here, then, is an arresting milestone upon the way.

[1] See "Lands of the Thunderbolt," chap. xxiii.

For another we have not to go far; for if from Bhubaneswar we travel some three miles to the north-west, we shall find ourselves at the foot of a low three-peaked hill rising to a height of 120 feet from a rolling stretch of arid laterite. The hill itself and the approaches to it are well wooded, mangoes, bamboos, and other forest trees affording welcome shelter from the rays of a burning sun. Its three peaks bear the names of Udayagiri or the sunrise hill, Khandagiri or the broken hill, and Nilgiri or the blue hill. The whole ridge is honeycombed with caves. In all there are sixty-six, the haunt during the centuries immediately preceding the Christian era of a flourishing colony of Jain monks. Amongst the carvings, which cover a wide range of subjects both secular and religious, is the image of Parsvanath and his symbol the serpent hood, an early preacher of whom little is known, but who is reputed, according to the chronicles of the Jains, to have lived two hundred and fifty years before Mahavira, and therefore seven hundred and fifty years before Christ. Here, too, there is an inscription of no small historic interest. It is engraven upon the smooth surface of the roof rock of a cave on Udayagiri, known as the Hatigumpha or elephant cave. It is dated the 16th year of the Mauryan era, and is a record of the reign of King Khāravela of Kalinga during the second century B.C., ascribing to him the title of Mahameghavāhana—one whose elephant is as big as a large cloud. The tables of the previous century were turned, for Khāravela is depicted as a powerful monarch who invaded Magadah, and, penetrating to Pataliputra, the capital of the empire, compelled the emperor to acknowledge his independence.

Bhubaneswar is another distinct milestone on the road. Its immense collection of temples—

there are still about one hundred—were built between the eighth and twelfth centuries A.D., at a time, that is to say, when circumstances were favourable to a great flowering of creative art. Architecturally they are elaborate, and in many cases vast. They are the product of a sectarian and an emotional age. At the time of their construction, Buddhism had lost its individuality, and had become more and more merged in Hinduism. The twilight period, marked by its decay as a living faith, when scepticism had struck a fatal blow at its roots and its lofty ethical teaching had been corroded by an erotic mysticism, had passed, and the era of religious fervour ushered in with the revival of Hinduism had set in. The emotional faith and devotion to the deity, characteristic of the Purānic renaissance, gave to these centuries that artistic importance which has led Mr. Havell, contrary to many Western critics, to describe them as "the great period of Indian art corresponding to the highest development of Gothic art in Europe," by whose achievements "India's place in the art history of the world will eventually be resolved."[1] "Moral principles, self-discipline, and introspection, the watchwords of Buddhism, were thrown into the background, and faith in God became the motto and the catchword of the Puranik renaissance."[2]

The visitor to-day is at once struck by the form of the great central towers which dominate the courtyards of the temples and which have given their distinctive character to the religious buildings of Orissa. They compel one's gaze from afar, and have excited the admiration of all who have beheld them. Of the great tower

[1] "The Ideals of Indian Art," by E. B. Havell.
[2] "History of Bengali Language and Literature," by Rai Bahadur Dinesh Chandra Sen.

of the Linga-raj temple, the central building of Bhubaneswar, Mr. Havell has said that "for purity of outline and dignity of its rich but unobtrusive decoration, as well as for its superb technique, the Linga-raj Sikhara must rank as one of the greatest works of the Indian builder." Nor is the purity of outline, which strikes one from afar, the only outstanding feature of this wonderful building. Closer inspection of the temples of Bhubaneswar discloses the fact that immense surfaces of stone are literally covered with minutely elaborate carving. So much so that another authority, Mr. Ferguson, has said of this feature of the tower of Linga-raj, that "if it would take, say, a lakh of rupees to erect such a building as this, it would take three lakhs to carve it as this one is carved." And he has added, what must be apparent to every one who visits these remarkable buildings, that "infinite labour bestowed on every detail was the mode in which he (the Hindu) thought he could render his temple most worthy of the deity; and whether he was right or wrong, the effect of the whole is certainly marvellously beautiful."

I have visited Bhubaneswar more than once, and each time as I have wandered from one temple to another, and gazed fascinated upon these amazing examples of man's handiwork, I have been struck with the same thought—the tremendous force of the impulse which has impelled him to devote so much labour, so much time, so much treasure, and such concentrated care to giving expression in wood and stone to the visions of his spiritual eye.

Yet another milestone of the Purānic age now stands in splendid isolation twenty miles up the coast from the town of Puri. The great black temple of Konārak, dedicated to Surya, the Sun god, is one of the most stupendous buildings in

India, and rears itself aloft, a pile of overwhelming grandeur even in its decay. At the present day the great highways pass it by—a striking reminder of the alterations which have taken place in the configuration of the country since the days when, seven centuries ago, at the command of King Narasinhadeva, twelve hundred carpenters and masons worked for sixteen years upon its construction. And it is, consequently, somewhat difficult of access. In a straight line up the coast it is probably not more than twenty miles from Puri; but by road it is nearer fifty. For twenty-five miles we travelled along the famous pilgrim road along which at certain seasons of the year stream families of pious Hindus on their way to the great shrine of Jaganāth. We then turned off, and for the next eighteen or twenty miles bumped over a country cart-track, and finally for six miles over what is known as a fair-weather road, *i.e.* a track across fields, which is a track during the slack season on the land only, being absorbed in the fields themselves when the crops are sown. At last we ran into the sandy soil upon which the temple stands, and the huge mass of its central building, representing the chariot of the sun, burst upon our gaze. It is profusely ornamented with sculpture—some of it of the curious erotic type which to the European seems so strangely incongruous in any place of worship, but some of it of a more edifying character, including some fine figures of the Sun God carved in deep relief in panels of green chlorite. At intervals round the base of the building are beautifully carved stone wheels. Detached groups of sculpture, consisting of figures of elephants, lions, and horses, stand facing the various entrances to the main building. To those who worshipped here it must have made an immense appeal; but it has equally elicited admiration from those having no sympathy with the beliefs to which it was raised up. Writing of it in his Ain-i-Akbari, Abu Fazl said: "Near Jaganāth is a temple dedicated to the Sun. Its cost was defrayed by twelve years' revenue of the Province. Even those whose judgment is critical, and who are difficult to please, stand astonished at its sight." The crowning stone slab of the temple is 25 feet thick, and is estimated to weigh not less than 2000 tons. Preserved within a shed close by is a massive architrave, with images of the nine planets, an immense cube 3 feet square and 19 feet in length, which was originally supported in its position over the eastern doorway by an iron beam 22 feet 10 inches in length and 10 inches square. The stone must have been brought from great distances, for there are no quarries near the site of the temple, and, in the case of the first of these two pieces, must have been hoisted up, at a prodigious expense of labour, on to the summit of a tower which was probably 190 feet high. This in itself was no mean feat, over the accomplishment of which the engineer of to-day may puzzle his head; but for the layman, the chief interest of this, as of the many other buildings which lie scattered over the land, will be the strength of the religious impulse which impelled men to devote so vast an amount of time, labour, and treasure to their construction.

Finally, there is the great temple of Jaganāth at Puri itself, a collection of buildings within a high-walled enclosure nearly 650 feet square, dominated by an immense tower 190 feet high, similar in design to those of the temple of Lingaraj at Bhubaneswar and of other Orissan temples. The images representing the gods are curiously unworthy of so magnificent an abode. They consist, in fact, of logs of wood crudely carved to

Plate 21.

THE CHARIOT OF THE SUN AT KONĀRAK.

"At intervals round the base of the building are beautifully carved stone wheels.

represent Krishna under his title of Jaganāth, "Lord of the World," Balabhadra his brother, and Subhadra his sister. So crude is the carving that they appeared to Mr. B. K. Ghose, the author of a volume entitled the "History of Pooree," as "bulky, hideous wooden busts." The two brothers, he said, had arms "projecting horizontally forward from the ears." The sister did not possess "even that approximation to the human form." There is, of course, an explanation of this strangely inadequate representation of so powerful and popular a divinity; and it has been extracted from the myths and traditions current about the place by the Abbé Dubois. Indra-mena, the mythical builder of the temple, had been told by Brahma that on the completion of the building Krishna would appear on the sea-shore in the guise of a tree-trunk. In due course the prophecy was fulfilled, and Indra-mena, the king, having worshipped the tree-trunk which had miraculously appeared, placed himself at the head of a hundred thousand men, and conveyed it with great pomp and ceremony to the shrine within the temple. The famous carpenter, Visvakarma, next appeared upon the scene, and undertook to carve the image of Krishna out of it in a single night, provided that no prying eye was permitted to be a witness of his work. Visvakarma worked so silently that the king's curiosity was aroused, and he peeped in through a chink in the door. This lapse on his part was disastrous, for Visvakarma, discovering that he was being watched, left the work little more than begun, and departed never to return.

This uncouth image of Jaganāth contains an article about which there is considerable mystery. The image itself is renewed from time to time, and it is at the consecration of a new one that the mystery comes into prominence. Various accounts have been given of this ceremony, the most reliable being, in all probability, that of the Manager of the Temple, supplied to Mr. L. S. S. O'Malley for incorporation in the district gazetteer. According to this account, the unknown article, called the *Brahma-padartha*, is transferred from the old image to the new by a priest, who is blindfolded and whose hands are swathed in cloth, so that he may neither see nor touch the sacred article.

The Abbé Dubois, who is responsible for the story of the origin of the images given above, is also responsible for perpetuating the stories told by early European travellers of the fanatical suicide of pilgrims by throwing themselves under the wheels of the ponderous chariots, in which the images are dragged from the temple in the town to the garden temple a mile or more away, at the time of the Rath Jatra festival. Whence the incorporation in the idiom of the English language of the phrase, "a car of Jaganāth." Cases of accident, when in the crush of pilgrims straining to catch sight of the god persons have been knocked down and run over, there undoubtedly have been. But wild statements, such as that of Bernier in 1667, that "persons are found so blindly credulous and so full of wild notions as to throw themselves on the ground in the way of its ponderous wheels, which pass over and crush to atoms the wretched fanatics," are now generally discredited. The car festival is the greatest and most popular of all the observances connected with the worship of Krishna. It commemorates the victorious drive of Krishna and his brother from Gokul to Mathura, where the divine hero slew Kansa, the demon king of Mathura, who stood for the principle of evil. It is attended by vast crowds of pilgrims and sightseers, numbering from fifty to a hundred thousand. The town is the scene of a large number of festivals throughout the year, the one which I have seen myself being the Holi, which takes place in the month of Phalgun, corresponding to February-March of the English calendar.

CHAPTER XXI

POPULAR HINDUISM

The Holi, the great spring festival, which in varying forms is celebrated all over India, provides an occasion, so far as the lower orders are concerned, for ribald and boisterous merry-making. The feature of the observance which at once attracts the notice of the onlooker is the indiscriminate throwing of red powder and the squirting from syringes of a red liquid, much as confetti is thrown at the mi-carème amongst the Latin races of Europe. For days after the celebration men may be seen going about with their white cotton clothes still stained with patches of scarlet or magenta. This display is accompanied by the singing of songs and the shouting of language in the streets which it requires no great intelligence on the part of the onlooker, even though unacquainted with the vernacular, to recognise as obscene.

In some parts of India the celebration of the Holi is combined with another ritual, namely, the swinging of images of Radha and Krishna in specially constructed swings. At Puri and in the villages around, the swings are of an elaborate character, the structure from which they hang being an ornamental archway of carved stone standing upon a raised stone plinth. Let me give a brief description of the setting of this great spring festival as I witnessed it at Puri, and then try to interpret what at first sight appears to be a not very intelligible display of buffoonery.

Large numbers of pilgrims have come into the town for the festival, and the streets and open spaces—to say nothing of the beach, where bathing is in progress—are thronged with a good-natured holiday crowd. The main thoroughfare, leading up to the square in front of the great temple, is lined with booths at which great quantities of the red powder thrown by the holiday-makers is on sale. Because there are many pilgrims in the town, there are also many sādhus. I have been to Puri on many occasions, but have never seen so many sādhus as now. These are not genuine sannyasis treading the "path of knowledge"; on the contrary, they are ignorant persons who are obviously here for gain—mountebanks who provide the side-shows of the fair. But even here one obtains an insight into the trend of Indian thought. These side-shows, though caricatures, are caricatures of that which India reverences and admires—renunciation, asceticism, mortification of the flesh.

There is a narrow winding street which runs from the square in front of the temple of Jaganāth away through the town—a long street, which for some distance runs between houses and shrines with picturesque lintels of carved wood, but later broadens out between walled enclosures and stretches of open waste land, before losing itself eventually in some rough ground giving on to the beach. It bears the attractive name, during some part of its length at any rate, of "Paradise Gate." It is this street which appears to be the favourite haunt of the sādhu, and the heat and dusty discomfort of a walk along it were more than compensated on this occasion by the novelty of the sights which it held in store.

One of the first examples of self-mortification

which we encountered was that of a gentleman, with little to cover his nakedness beyond a coating of wood ash smeared all over his body, standing motionless upside down. The posture must certainly have been one of considerable discomfort. His whole weight rested on his head and elbows, the hardness of the ground being mitigated only, if at all, by a leopard skin spread upon the street. His legs were crossed in the air and the sun beat down upon him with unrelenting fierceness. It was said that he had already been in this unconventional posture for two hours. Farther along, another exponent of the doctrine of the mortification of the flesh reposed upon a bed of spikes. He had been lying thus in the sun for three hours. But the most popular practice appeared to be that of being buried alive. On patches of waste land along the road were rows of human arms which had the appearance of strange plants growing from the soil. These marked the graves of living sādhus, the object being, so far as I could gather, to illustrate the efficacy of the system of breathing which forms part of the training of a Yogi—a training which, it is claimed, ends by giving a man complete control over all the functions of the body. We took hold of one such pair of protruding hands whose owner allowed us willingly enough to raise him up from his temporary grave. He had been buried, we were told, for half an hour. Into other such hands we placed small coins. These, too, so far as we could judge, were accepted gratefully. Besides performing sādhus, there were numbers of ordinary beggars, containing a large sprinkling of the maimed, the halt, and the blind, exhibiting their physical imperfections for the purpose of exciting the compassion of the passer-by.

We completed our inspection of the outward and visible signs of the Holi festival when we

Plat 22.

A SADHU ON A BED OF SPIKES AT PURI.

". . . another exponent of the doctrine of the mortification of the flesh reposed upon a bed of spikes."

witnessed the swinging of Krishna in an open space not far from the temple.

The disentanglement of the meaning of these observances is not rendered easier by the variations in the ritual in different parts of India, and the confused medley of legends which has gradually become associated with the festival in the minds of the people. But there seems little reason to doubt that the origin of the festival is to be traced back to very early days, when primitive man sought to give expression to the feelings of exaltation which he experienced at that season of the year when the pulse of life is quickened and all animate existence receives a stimulus towards growth and reproduction. The Indian month of Phalgun—itself signifying fructifier—falls at the time of the vernal equinox, when the sun with its life-giving warmth is well on its northward course, a season at which a quickened vitality stirs the emotional impulses which seek expression in love and worship. In its earliest form the festival was, in fact, nothing more than man's welcome to returning spring, and it is referred to in early Sanskrit poetry as Basanta-utsava, or the Festival of Spring. The universal tendency of primitive man to endow anything which called forth his worship with his own image would of itself be sufficient to account for the intrusion of a personality into a celebration which began as a mere expression of gratification at the effects of a seasonal change. The nature of the personality would naturally enough be determined by the type of worship called forth. The feelings of joy and gladness excited by seasonal change at the time of spring, having their root in a quickening of the physical organism and a consequent impulse towards reproduction, would inevitably suggest a god of love; and one would expect what, in fact, one finds, namely, mention in the ancient poetic and dramatic literature of another festival, the Madana-utsava, or Festival of the Indian Cupid.

Festivals such as the Basanta-utsava and the Madana-utsava, containing, as they did, such obvious elements of popularity, were not likely to be cast aside by theologians bent upon popularising their own particular sect; and the Holi in its present form seems to be the outcome of sectarian effort of this kind. The cult of Krishna, with its origin deep-rooted in the great epic of India, the Mahabharata, was seized upon by Vaishnavite theologians, who in their handling of the Purānas—those famous religious poems which for centuries past have been the Bible of the people—evolved an idyll which gripped the popular imagination. With Krishna the very incarnation of love, little difficulty was to be expected in absorbing the primitive festivals and re-incarnating them as an episode in the idyll which served as so admirable a vehicle of sectarian teaching. In the Purānas, Krishna becomes the hero of an incident which is now generally accepted as the particular event the memory of which is perpetuated by the Holi festival.

The story is of the Saint George and the Dragon order. A she-demon named Holi or Holika scourged the land of the Jumna, devouring children, each family in the stricken area having to take its turn in sacrificing a child to the blood-lust of the monster. From this scourge Krishna delivered the people, vanquishing the demon and her armies on the banks of the Jumna. Here one finds a clue to the significance of the red powder scattered broadcast at the time of the celebration. It is symbolical of the sands of the Jumna stained red with the blood of the demon whom Krishna slew; while the swinging of Krishna as a method of celebrating his victory may well be derived from the prevalence of this particular form of merry-making at the earlier and more primitive celebrations.

There remains the practice of shouting obscene language to be accounted for. This custom dates back in all probability to the early pre-Hindu days of the primitive spring festival, for a belief in the efficacy of obscene acts and language in warding off evil spirits was, apparently, common amongst primitive peoples; and the season when the thoughts of men were turning expectantly towards a quickening of the great life principle in the animal and vegetable world alike would naturally be one at which fears of famine would be mingled with hopes of abundance, and when precautions would, consequently, be taken to guard against the advent of evil influences bent upon checking fertility during the coming months. Here again the theologians stepped in with an explanation which they popularised through the agency of the Purānas. The story in this case is a variation upon that given above in which Krishna appears as the hero. The demon is still Holika, but her destruction is brought about by other means. According to this version a holy sādhu, when passing through a village afflicted by the monster, was attracted by the lamentation of an old woman, and on learning that the cause of her grief was the impending loss of her only grandson, gave himself up to meditation. In due course he announced that Holika could be destroyed in one way only, namely, by being made to listen to vile and obscene language. The people took the holy mendicant at his word, and when Holika arrived to demand her due she was greeted with such a chorus of filthy abuse that she straightway fell down and expired.

I have laid stress in the previous chapter upon the reality and the strength of the religious impulse which has covered the face of the land with great temples. A question which, at first sight, is a puzzling one will probably arise as a result of what has been written above of the uncouth nature of the idols at one of the most famous and most popular temples in India, and of the primitive character of the great festival which has been described. The reader will be inclined to ask whether, in her long quest after God, India has not failed; whether the road she has taken has not led her into a morass of idolatry and superstition rather than to the threshold of the divine. In a country in which the percentage of illiteracy is so high as it is in India, the gulf between the intellectuals and the masses is a wide one. I have vivid recollections of a ceremony which I once attended at a temple in the south of India, at the invitation and in the company of a cultured Brahman gentleman. The images were brought out from their shrines in the building and were carried in procession round the temple in the sight of a large crowd. The procession was headed by a company of nautch girls dancing, and was brought up by a choir of temple attendants, chanting passages from the holy books. As darkness fell and the moon rose over the still water of the temple tank, the whole scene assumed a picturesqueness which it would scarcely have worn in the broad light of day, for the light from the torches served to hide rather than reveal the tawdriness of the trappings. My host, I think, divined something of what was passing in my mind. "The display is for the people," he said; and we left it at that. He was himself one of the highly intellectual and cultured Brahmans of southern India, the type of man whose mind penetrates without difficulty the complexities of the Vedanta philosophy in its most intellectual form, as set forth, for example, by Sankara, the great commentator of the eighth century A.D. Elsewhere I have described the attitude of a famous priest and hermit of the eastern Himālayas towards this same question, and have set forth his frank avowal that all formalism in religion was meaningless to those who had risen above the level of the comparatively primitive, and was of value only in so far as it drew the minds of the uneducated from earth towards heaven. If, then, in India one finds side by side not merely different races and different creeds, but also, as has been pointed out in Chapter XVII., different epochs, is it surprising that one should also find widely differing stages in the evolution of religious thought? It is one of the main contentions of the Vedanta philosophy, as I shall hope to show in another volume, that all human truth is relative and not absolute; that as the veil of ignorance is gradually drawn aside, the truth of yesterday is seen to be but partial truth in the greater light of the knowledge of to-day. Will not the truth of to-day in its turn be seen to be relative only in the still greater light which will assuredly be shed upon the darkness of the human mind by the greater knowledge of to-morrow? The Indian intellectual of to-day perceives the relative nature of that which appears as truth to the masses of his less highly developed fellow-countrymen. I asked a cultured Hindu gentleman at Puri what he saw in the swinging of Krishna and the squirting of red liquid at the Holi festival which I have described. His reply was both interesting and instructive. For him the forward and backward motion of the swing stood for the life-giving action of the systole and diastole of the heart, and was emblematic of the function of the Deity as Preserver of mankind. In the squirting of the red liquid he saw the offering of one's life-blood to God. Similarly there is the authority of Mr. Havell for the statement that while the lingam of Shiva is undoubtedly a phallic emblem in the eyes of the masses, "to the cultured Hindu it is only suggestive of the philosophic concept that God is a point, formless, or that He is the One."[1]

There is no more marked characteristic of the cultured Hindu than that of idealising the formalism of popular Hinduism, of seeing in the stories around which have sprung up the manifold modes of popular worship great spiritual truths clothed in a form suitable to the understanding of the people to whom they were first presented. No legend has excited greater discussion than that of the early days of the life of Krishna, when he is represented as playing with the gopis[2] in the meadows of Brindaban, out of which arose the story of the love of Radha, the daughter of a king, already given in lawful wedlock to a husband of suitable standing, for Krishna. The story is a simple one of love at first sight. Shown a picture of Krishna by one of her attendants, Radha felt a strange emotion and experienced an overpowering desire to see the original. The sight of him was in due course vouchsafed to her, standing with his flute in the shade of a kadamba tree. Meetings follow, and the emotions of the lovers form the subject of a considerable literature. The story makes an immense appeal to the cultured Vaishnava even to-day. I have in my possession a painting by one of the most inspired of the younger generation of Indian artists—himself a devout Vaishnava—representing Radha, disconsolate, caressing the trunk of the kadamba tree. The picture is full of pathos; one sees written on her features and in her gesture a great yearning after that for the attainment of which she would

[1] "The Ideals of Indian Art," by E. B. Havell.

[2] Gopis = milkmaids. See forward the quotation from Dr. Coomaraswamy's "Sahaja."

sacrifice all else. And this, indeed, is the meaning which the cultured Vaishnava of to-day reads into this centuries-old story. He sees in it a representation in terms of emotion of the agelong ideal of India, that of renunciation, presented so often in India in other terms—those of asceticism. " A person who yearns for God shall not care for home, for fame, or for any earthly consideration; he must renounce all. This idea is best expressed by the allegory of Radha and Krishna; for a woman, peculiarly situated as she is in Hindu society, cannot contract love with a stranger without risking all that is near and dear to her. The spirit of martyrdom in this love is kindred to that for which the soul of a true devotee is always ready." [1] Or, as another writer has put it, " Because the stages of human love reflect the stations of spiritual evolution, it is said that the relationship of hero and heroine reveals an esoteric meaning, and this truth has been made the basis of the well-known allegories of Radha and Krishna, which are the dominant motif of mediaeval Hinduism. Here, illicit love becomes the very type of salvation; for in India, where social convention is so strict, such a love involves the surrender of all that the world values, and sometimes of life itself. . . . All this is an allegory—the reflection of reality in the mirror of illusion. This reality is the inner life, where Krishna is the Lord, the milkmaids are the souls of men, and Brindaban the field of consciousness. The relation of the milkmaids with the Divine Herdsman is not in any sense a model intended to be realised in human relationships, and the literature contains explicit warnings against any such confusion of planes." [2]

[1] Rai Bahadur Dinesh Chandra Sen in his " History of Bengali Language and Literature."

[2] Dr. Ananda Coomaraswamy in an essay entitled " Sahaja," published with others in a volume " The Dance of Siva."

Innumerable examples of this widespread and strongly-marked tendency could be given did space permit. The evolution of the idea of Shiva as Nataraja, "Lord of Dancers," may be taken as a further illustration. In Chapter II. I have referred to the sculpture of Shiva engaged in a cosmic dance which is to be seen in the Caves of Elephanta, and I have mentioned the bronze images of southern India which embody the same idea. I have a beautiful specimen of a bronze Shiva Nataraja, made by a temple image-maker of southern India of the present day, a remarkable suggestion in metal of boundless energy displaying itself in rhythmical and tireless motion. The sculptures at Elephanta, Ellora, and Bhubaneswar are said to represent a dance of Shiva called Tandava, performed in cemeteries and burning-grounds. It is said by Dr. Coomaraswamy to have its origin in the revels of a pre-Aryan divinity, half-god, half-demon, who made of the burning-ground a theatre for his wild performances. And the same writer points to the meaning to be read into this dance of Shiva. The burning-ground is the human heart into which Shiva has entered; a burning-ground indeed, though not of the body, but of that which separates man from God—the illusion produced by false knowledge, the illusion, that is, which is this world and all that appertains thereto. And he quotes a Bengali poem addressed to Shiva in his aspect of the Great Mother of the universe, in which he is known as Kali:

> Because Thou lovest the Burning-ground,
> I have made a Burning-ground of my heart—
> That Thou, Dark One, haunter of the Burning-ground,
> Mayest dance Thy eternal dance.
> Nought else is within my heart, O Mother:
> Day and Night blazes the funeral pyre:
> The ashes of the dead strewn all about,
> I have preserved against Thy coming.

To the metaphysically-minded the bronze Nataraja conveys another idea contained in the Vedanta philosophy. A system which conceives of all ultimate reality as that which is above and beyond all attributes cannot attribute the creation to God's desire; for desire postulates a want, and the God of the Vedanta is *ex hypothesi* lacking in nothing. The universe, therefore, is God's *līla*, a word which is usually translated *play*; the inference to be drawn from this description being that the phenomenal universe and all that there is in it is of God's Nature, being the product neither of His necessity nor of His desire. Of this difficult subject, more elsewhere. To a person steeped in the philosophy of the Vedanta the Nataraja stands for this idea of spontaneous energy which is the cause of the universe as we know it. The idea conveyed to such an one by these striking and beautiful images is that of primal energy employed of no necessity and for no purpose, but providing incidentally the basis of all human existence. Without a considerable measure of familiarity with the main concepts of the monistic philosophy of the Vedanta it is difficult to grasp the ideas contained in such words as *līla*; it is still more difficult to give intelligible expression to them. My object here is not to attempt to do so, but merely to illustrate the facility with which the cultured Hindu perceives the process of evolution at work in the realms of thought. And no more striking example, surely, could be found than his perception, in that which has its origin in the corybantic revels of a primitive deity, of an emblem of the most abstruse conceptions of which the human mind has hitherto proved capable.

It will help, perhaps, towards an understanding of this attitude of the cultured Hindu towards the evolution of religion if I quote the words of an English scientist which contain views corresponding closely with those of the Vedantist. For when Professor Benjamin Moore wrote that the progress of science "added a new beauty to religion, or rather revealed a beauty that was there all the while, but concealed by misconception or lack of knowledge," he was, albeit quite unconsciously in all probability, stating the position of the Vedantist; and when adding that "the eternal truths of science and religion were the same one hundred years ago as they are today, and as they will be a hundred years hence," and that "it is our knowledge and powers of conception that have changed and not the eternal verities,"[1] he is—equally unconsciously, no doubt—drawing a picture of the *maya* used in the sense of *avidya* (ignorance) of the followers of Sankara.

[1] "Origin and Nature of Life," by B. Moore, D.Sc., F.R.S.

CHAPTER XXII

PESSIMISM AND ITS CAUSES

The Physical Cause

IN the first chapter of this volume I have said something about generalisations—of the caution with which, in the case of so vast and varied a land as India, they should be made; of the fact, nevertheless, that the observer finds himself forming certain conclusions which seem to possess general applicability. A generalisation which has often been made is that a certain submissive sadness is characteristic of the people of India. One often hears the joyousness of the Burmese contrasted with the taciturnity of the Indian; and if one travels from the plains of India to the hills—at any rate those parts of the hills peopled by men of Mongol stock—one cannot fail to notice amongst the people of the latter a cheerful vivacity which one does not recall amongst the inhabitants of the former. Writers upon India whose works are world-famed have given expression to this generalisation—Sir Edwin Arnold, for example, in the oft-quoted lines:

> The East bowed low before the blast in patient, deep disdain;
> It let the legions thunder past, then turned to thought again.

If one searches for causes one has little difficulty in discovering them—physical causes, which are always the first to catch the eye, since they lie upon the surface; and, later, causes of a more subtle kind, which are not so easily perceived because they are internal rather than external—things not of the body but of the mind. First, then, as to the former.

In many parts of India, especially those afflicted with the damp and heat-laden atmosphere of the tropics, the lassitude due to climatic enervation is evident enough. It is equally apparent that man's physical organism in its relaxed condition falls an easy prey to disease. Bubonic plague, which made its appearance in Bombay in 1896, has been responsible for a prodigious mortality, over 10,500,000 deaths having actually been recorded from this cause in something less than a quarter of a century after it first made its appearance. The great influenza epidemic which swept across the continent in 1918 carried off at least 7,000,000 persons.

Another form of disease to which peoples inhabitating lands situated in tropical and semi-tropical zones seem to be peculiarly liable, but which remained for long undetected, has recently been shown to be almost incredibly widespread. Mention of a disease known to the medical profession as ankylostomiasis was made at the first Indian Medical Congress held in Calcutta in 1894. Its symptoms were said to take the form of dyspepsia and anaemia, accompanied by chronic apathy and a general lowering of the vitality; its cause, the presence in the human intestine of a parasite about half an inch in length, commonly known as hook-worm. Sporadic investigation suggested that it was widely prevalent in India. An examination of the inmates of the jails in Darbhanga by Colonel Calvert a few years later gave startling results, the presence of the parasite being detected in no less than 83 per cent of those examined. An examination of 600 coolies engaged on the tea gardens of Assam made by

Dr. Bentley in 1904 proved to be still more alarming, only one of the whole number being free from contamination. Some years later an investigation on a much larger scale carried out among the labourers on the tea gardens in the district of Darjeeling by Colonel Clayton Lane drove him to the amazing conclusion that there were large areas where the extent of the infection must amount to at least 80 per cent. This pessimistic conclusion unhappily found support in the result of a systematic examination of the jail population throughout Bengal in 1917, which showed that more than 71 per cent of 12,570 persons examined was infected. Here then was a sufficiently potent cause of pessimism; yet the hook-worm is but one of the sinister performers in the grim tragedy of endemic disease played out upon a stage upon which no curtain ever falls. An even more malignant figure in the remorseless dance of death is the parasite discovered by Professor Laveran in 1880, and conveyed to man—as was proved by the patient and brilliant work of Sir Ronald Ross brought to a conclusion in 1897–98—by the female of the *Anopheles* mosquito.

A perusal of the vital statistics of British India in recent years shows that of a normal annual death-rate of from 7,000,000 to 7,500,000, from 4,000,000 to 4,500,000 are attributed to fever. How great a proportion of this latter figure should be assigned to malarial fever in particular it is difficult to say. But recent estimates of the extent of the ravages of the malarial parasite in Bengal, arrived at after much painstaking work by the Director of Public Health, Dr. Bentley, discloses a state of affairs before which one stands appalled. Every year there occur in the Presidency from 350,000 to 400,000 deaths from this cause alone. But a mere enumeration of the deaths gives only a faint idea of the evil wrought by the disease. It is probable that at least a hundred attacks of malarial fever occur for every death for which it is responsible, and it is estimated that this disease alone is accountable for 200,000,000 days of sickness in the Presidency every year. This gives some idea of the damage done, from a purely economic point of view. Its leprous touch may also be traced in a diminution of the birth-rate as well as in an increase in the death-rate, for in the worst malarial districts the population shows a serious decline. The tragic meaning of such statistics is summed up in the Bengal Census Report of 1911 in a few sentences, whose brevity detracts in no way from their impressiveness: "Year by year fever is silently at work. Plague slays its thousands, fever its ten thousands. Not only does it diminish the population by death, but it reduces the vitality of the survivors, saps their vigour and fecundity, and either interrupts the even tenor or hinders the development of commerce and industry. A leading cause of poverty —and of many other disagreeables in a great part of Bengal—is the presence of malaria. For a physical explanation of the Bengali lack of energy, malaria would count high."

I believe this to be an accurate picture. I am of course aware of the caution with which statistics, and particularly vital statistics, must be accepted in India, on account of the unreliability of the reporting agency. The village watchman, who is charged with the duty of reporting such occurrences as births and deaths, is by temperament unappreciative of the value of accuracy in such matters. In a small town in Bengal an enterprising inspector who went from house to house to verify the returns made in his area found that out of twenty deaths ascribed to fever three only were actually due to malaria.

Of the others, two had not, in fact, died at all, one had died of convulsions, one of dropsy, one of bronchitis, and the remainder from various causes, including old age. Another investigation carried out by an officer of the Indian Medical Service showed that one reported death from fever was, in fact, a birth (registered as a death by mistake), four others were still-births, five others were due to dropsy, two to carbuncle, two to old age, and one to burning. No wonder that in a recent report the Director of Public Health observed that "in Bengal the record of deaths is not complete, neither is the statement of cause accurate," or that it should be on record that "the term *fever* commonly used in the official returns is really of little greater value as affording an idea of the actual cause of death than the heading 'other causes.'" But such statistics as I have given represent the considered conclusion of the best expert opinion after allowance for all possible inaccuracies has been made.

So much for the disease in its endemic form, in which it gnaws ceaselessly and unrelentingly into the vitality of the people. But it also sweeps down in sudden savage fury in epidemic form, and marks its visitation with a virulence more dramatic and more immediately fatal by far than the steady persistence which characterises it in its endemic form. Here is a description by Dr. Bentley of a visit which he paid to a village in Faridpur on the occasion of an outbreak in epidemic form in the autumn of 1912. "In many cases," he wrote, "every member of a household was prostrated at the same time, and in other cases perhaps one member had escaped. . . . Systematic investigatory work was difficult, owing to the scores of people who besieged the camp seeking treatment. In a comparatively short time over 30,000 quinine tablets were distributed.

The mortality was considerable. In one case a whole family had died. Another family of eleven lost seven members in two months. A remarkable feature was the hopeless attitude of the people, who appeared cowed, not so much by the acuteness of the fever as by the succession of the relapses." Grim tragedies such as these may well breed a brooding melancholy amongst those in whose midst they are constantly enacted.

This brief picture of the fierce and unceasing warfare waged by disease against the people of India points clearly enough to the physical source of Indian pessimism. There remains that more subtle source of which I have spoken—the mental attitude of Hinduism towards human existence and the problems arising therefrom. But before touching upon this I am tempted to inquire whether this remorseless enemy may not be successfully fought—whether in the scientific knowledge which is in special degree the property of the peoples of the West we do not possess a golden gift which we can offer to the peoples of the East. In these days, when there is a disposition in some quarters in India to decry the civilisation of Europe as a thing accursed,[1] such questions demand an answer.

The discoveries of Professor Laveran and Sir Ronald Ross have at least made plain what has to be done if malaria is to be driven from the land. They have disclosed the cause of the disease and the manner of its propagation. They

[1] European medicine has been singled out for special attack by Mr. Gandhi, the dominant figure among Indian Nationalists from the early months of 1919 until his arrest and conviction of sedition in March 1922. In a small volume entitled "Indian Home Rule," a second edition of which was issued with Mr. Gandhi's approval in May 1919, he wrote of hospitals that they were "institutions for propagating sin," and of the medical profession that, far from being of real service to humanity, it was "injurious to mankind." The whole volume well repays perusal, for it contains the key to Mr. Gandhi's attitude towards the West, which to many has proved so profound a puzzle.

have swept away the erroneous beliefs upon which, until less than half a century ago, all previous theories as to the nature and origin of the disease were built up, namely, that it was caused, as its name implies, by bad air. When we know, as we now do, that the cause of the disease is not the inhalation of bad air but the introduction into the blood of a minute unicellular animal parasite, and that this introduction is effected solely by the bite of the *Anopheles* mosquito, we perceive with certainty what it is that we have to do to extirpate the disease. We have to get rid of the *Anopheles* mosquito. It is, however, one thing to know what has to be done, but quite another thing to know whether it can be done. The destruction of an insect so widespread and so prolific as the mosquito is clearly a formidable task, and one which is only likely to be accomplished if it is found possible to bring about conditions which are unfavourable to its breeding. The fundamental question, then, resolves itself into this—can an environment in which the mosquito now multiplies freely be so changed as to render it unsuitable to continued breeding? The answer to that question is of momentous import to the Indian people.

The mosquito breeds in water, and in particular in small pools of stagnant water; and in a country which is naturally dry, but which experiences seasonal inundations, such as the Punjab, for example, the obvious thing to do is to drain the country so that, as the water brought by the monsoon subsides, it does not leave behind it stagnant pools as breeding places. Ismalia provides an admirable example of the efficacy of this method where conditions admit of its employment. In 1891 malarial fever in the town was acute, 2500 cases being reported. In 1902 effective measures were taken to dry up the town, and by 1906 the disease had disappeared, no case having been reported since then.

In a country which is naturally a wet country, like Bengal, this method is obviously out of the question. In some of the low-lying lands of Eastern Bengal the amount of water even in the dry season is phenomenal. In the district of Bakerganj, for example, with a total area of 4890 square miles, there are 1400 square miles of water; and a picture of the country during the monsoon has been given in Chapter XII. As well try to dry up the ocean as to dry up Bengal. The problem is further complicated by the fact that there are three varieties of *Anopheles* in Bengal, each of which is a carrier of malaria and each of which breeds under dissimilar conditions. Thus the *Anopheles Listoni* breeds in running water, such as small streams, and is found in the Duars. Another variety, known as *Anopheles culicifacies*, breeds in water having a mild current, and is found in undulating country; while the third variety, namely, the *Anopheles fuliginosus*, breeds in stagnant water and is common throughout the deltaic tracts of the Presidency. Experiments for destroying the first two varieties have been in progress for some years; but since the *Anopheles fuliginosus* is by far the most widespread, I shall confine myself here to the measures required in a war of extermination against this particular variety.

A study of observations made in different ages in many different countries results in a conclusion which at first sight reads like a paradox, namely, that in wet countries malarial fever diminishes with an increase in the quantity of water upon the land. This has been the experience in the case of all the chief malarious regions of the world which are subject to periodical inundation, such, for example, as the lands within the flood zone of great rivers like the Nile, the Indus, the Euphrates, the Ganges, the Niger, and the Mississippi. A striking example is provided by Holland, where in the year 1748 the Dutch defended their land against attack by letting in the water. After the conclusion of peace the water was removed and there followed a serious outbreak of malaria. Not until the land was again submerged was the outbreak checked. It is only in recent years that, following upon the discoveries of Sir Ronald Ross, an explanation of this widely observed phenomenon has been forthcoming.

Experiments carried out by Captains Hodgson and King of the Indian Medical Service, and described by them at the Lucknow Sanitary Conference in 1914, showed that the larvae of mosquitoes flourished in water of certain temperatures only; that as the temperature of the water rose above 80° F. the larvae suffered until at 95° and upwards it rapidly ceased to exist. Their observations showed something more, namely, that owing to rapid evaporation small pools of water remained much cooler than large expanses, a notable case in point being that of small hoof-marks in grass, where the water was nine degrees cooler than that in a large pool close by. Here then was an explanation of a phenomenon already widely observed, and a key to the problem of what was to be done. If conditions are such that you cannot get rid of the water, the alternative is to alter its character; that is to say, to convert the numberless small shallow pools with a maximum of edge and a comparatively low temperature, which form with the rise of the flood level at the beginning and its fall at the end of the rainy season, into large expanses of water with a minimum of edge and a higher temperature. This can only be done with the assistance of the irrigation engineer, whose aim must be to cover the land with carefully devised systems of embankments and sluices, by means of which he can hold up the water upon the surface of the country at convenient levels during the wet season, and flush the land clean with the approach of the dry months. By a fortunate dispensation of Providence the staple crops of Bengal—jute and rice—are crops which grow in standing water, so that if the inflow and the efflux of the water be regulated scientifically it should be possible not only to destroy the mosquito larvae and maintain a level of water suitable for the production of good crops, but actually to improve the fertility of the land by compelling the inflowing water to deposit its silt upon the fields.

It was before the experiment of Captains Hodgson and King provided an explanation of the disappearance of malaria as a result of the submersion of the land, and primarily with the object of protecting the crops from unregulated floods, that a scheme of this kind was carried out in Bengal in the neighbourhood of the Hughli river at Diamond Harbour, which provides a valuable object-lesson. The conditions of the country which called for treatment were described by an engineer, Mr. Whitfield, as follows: "For want of drainage and protection the production of the locality is only a fraction of what it should be"; and he added incidentally, "Fever is constantly present in every village." For long, however, Mr. Whitfield's was the voice of one crying in the wilderness, and it was not until the intervention of a devastating calamity of the kind referred to in certain legal documents as "the act of God" that action on comprehensive lines was taken. In September in the year 1900 the heavens were opened and the rains descended upon the earth much as they must have done in the days of Noah. Sixteen inches were measured at Diamond Harbour in twenty-four hours, and in all 39 inches fell in seven days. Not only the crops but the village sites were totally submerged; so that where there had been dry land and happy villages there was to be seen nothing but a bleak wilderness of water.

The reclaiming of this watery waste provides one of the many romances of which the annals of the irrigation engineer are full. Let me recite the bald facts and then relate briefly the story of construction as it was told to me while I stood on the great cross dam at Diamond Harbour, which with its sluice-gates regulates the level of the water over 283 square miles of fertile land and wards off the influx of the destructive saline water which sweeps up the Hughli on the tides. The first sod of the drainage works was cut in November 1904. In June 1909 the Diamond Harbour sluice was opened for drainage and the whole area cropped for the first time. The capital cost amounted to £137,000. A fair proportion of this sum found its way into the pockets of the people of the locality themselves, for the majority of the 5000 hands employed upon the work of construction was recruited from the villages within the area affected. And seldom, surely, can money have given a better return; for while the people benefited were called upon to pay a modest sum of ninepence per acre for a period of thirty years, they obtained in return enormously improved health, excellent communications in the shape of a number of navigable channels, and an increased return from their crops estimated at no less than £310,000 a year. In face of these figures a capital expenditure of £137,000 appears paltry.

From the dam and sluice-gates at Diamond

Harbour I looked back over a limitless expanse of gently-waving rice, whose vivid green paled off in a light haze where it cut the horizon. The whole world was filled with colour—blue and green, blended into perfect harmony by the all-pervading sun. And I should have been of a singular disposition indeed if I had not been affected by the enthusiasm of the engineer at my side as he told the story of the building of the sluice and the dam on which we stood. Work had not progressed far when the top stratum of blue clay at the site selected for the sluice-gate was discovered to be inconveniently shallow. Worse still, it rested upon a quicksand which, when uncovered, seethed and bubbled like the murky matter in the pit of a live volcano—a lid upon a boiling cauldron. A complete revision of plans became necessary. Open foundations were no longer practicable, and 164 masonry wells had to be sunk as a foundation for the superstructure. The work was long and laborious, but by the end of 1908 was sufficiently far advanced to justify the engineers in closing the Diamond Harbour creek alongside of the sluice-gate, an operation which involved the construction of a dam 450 feet long and the movement of 6,000,000 cubic feet of earth. The season available for the work was a short one; but preliminary work had been completed during the previous three years, and in January 1909 the first attempt to close the creek was made. It was a fight against time and tides. The first attempt failed. A second attempt, made a fortnight later, came within measurable distance of success. A dam was actually constructed from bank to bank, but breached on the very day of completion. The third attempt was made in the middle of February. An army of coolies worked day and night, and as the river rose with the rising tides, 3000 men kept a ceaseless flow of earth pouring on to the dam as it gradually settled under pressure of the battling waters. For six days they held the waters—right up, in fact, to the night of the highest spring tide, when one supreme effort was required to hold the work against the final onslaught of the river. Darkness descended upon a scene of restless struggle. The tide rose inexorably, biting into the dam with ever-increasing pressure, while a groaning and perspiring army strove with taut sinews against it. Slowly but surely the earthwork settled until the waves washed the top. It was within a quarter of an hour of midnight when the supervising engineers were called hurriedly away to deal with a leak at one end of the rampart. Success and failure hung evenly in the balance. Another fifteen minutes of breathless labour along the length of the dam to keep up the height as the earth settled, and victory was sure. But it was precisely the strain of the final fifteen minutes that proved too great. With the hurried departure of the supervising engineers to meet the menace of the leak, and the consequent removal of their compelling presence from the direct control of the main working party, the determination of the exhausted coolies wavered. As their courage ebbed their movements slowed down, and finally ceased. A huge tidal-wave, sweeping up the stream, topped the embankment, and, to quote the words of the narrator of the desperate story, " In two minutes twenty thousand rupees' worth of embankment was racing down the river."

The fourth attempt, made during the following month, was crowned with success. Some idea of the nicety of the calculations necessary in the planning of works of this kind in the flat, alluvial stretches of Bengal may be gained from a study of this, the Magra Hāt drainage scheme. The water from the whole area concerned had to be drained into the Hughli river. But the slope of the land was not towards, but away from the river; and drainage had consequently to be to a central basin, whence it was trained *back*, along a specially constructed channel with a slope of only 4 inches in the mile, to the great sluice-gate with its thirty vents, the building of which has been described.

The Magra Hāt drainage project was devised, as has been mentioned, for the protection and improvement of crops. It resulted not only in a tremendous increase in the agricultural value of the land affected, but in a vast improvement in the health of the people. Schemes on similar lines have been undertaken since, and many more have been planned and await only the provision of the necessary engineering staff and funds, in the shape of capital outlay, before being undertaken. They are devised now primarily with the object of ridding the land of disease, though, with the object-lesson of Magra Hāt available, the improvement of agriculture is kept in view as a parallel objective.

Many years must necessarily elapse before any very great impression can be made upon the *Anopheles* mosquito by means such as these. And in the meantime effort must be concentrated upon the alleviation of the fever by the widespread distribution of quinine. It is curious that though the value of the bark of the cinchona tree as a cure for malarial fever was discovered nearly three hundred years ago—it obtained its name from the Condesa del Cinchon, wife of the Spanish Viceroy of Peru, who was cured of fever by it in 1638—it has only been widely administered in India in comparatively recent years. At one time its price was prohibitive. It is said, for example, that King Louis XIV. of France, who was cured with quinine by Sir Robert Talbot in

1679, purchased the secret of the cure for £48,000, and a pension of £2000 a year.[1] The modest price of the drug in India to-day is due to the action of the Government of India in cultivating the tree in different parts of the country. Tucked away on the hill slopes above the valley of the Tista river, where it flows through the district of Darjeeling, may be seen carefully tended plantations of the shrub. The journey to that above the right bank of the river at Mungpo may be made from Darjeeling on foot or on a hill pony, the track leading through magnificent forest containing fine specimens of cryptomerias, tree-ferns, bamboos, and sago palms, amongst many other varieties, and displaying not a few specimens of the pothos, a giant-leaved creeper, which winds itself round the trunks of trees and eventually strangles them. The cinchona trees are planted in rows, 1700 to the acre, on the hillside 4000 feet above sea-level. At the age of ten the trees are uprooted, and bark and root treated at the factory, where from 40,000 to 50,000 lb. of quinine are produced each year. Across the valley, high up above the left bank of the river at Munsong, a further 2000 acres have been planted, with approximately 3,500,000 trees. Other plantations are to be found in Madras and in Ceylon, and a project for the cultivation of the tree on a large scale amongst the hills in Burma, which has for some time been under consideration, has been begun.

[1] For this story and for most of the facts about malaria and its cause I am indebted to the painstaking research of Dr. Bentley.

CHAPTER XXIII

PESSIMISM AND ITS CAUSES

The Intellectual Cause

ONE obtains one's first clue to the more subtle cause of Indian pessimism by observing the leisurely habits of the people. One sees around one an immense stock of patience, and on all sides a contemptuous disregard for time. There is no need to enlarge upon this latter characteristic in its ordinary manifestations. The daily inconveniences arising out of it are in themselves more than sufficient to ensure its being kept constantly in mind. But it is worth noting in passing that the complete indifference to time exhibited by the Indian mind is more far-reaching in its consequences than is at first apparent. It carries with it an equally complete indifference to order in the sequence of events. Before the advent of Western education the average Indian was constitutionally incapable of appreciating the meaning of the word chronology. European writers of history, with their passion for precision in such matters, have found themselves baffled over and over again by this trait when endeavouring to assign dates in the story of India. The sort of attitude of mind towards chronology, for which it is responsible, is well illustrated by the following dialogue which took place between an inspector of schools and an Indian school-teacher :

Inspector : "Can you tell me the date of the arrival of Alexander in India ?"

Teacher : "Three hundred and thirty-two B.C."

Inspector : "And the date of Muhammad ?"

Teacher : "The Hegira, Sir, A.D. 618."

Inspector : "What was the religion of Alexander ?"

Teacher: "A follower of the Prophet" (*i.e.* a Muhammadan).

Comment is superfluous.

Patience is of two kinds. In its more ordinary form it is little more than another name for indifference to time. The traveller may notice an example of it at almost any railway station of importance. At any hour of the day or night he may observe groups of blanketed figures squatting on the ground in some portion of the station precincts, which serves the purpose of a third-class waiting-room. These are folk who purpose taking a journey, but to whom the idea of first ascertaining the time of departure of their train does not occur. They arrive at the station when it suits them, and they are perfectly content to spend a day or a night, or a day and a night on the platform, pending the arrival of their train.

This kind of patience, which I may perhaps style common patience, if traced to its root causes, would probably be found to be due to a great extent to inertia resulting from the influence of climate.

But there is another form of patience which is due far more to certain fundamental beliefs and tenets governing the Hindu's outlook upon life—a form of patience which amounts to an almost complete indifference to all external phenomena whatever. The observant traveller will discover that patience of this kind is an immemorial possession of the Indian peoples, for he will find it embodied in wood and stone, notably in the images of Buddha, both ancient and modern, whose attitude and expression—however crude their execution—never fail to convey a suggestion of extreme other-worldliness and indestructible repose. He will find it even more strikingly exhibited in the living disciples, not of Buddha only, but of all the great Indian thinkers of the past who have preached the gospel of renunciation. Asceticism always has been, and still is, practised widely throughout the continent. In particular, it is the ostentatious profession of the vast army of religious mendicants, officially estimated at 700,000, who wander homeless over the land. At any moment, and in any part of India, the curiosity of the visitor may be excited by the novel spectacle presented by the strange figure of some itinerant member of one or other of the many orders of Indian ascetics. With staff and begging-bowl he haunts the great religious fairs, and is to be seen living a life of studied inaction in the neighbourhood of all the more famous Hindu temples and places of pilgrimage.

I first encountered one of these folk in the neighbourhood of Lake Pushka in Rajputana, within a few days of my first landing in India. The spectacle he presented did not seem to me to be an edifying one. His entire clothing consisted of a microscopic loin cloth. His limbs were shrunken and his body emaciated; and the general uncouthness of his appearance was heightened by the grey pallor of his skin, caused by the coating of wood ash with which he had freely smeared himself. He was pointed out to me as a *sadhu* or "holy man of dubious morals, who lived on charity at the expense of an easy-going public." I was perfectly content at that time to accept this estimate of his character and mode of life. Later on, I began to take an interest in these folk. After all they were some-

Plate 23.

A RELIGIOUS MENDICANT.

"With staff and begging bowl he haunts the great religious fairs.

thing outside one's experience in Europe, and to brush them aside as common beggars and impostors was, to say the least, unenterprising.

I have since encountered many religious mendicants under different designations—fakir, sadhu, yogi, sannyasi—and I am ready to admit that fraud and immorality are widely practised under cover of holiness, and that the number of educated men now to be found within the ranks of these homeless wanderers is small. Yet to pass an universally unfavourable judgement upon Indian asceticism, because of the delinquencies of many of those who profess it, would be both misleading and unfair. It is far more profitable to make some attempt to understand what it is that lies behind these outward evidences of a practice which is in intention, if not necessarily in fact, highly meritorious; and one's trouble is well repaid, for one discovers in the members of this strange fraternity the outward manifestation of much that is fundamental in the thought and outlook upon life of the peoples of India.

For the origin of asceticism one must peer far back into the dim and shadowy twilight which broods darkly over the thought and doings of the early settlers in the northern plains of the peninsula, long before that which in India passes for history dawned to throw a fitful light upon a venerable civilisation wrapped in obscurity. The existence of a religious order of ascetics is referred to in the Buddhist traditions, themselves dating back some centuries before Christ, "as something of which there is no recollection that it had ever been otherwise."[1] And the religious and epic literature of India shows us that from the earliest times into which we are able to thrust our gaze down to the present day, there have passed in uninterrupted procession across the centuries not

[1] "Buddha," by H. Oldenberg.

merely persons, but communities of persons, who have given up home to become homeless, who have renounced the world and all that appertains to the world, that life in the world for them might cease—finally, irrevocably, eternally. What has been the driving force behind such strange behaviour? It is the answer to that question that we have to seek.

The earliest literature of the race consists of a collection of hymns in honour of the gods, themselves impersonations of the forces of nature. The greatest of the gods was Indra, the god of the sky, the heroic but kindly deity who hurled himself with thunder and lightning against the malevolent spirits entrenched behind their dark fortifications of cloud, and compelled them to release the life-giving waters so that they might descend to earth in rain for the benefit of man. Sacrifices were offered to the gods to appease or please them, and the hymns in their honour were sung at the performance of the sacrifice. For how many generations these hymns were handed down without method or classification, it is impossible to surmise, but a time came, about 1000 B.C. in all probability, when an effort at collection was made and the compilation known as the "Rig Veda" was achieved. These early works are occupied with the ritual of the sacrifice; they contain nothing in the nature of a philosophy which would induce men to renounce the world, and it is probable that austerities were practised in these early days for the same purpose for which sacrifices were offered to the gods, namely, to secure their aid, for it is an ancient and deep-rooted belief in India that spiritual power can be acquired by mortification of the flesh; that the man who practises austerities upon himself can compel the attention of the gods.

But as time went on the simple beliefs which

shine forth in the "Rig Veda" ceased to satisfy. It is easy to believe that the dwellers in the warm plains of the Ganges Valley found themselves amid an environment conducive to speculation. The vast forests which covered the land afforded them protection from sunshine and storm; food and shelter were to be had for the asking; the fierce fight with nature, which consumes the energy of man in less hospitable climes, was absent. And under such circumstances man found both time and opportunity for meditation. And then upon the horizon of his meditative gaze vague questionings took shape. The "how" and the "why" of the universe, the "whence" and the "whither" of man, these were the eternal problems which began to beat at the door of his mind and imperiously to demand admission. Living as he did in close communion with the mysteries of nature by day, and scanning the vast and majestic star-strewn vault of heaven by night, he became consumed with a passionate desire to fathom the meaning of things—of the universe, of human existence, of life and death, of time and space, of right and wrong, of pleasure and pain, of all the multifarious phenomena arising out of human consciousness. Inspiration born of such ponderings soon became clothed in words. To the Vedic hymns were added works of a different kind containing strange and abstruse speculations upon the nature of things to which was given the name *upanishad* or books of secret knowledge.

This remarkable mnemonic literature, which was handed down from generation to generation, constitutes the *fons et origo* of the deep reservoir of mingled religious and metaphysical thought whence the daring systems of Hindu philosophy, which flowed forth freely over the intellectual soil of India during the succeeding centuries, found their source. And permeating the whole, and colouring not only the six orthodox systems of Hindu philosophy based upon the upanishads but the heterodox systems of Buddhism and Jainism as well, is a doctrine which has exercised a profound, a widespread, and an enduring influence upon Indian thought for at least two thousand five hundred years. That doctrine is known as the doctrine of Karma. Its sombre shadow spreads far and wide over the Indian continent, impregnating men's minds with the germs of an enervating fatalism. Proof of the doctrine never seems to have been—and certainly never is—demanded. It is accepted as axiomatic. It dominates Hindu thought and is so universally accepted that it has been held that a belief in it is the sole criterion which need be taken to determine whether a man is a genuine Hindu in the popular acceptation of the term.[1] It is, according to a learned Hindu, "the every-day working belief of every Hindu from the man in the street to the pundit in his study, the sage in his cloister and the recluse in the forest."[2]

And this all-pervading doctrine, which finds no place in the early Vedic hymns, but which was boded forth in the upanishads, gave a new impetus to, and provided a rational basis for, asceticism. A belief in reincarnation was a necessary corollary of a belief in the doctrine of Karma, and herein are to be found the roots of that more subtle form of Indian pessimism of which I have spoken. Let the Hindu speak for himself. "That our present life is a thing to be avoided and that release from this round of births and rebirths in lower and higher orders of being is to be sought after, is what lies at the root of all that renunciation, all that self-denial,

[1] In the Census Report for 1911 for example.
[2] Rai Bahadur Lala Baijnath. See "The Essentials of Hinduism."

all that asceticism . . . which plays such an important part in our religion. Every one is anxious to get rid of the present condition of life for a better one hereafter." And he adds that the practical result of this is "a spirit of renunciation, of self-denial, of distaste for the things of this world seldom found in any other people of this world."[1] I once received a startling illustration of the tired pessimism which this belief is apt to induce. I was questioning a young Bengali who was believed to have taken part in the assassination of a police officer. Towards the close of the conversation he brushed his past aside, as it were, with a tired gesture and with the words, "Perhaps in my next incarnation I shall not be born a Bengali." It was the tone of the words as much as the words themselves which was significant, suggesting a complete repudiation of responsibility for his present lot—which was the product of previous karma—and the hopelessness of trying to exercise control over what lay before him.

What, then, is the doctrine and how did it arise? It finds no place, as has been said, in the hymns of the "Rig Veda"; it is not the product of a simple religious faith, but of a fierce intellectual struggle. For it was when the ritual of the sacrifice ceased to satisfy man's intellectual hunger, and in its insufficiency drove him to speculation, that this new idea arose, and having arisen, determined for all time the trend of Indian thought.

[1] Rai Bahadur Lala Baijnath.

CHAPTER XXIV

PESSIMISM AND ITS CAUSES

The Intellectual Cause (*continued*)

It is easy enough to follow the lines of thought along which the early philosophers of the upanishads travelled. All round them men saw inequality and suffering. Whence came this inequality and this suffering? That section which predicated a Creator of the universe—necessarily Almighty and presumably All-merciful—could not attribute them to him. What, then, was the solution of this perplexing riddle? The reply of the philosophers of the upanishads was unanimous—to the deeds of men themselves; a reply equally well suited to those schools of thought—the majority—which dispensed with a Creator altogether. And having arrived at this conclusion, they did not hesitate to face the full and, as will be seen, momentous consequences of their belief, namely, that every action good or bad meets automatically with a recompense that is inexorably just; that this recompense in its turn involves the individual in further action (karma) which again calls forth in due time its necessary recompense. The doctrine of transmigration or rebirth was of course a necessary corollary, for since men died and the automatic sequence—action and reaction—went on, they must be born again.

That the recompense of men's deeds should

necessarily involve them in further activity is not perhaps, at first sight, apparent. Why, one is inclined to ask, should not the recompense—whether reward or retribution—balance precisely the account, completing the transaction and leaving nothing over? But a little thought shows that this cannot be. For if this were so, whence arose the deeds which called forth the punishment or the reward? They must have had some cause, and no cause could be found except still earlier deeds; and so on *ad infinitum*. And if this reasoning held good in respect of the past, it must equally hold good in respect of the future, for the future of to-day is the past of to-morrow. This may be tested by a concrete example. I was once discussing the question of karma with a Buddhist monk. He referred to the duties devolving upon me by virtue of the office which I held. He did not consider it necessary to discuss the causes which had led to my holding the office. From his point of view no such discussion was necessary: my tenure of office was the fruit of past action—a fruit, he intimated with fine courtesy, bearing witness to the meritorious nature of my previous activity. But it must be obvious—this was not said in so many words, but was implied—that the reward which I was enjoying now was not an actionless passivity. Far from it. Could I think a thought, or say a word, or do a deed which would not sooner or later be followed by some effect—not necessarily in the world of affairs, but inevitably upon the credit or debit side of my own moral ledger? The theory, in short, may be said to be the equivalent in the domain of morals of the modern theory of the conservation of energy in the physical sphere.

And when one considers the doctrine in all its implications, one realises in what a terrible and remorseless net those who held it found themselves enmeshed. For if the doctrine were indeed true, human existence must be eternal. There could apparently be no escape. Man was constrained by inexorable fate to pass through a never-ending succession of births and deaths, fulfilling the effects of former causes and simultaneously creating new causes which must lead to subsequent effects. He was the impotent victim of an inflexible and automatic system. "As soon as the clock of retribution ran down," in the words of a distinguished scholar, "it wound itself up again."[1] There could be no real evolution, merely repetition. Good deeds might meet with a relatively desirable reward, certainly. A man whose actions had been highly meritorious might for a time be reborn a god. Yet would he not have freed himself from the eternal cycle of existence, for gods, like men, are bound by the iron law of karma. Indeed, according to the teaching of one system—that of the Jains—a god cannot attain *siddhahood*, the Jain equivalent of *nirvāna*, without first being reborn a man.[2]

The prospect of this eternity of repetition was sufficiently appalling. Life was not so joyous a thing that its extension to infinity could be regarded with composure. Moreover, Indian imagination, conscious perhaps of the comparative meaninglessness of the picture conjured up by the word "eternal," was not slow to invent aids to the mind towards grasping something of its overwhelming significance. At the end of vast aeons of time (*kalpa*), it was asserted, the universe fell into a state of dissolution. One would have thought that this comparatively happy solution

[1] Professor Deussen.

[2] To speak of *siddhahood* or *nirvāna* at this stage is to anticipate, since to do so is to assume a way of escape from a succession of existences which has been described as eternal. It is necessary to anticipate further, therefore, by saying that the object of the Indian systems of philosophy is to find a way of escape, and that in this they claim to have been successful.

of so perplexing a problem as that of existence having been achieved, speculation might have ceased and the troubled soul of man been allowed at last to share annihilation in this cosmic cataclysm. But the Indian metaphysician refused to allow himself to be beguiled by even so alluring a prospect as this, from the path which the inflexible logic of his mind compelled him to pursue. The universe might fall asunder and vanish as completely as mist before the morning sun, but there would still be a vast stock of unrequited action which not even the dissolution of the universe itself was able to destroy. So the disappearance of the heavens above and the earth beneath was only temporary, and the cataclysm having been achieved, there issued from Brahman[1]—the one eternal and absolute reality—a remanifestation of the universe. Matter reappeared, the worlds renewed their interrupted race through space, souls were re-embodied, and the recurring cycle of human birth and death proceeded as before, until at the termination of further aeons dissolution again took place. Thus with a sort of morbid satisfaction did the metaphysicians set up inexorable milestones along the unalterable path of eternity.

This attempt at a reconciliation between the two apparently antagonistic conceptions denoted by the words "time" and "eternity" is encountered in slightly different forms in the various schools of thought which have become entangled in the maze of karma. A favourite illustration of the nature of time is that of a wheel revolving eternally, the upward motion representing the evolution of all things, and the downward the corresponding involution which sets in when the evolutionary process has reached its limit. Each process is divided into periods. The first

[1] Not to be confused with the same word denoting the priestly caste.

period of the involutionary process, which is now in full swing, lasted according to Jain chronology for four crores (40,000,000) of crores (10,000,000) of *sāgaropama*. The *sāgaropama* consists of one hundred millions of *palya* multiplied by one hundred millions, and the *palya* itself consists of countless years.[1] We are apt to think that we are dealing in time on a vast scale when we talk of geologic time. Even the geologist must feel chastened when confronted with this specimen of time chipped off from eternity by the meticulously minded Jain.

But though the Indian thus boldly faced the consequences of the train of thought which he had set in motion, he none the less felt acutely the intolerable nature of the conclusions which he had been compelled to draw. The net result of all his speculation up to this point was only too painfully apparent. Man was caught helplessly "in the teeth of a machine which was unerringly moral, but as rigidly Godless."[2] Was there no way of escape? Henceforth it was upon this all-absorbing problem—how to win emancipation—that men's minds turned with fierce determination. The desperate need acted as a powerful stimulus to thought. Great thinkers arose who declared that they had found the way of release. Buddha was such a one, and his teaching, as we know, is to-day the consolation of millions of the human race. Mahavira, the founder of the Jain religion, was another. Men like these were striking personalities who drank deep from the great well of quickened thought around them, and fashioned from it systems of their own. But from the ferment of ideas which was the common property of the intellectuals of the time, there gradually emerged great systems which could

[1] Mrs. Sinclair Stevenson in "The Heart of Jainism."
[2] J. N. Farquhar in "The Crown of Hinduism."

claim no single individual as their author, but which rather grew spontaneously, to be associated only in later times with the names of men who collected and collated, rather than evolved, the ideas composing them. Thus came into being the Six Systems of Indian philosophy.[1] All these are remarkable productions, bearing unimpeachable testimony to the astonishing heights of thought reached by the Indians of those early days. They contain ideas of great originality, but though they differ in their methods they, no less than the religions of Buddha and Mahavira —if, indeed, the word religion can properly be applied to doctrines which take no cognisance of a deity—owe their existence in the main to a common inspiration—that derived from the rebellion of the human mind against the desolating effects of the law of *karma.*

Since karma, or action, was the cause of all the trouble, the avoidance of action was the most obvious way of escape. But before a way of avoiding action could be discovered, it was necessary to ascertain what it was that impelled men to action at all. An answer to that question became imperative, and the answer that was found was *desire.* Desire sprang up in the heart of man. He took thought how to satisfy his desire, and, having done so, he translated his thought into action. So it was argued. Thus we find it stated in the sacred books that: "Man verily is desire-formed: as is his desire, so is his thought; as is his thought, so he does action; as he does action, so he attains." And again:

[1] The six Vedic systems are:
(i.) The Vedanta or Uttara-Mimamsa set forth in the Sutras of Badarayana.
(ii.) The Purva-Mimamsa of Gaimini.
(iii.) The Samkhya embodied in the Sutras ascribed to Kapila.
(iv.) The Yoga contained in the Sutras of Patangali.
(v.) The Nyaya in the Sutras of Gotama.
(vi.) The Vaiseshika in the Sutras ascribed to Kanada.

"When all the desires hidden in the heart are loosed, then the mortal becomes immortal, then he here enjoyeth Brahman." It is true that the Bhagavad-Gita, from which these quotations are taken, taught that a literal abstention from all activity was not necessary, that action performed simply because duty demanded, and with no other motive, had no power to tie men to earth; but the very fact that the Bhagavad-Gita came into existence to teach this lesson bears witness to the widespread belief in the efficacy of a literal abstention from all activity. This at least seems to me to be the root idea lying at the back of Indian asceticism.

It must not, of course, be assumed that the idea presented itself in a precisely similar form to everybody. If it had done, there would have been one system instead of several, and one order of ascetics in place of many. The danger of generalisation is as great here as in most things Indian. This can be seen from a cursory glance at the distinctive features of the principal schools of thought.

The most literal view of what is meant by abstaining from action is held by the followers of Mahavira. For the Jain ascetic the mere fact of doing is a tie binding the doer to the weary cycle of existence. Thus the parents of Mahavira refrained from eating lest, by the mere action involved in doing so, they should spin the web of karma more closely about them, and died gloriously of starvation. So are there Jains to this day who, when death is seen to be approaching, abstain from food. Not only is a further accumulation of karma thus prevented, but by this austerity karma already in stock, so to speak, is destroyed. For this is one of the outstanding features of the teaching of Mahavira—and one dividing his teaching fundamentally from that of Buddha—that by the fierce fire of self-mortification is karma consumed. Mrs. Sinclair Stevenson records a remarkable case of death by voluntary starvation as occurring at Ahmedabad in 1912, where a sadhu named Chaganalalaji took a vow to fast for the rest of his life, and died at the end of forty-one days. The literal interpretation which the Jains place upon the teaching that the avoidance of action is the way of escape is further illustrated by the practice of the Digambara sect, which requires in the case of its ascetic members a complete abandonment of their possessions, including their clothes. The Digambara, or sky-clothed ascetic, must live stark naked, and by doing so he proves that he has conquered not only the sensations of the flesh, but also the emotions arising therefrom. Bodily indifference to heat and cold renders clothes unnecessary from an utilitarian point of view; absence of all emotion, including shame, renders them unnecessary from other points of view. According to this view he is no true ascetic who has not regained that state of innocence which was the happy lot of our first ancestors, before they ate of the tree of knowledge and knew that they were naked and were ashamed.

These more severe forms of asceticism were condemned by Buddha after he had tried them and found them wanting. The way of life which he taught was a middle way. Those who sought release must find it in the extinction of *desire*. But if *desire* grew and flourished amid worldly surroundings, it was not to be eradicated by the practice of extreme austerities. It was to be killed rather by the gradual realisation on the part of the individual of the impermanence of the world and all that appertained thereto. Such realisation, it was urged, could best be achieved by contemplation amid the peace and quiet of a secluded life. Hence, monasticism became a distinctive feature of the Buddhist way of life.[1]

Nor was an injunction to abstain from action in a literal sense contained in the Vedic philosophies. The main contention running through the six systems is that man is tied to earth by ignorance or false knowledge. Ignorance of what ? Ignorance, according to the Vedanta, of the ultimate truth that the *self* of man is identical with Brahman—the sole and absolute reality lying behind all phenomena. Assuredly ignorance of this stupendous thought was scarcely likely to yield to casual effort. To ponder on—still more to grasp—the conception here set forth might well demand of man a complete renunciation of all ordinary avocations, an uninterrupted course of mental and spiritual concentration, to the exclusion of all else.

The Yoga philosophy, on the other hand, definitely prescribes a system of ascetic discipline for the purpose of obtaining the greatest possible concentration of thought. The Yogi, by constant discipline of his body, aims at the complete subjugation of the senses, so that he becomes indifferent to pain and pleasure, heat and cold, hunger and thirst. Success in this respect is not, however, the object which he has in view, but the means by which the object may be attained. And the object is again the destruction of ignorance. In this case it is ignorance of the difference between the seer and that which is seen, the subject and object, the self and the phenomenal universe.

The Yogis have become famous in popular estimation by reason of the supernatural powers with which they have been credited, and which they are supposed to have acquired as a result

[1] I have dealt with Buddhism at some length elsewhere. See "Lands of the Thunderbolt."

of the complete control which they obtain over the body. Stories of miracles performed by them abound. But it would be a mistake to suppose that the manifestation of supernatural powers was more than incidental to the career of the true Yogi. The sole aim and object of the followers of Patanjali was the severance of the ties which bound the soul to earth, and that severance could only be effected by the acquisition of true knowledge. Such knowledge was accompanied by a complete cessation of desire, and the bonds of karma were thenceforth loosed. " Though, as a rule, whatever a man does has its results, whether good or bad, the act of a Yogi," we are told, " is neither black nor white; it produces no fruit, because it is performed without any desire." [1]

This, the annihilation of *desire*, is the great teaching common to all the religions and all the systems which the intellectual genius of India has given to the world. It is the essence of the wisdom of the East. It is summed up concisely in the words of the Bhagavad-Gita in passages like the following:

> Whose works are all free from the moulding of desire, whose actions are burned up by the fire of wisdom, him the wise have called a sage.
>
> Having abandoned attachment to the fruit of action, always content, nowhere seeking refuge, he is not doing anything although doing actions.
>
> Hoping for naught, his mind and self, controlled, having abandoned all greed, performing action by the body alone, he doth not commit sin.
>
> Of one with attachment dead, harmonious, with his thoughts established in wisdom, his works sacrifices, all action melts away.[2]

It may now be asked: " If life and death, sorrow and joy, tears and laughter, and every-

[1] Max Müller.

[2] From Mrs. A. Besant's translation of the Bhagavad-Gita.

thing else that comes within the compass of human experience, are the fruit of previous actions, how and when did the earliest of these actions or causes arise?" To that question we are vouchsafed no answer. The nearest approach to an answer is to be found in the daring theory propounded by Sankara, the famous commentator on the Vedanta Sutras of Badarayana. His doctrine was an uncompromising monism. There was one absolute reality, and one only—Brahman. All else was unreal. The whole phenomenal universe was maya—illusion—and the conception of the in reality non-existing universe was due to ignorance (avidya). This might be said in a sense to answer the question, since if the world and all that was therein was nothing but a cosmic fantasy—a dream obscuring for an infinitesimal moment the absolute knowledge of Brahman and passing away again with the return of complete knowledge—no first cause would be required. But this in reality does not get over the difficulty, it merely postpones it, for we are still left without an explanation of the origin and cause of the ignorance (avidya) which is responsible for the illusion of the universe. Here we seek in vain for an answer—and when one thinks of it, necessarily so. We have travelled back step by step towards the beginning of things, and we have reached a point beyond which a finite understanding cannot go. As well may the human mind conditioned by time and space endeavour to grasp the meaning of eternity. So we must rest content and cease striving after the unattainable.

All great religions have laid stress upon the permanence—and, consequently, the reality—of the spiritual as compared with the impermanence of the physical or phenomenal universe. Christianity provides a striking example of this teaching in the words of Our Lord, "Before Abraham was

I AM." But no philosophy of East or West has gone further in asserting the impermanence and, therefore, the unreality of the material universe as compared with the permanence and, therefore, the absolute reality of that which lies behind it than the Vedanta as set forth by Sankara. He realised the almost insuperable difficulties which stood in the way of his teaching obtaining any general acceptance; and he faced the situation with characteristic courage and ingenuity. He granted the actual existence of phenomena for those who had not reached the altitude of thought necessary for the understanding of ultimate truth. To the dreamers, the dream was real; and in their case he even granted the existence of a God or Lord, corresponding to the monotheistic conception of a personal God.

But, singular though he be in the iconoclastic severity of his teaching, it is, as it seems to me, the fact that he carried his reasoning further than others that differentiates him from those whose beliefs have been inspired by a similar ideal. There is something akin to the Vedanta philosophy of Sankara, surely, in the idealism of Bishop Berkeley.

Bishop Berkeley proved step by step to his own complete satisfaction that matter in the ordinary acceptance of the word did not exist. Colour, extension, sound, motion—all the attributes with which we clothe the objects which we perceive all round us, exist only in the mind. Were there no perceiving mind, all these objects would cease to exist. In other words, there is no such thing as matter as a-thing-in-itself. Then when I cease to perceive the trees in my garden, do they cease to exist, one naturally inquires? Not at all, replies the Bishop, they are still perceived by other minds. But if all men ceased to perceive the trees in my garden would they then cease to exist? Certainly not, we are told once more, they are still perceived by the all-pervading mind —the mind of God. The universe and all that is in it are merely ideas in the eternal mind of God, and are reflected by His will in the minds of men.

Berkeley, of course, assumed a plurality of minds. Sankara's conception of one unconditioned reality—Brahman—finds no place in his philosophy; and in this respect his ideas find a closer analogy in the Samkhya philosophy of Kapila, where the real eternal spirit corresponding to Brahman of the Vedanta, and known as Purushu, is not one but many. But the Samkhya system assumes something separate from Purushu, which corresponds to matter, and which is the basis of the phenomenal universe, but which at the same time only operates when perceived by Purushu, the eternal subject. In this case the universe is not explained as being due to ignorance in the sense in which the word is used in the Vedanta, but to the failure of Purushu to discriminate between itself and the whole gamut of sensations which it perceives, summed up by the word Prakriti, which is usually translated Nature —the "Magic Shadow-show played in a Box whose Candle is the Sun round which we Phantom Figures come and go," of Omar Khayyam. In so far, then, as Berkeley's conception of the universe can be said to resemble those of the orthodox Hindu systems, it agrees with the Samkhya in postulating a plurality of spiritual entities, but differs from it fundamentally in that it rejects the dualism which is the basis of the latter. In this respect it is closer to the Vedanta of Sankara; but it parts company with it when, under the influence of the famous commentator of the eighth century, it assumes its rigorously monistic character. There is, however, another interpretation of the Vedanta Sutras, of which the most famous exponent is Ramanuja, a great commentator of the twelfth century; and it is to the Vedanta as explained by Ramanuja that the conception of Bishop Berkeley is most closely related. The philosophy of Ramanuja is monistic in the sense that it rejects the dualism of the Samkhya. But it is monism with a qualification, and is described technically as *visishta advaita*, *i.e.* "non-duality with a difference." The Brahman of Ramanuja, far from being devoid of attributes, has *all* attributes; and the souls of men, far from losing individuality as a result of the destruction of ignorance, consciously enjoy eternal bliss. They *are* Brahman, but the latter "contains in himself the elements of that plurality which Sankara regards as illusion."[1] While the personal god of Sankara exists "only by collusion with illusion,"[2] and his ultimate god can only be described negatively, the God of Ramanuja can be and is described positively as an omnipotent and omniscient Lord of a spiritual world which is of his own nature. "The characteristics of the released soul," according to Ramanuja, "are similar to those of Brahman; it participates in all the latter's glorious qualities and powers, excepting only Brahman's power to emit, rule, and retract the entire world."[3] The two conceptions of God—those of Berkeley and Ramanuja—are not dissimilar; but if we seek an answer to the question why an omniscient and omnipotent being should impose restrictions upon himself, we discover an interesting difference in the point of view from which this question has been regarded in the case of Europe and India respectively. True it is, declares the Bishop, that the ideas which constitute the universe are impressed upon

[1] Professor E. W. Hopkins, in "The Religions of India."
[2] *Ibid.* [3] "The Vedanta-Sutras," by George Thibaut.

the human mind in a way which suggests a regular sequence of cause and effect, and this, he adds, "sufficiently testifies the wisdom and benevolence of its author," for were it not so, "we should be all in uncertainty and confusion, and a grown man no more know how to manage himself in the affairs of life than an infant just born." This may be said to answer the particular question why the Almighty has drawn up a code of rules which we call the laws of Nature, to which He subjects His omnipotence in His dealings with man. It is the answer of the thinker who is looking at the matter from a restricted point of view—that of man. It starts from the premise that God has decreed a creation, and it puts forward a reason for His voluntarily imposing restrictions upon His omnipotence in the interests of that which He has created. It does not pretend to offer any explanation of the reason for a creation itself. It does not aspire, that is to say, to look at the question from the point of view of the creator. Thinkers in India have not thus limited their outlook. To Sir Rabindra Nath Tagore, for example, it seems obvious that if the Almighty is to exercise His power at all, He must of His own will impose limitations upon Himself; and he illustrates his meaning by pointing to the limits which the chess player must perforce impose upon his freedom of action if there is to be a game at all. "The player willingly enters into definite relations with each particular piece and realises the joy of his power by these very restrictions. It is not that he cannot move the chessmen just as he pleases, but if he does so, then there can be no play. If God assumes His rôle of omnipotence, then His creation is at an end and His power loses all its meaning." [1]

And it is precisely this latter consummation

[1] In "Sādhana."

Plate 21.

DISCIPLES OF BUDDHA.

"Whether is more, the water which is in the four great oceans or the tears which have been shed by you while you strayed and wandered on this long pilgrimage . . ."

which is arrived at by so many of the Indian schools of thought. The Brahman of Sankara's Vedanta and the nirvāna of the Buddhists seem to correspond exactly to the expectations of Sir Rabindra Nath Tagore, under the circumstances suggested in the final lines of the passage just quoted. With all their subtlety of intellect and all their undeniable powers of clothing their ideas with words, the Indian philosophers have never been able to paint any positive picture of the final bliss which may be supposed to await those who obtain emancipation. "All speech," we are told, "turns away from the bliss of Brahman unable to reach it";[1] and, as Professor Max Müller has remarked, "when language fails, thought is not likely to fare better."

And so we are brought back to the inherent pessimism which darkens the outlook of the Indian upon life—a pessimism which was voiced by Sidhartha Gautama two thousand five hundred years ago when he uttered the first of the four great truths which he preached to men: "Birth is suffering, old age is suffering, death is suffering, to be united with the unloved is suffering, to be separated from the loved is suffering, not to obtain what one desires is suffering, in short the fivefold clinging to the earthly is suffering," and when he asked of his disciples "whether is more, the water which is in the four great oceans, or the tears which have flowed from you and have been shed by you, while you strayed and wandered on this long pilgrimage (earthly existence) and sorrowed and wept, because that was your portion which ye abhorred and that which ye loved was not your portion?" Sorrow and suffering, these are the ingredients of earthly existence to which the harassed mortal is tightly bound, and from which he is urged at all costs to endeavour to

[1] Taitt. Up. ii. 4. 1.

escape. What need to paint the joys of that which lies beyond the pitiless state of suffering which looms so large within the prison gates? No more powerful incentive can be devised than the incentive to escape. The way to freedom is, in all sooth, difficult enough; and those who are so fortunate as to find it may rest content, satisfied that the summit of human endeavour has been reached.

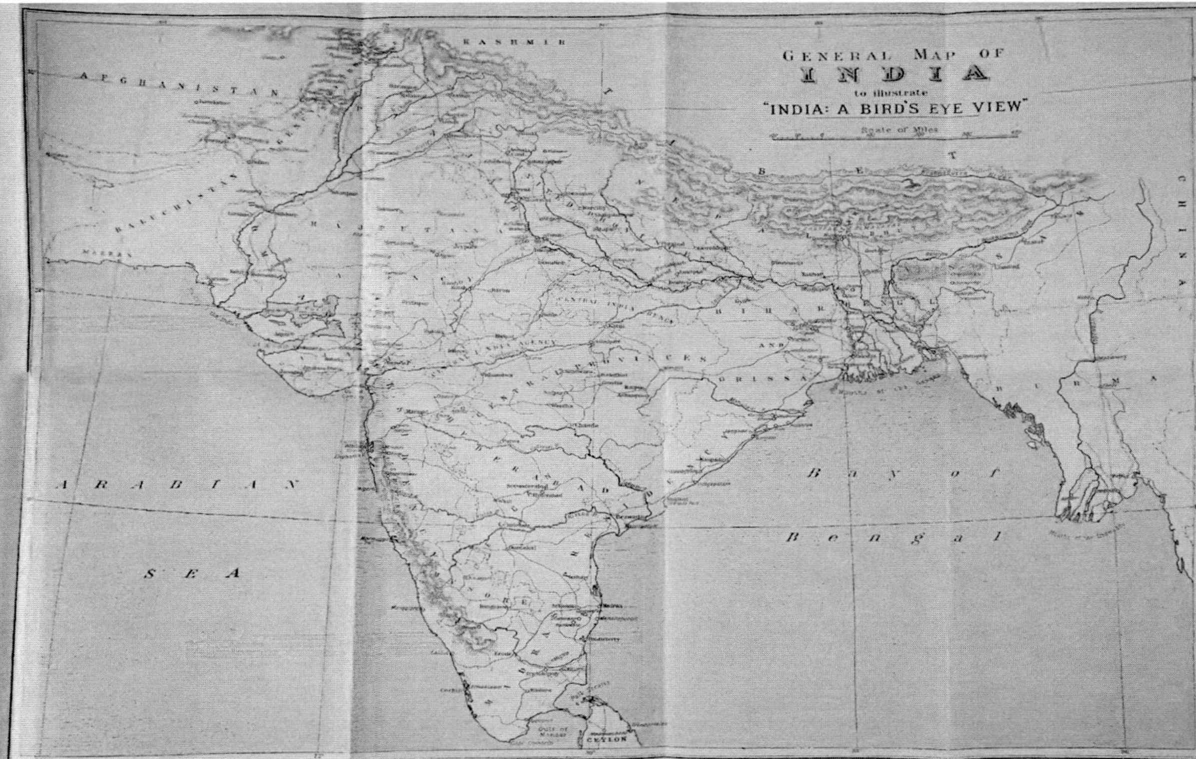
GENERAL MAP OF
INDIA
to illustrate
"INDIA: A BIRD'S EYE VIEW"
Scale of Miles
KASHMIR
AFGHANISTAN
BALUCHISTAN
RAJPUTANA
TIBET
CHINA
CENTRAL INDIA AGENCY
CENTRAL PROVINCES
BIHAR AND ORISSA
BURMA
ARABIAN SEA
Bay of Bengal
CEYLON
Gulf of Manaar

INDEX

THE END